D1175262

Partnerships for Service-Learning

Partnerships for Service-Learning

Impacts on Communities and Students

Todd Kelshaw, Freyda Lazarus, Judy Minier, and Associates

Foreword by Frank Alvarez

JOSSEY-BASS
A Wiley Imprint
www.josseybass.com

Copyright © 2009 by John Wiley & Sons, Inc. All rights reserved.

Published by Jossey-Bass
A Wiley Imprint
989 Market Street, San Francisco, CA 94103-1741—www.josseybass.com

No part of this publication may be reproduced, stored in a retrieval system, or transmitted in any form or by any means, electronic, mechanical, photocopying, recording, scanning, or otherwise, except as permitted under Section 107 or 108 of the 1976 United States Copyright Act, without either the prior written permission of the publisher, or authorization through payment of the appropriate per-copy fee to the Copyright Clearance Center, Inc., 222 Rosewood Drive, Danvers, MA 01923, 978-750-8400, fax 978-646-8600, or on the Web at www.copyright.com. Requests to the publisher for permission should be addressed to the Permissions Department, John Wiley & Sons, Inc., 111 River Street, Hoboken, NJ 07030, 201-748-6011, fax 201-748-6008, or online at www.wiley.com/go/permissions.

Readers should be aware that Internet Web sites offered as citations and/or sources for further information may have changed or disappeared between the time this was written and when it is read.

Limit of Liability/Disclaimer of Warranty: While the publisher and author have used their best efforts in preparing this book, they make no representations or warranties with respect to the accuracy or completeness of the contents of this book and specifically disclaim any implied warranties of merchantability or fitness for a particular purpose. No warranty may be created or extended by sales representatives or written sales materials. The advice and strategies contained herein may not be suitable for your situation. You should consult with a professional where appropriate. Neither the publisher nor author shall be liable for any loss of profit or any other commercial damages, including but not limited to special, incidental, consequential, or other damages.

Jossey-Bass books and products are available through most bookstores. To contact Jossey-Bass directly call our Customer Care Department within the U.S. at 800-956-7739, outside the U.S. at 317-572-3986, or fax 317-572-4002.

Jossey-Bass also publishes its books in a variety of electronic formats. Some content that appears in print may not be available in electronic books.

Library of Congress Cataloging-in-Publication Data
Kelshaw, Todd Spencer.
  Partnerships for service-learning : impacts on communities and students / Todd Kelshaw, Freyda Lazarus, Judy Minier, and associates ; foreword by Frank Alvarez.
    p. cm.
  Includes bibliographical references and index.
  ISBN 978-0-470-45057-4 (cloth)
  1. Service learning–United States. 2. College-school cooperation–United States. I. Lazarus, Freyda. II. Minier, Judy. III. Title.
  LC221.K45 2009
  361.3'7–dc22

2009011614

Printed in the United States of America

FIRST EDITION

HB Printing   10 9 8 7 6 5 4 3 2 1

The Jossey-Bass
Higher and Adult Education Series

Contents

Foreword   ix
Frank Alvarez

Preface   xiii
Todd Kelshaw, Freyda Lazarus, and Judy Minier

About the Editors   xxiii

About the Contributors   xxv

Part I: Service-Learning Partnerships in Community Contexts

1. The Student Coalition for Strengthening Communities: A Service-Learning Partnership Between P–12 Schools and a Preservice Teacher Education Program   3
   Jeffrey B. Anderson, Christopher Daikos, Jon Granados-Greenberg, and Audra Rutherford

2. Reflections on University-School Partnerships at Providence College's Feinstein Institute for Public Service   37
   Keith Morton and Jane Callahan

3. Metropolitan State University: Connecting with
    Community Through a University-Public Library
    Partnership   75
    Robert Shumer, Susan Shumer, Rebecca Ryan, Joanna Brookes,
    M. Alejandra Reyes Cejudo, and Karin DuPaul

4. Advancing Service-Learning Through Program
    Evaluation   103
    Nancy Nisbett, Sally Cahill Tannenbaum, and Brent Smither

5. Project ACtion for Equity: Service-Learning with a
    Gender Equity Focus on the U.S.-Mexico Border   129
    Judith H. Munter, Joesefina V. Tinajero, Sylvia Peregrino,
    and Reynaldo Reyes III

Part II: Learning Processes and Outcomes of Service-Learning Partnerships

6. STEM Literacy, Civic Responsibility, and Future
    Vision: Examining the Effects of the Lawrence
    Math and Science Partnership   165
    Linda C. Foote and Julie E. DiFilippo

7. School-Based Service-Learning as Action
    Research   206
    Deborah S. Yost and Elizabeth Soslau

8. Experiencing Engineering While Helping Others:
    UMass Lowell's Assistive Technology Design Fair   235
    Douglas Prime and Donald Rhine

9. Program Theory: A Framework for Collaborative
    Measurement of Service-Learning Outcomes   267
    Joannie Busillo Aguayo and Joyce Munsch

Afterword   285
    Ira Harkavy

Index   289

Foreword

Frank Alvarez

High fives, a pat on the back, a smile, a wave hello from across the room. These are part of the exchanges as two college interns, two teachers, and a dozen students begin to settle into an after-school program at a local church on a blustery fall day. Backpacks are scattered around the room, computers chime as students log on, books are swung open, and math manipulatives spill out onto a worktable. The energy is palpable. Everyone is focused and eager to work. And so begins an after-school program aimed at assisting students who are struggling to learn math. The students, who are recommended for this program, work alongside two classroom teachers and two college students or preservice teachers from a nearby university. A similar scene is playing out in several community sites across the school district.

For some time now, a tension has existed between elementary/secondary public education and higher education. It is the tension between practice and theory—the notion that what occurs within the confines of a classroom, such as content knowledge and classroom management techniques, may differ from the philosophical discussions and pedagogical methodologies espoused by academicians. This *disconnect* often creates a divide between current-day practitioners and those who are responsible for training future teachers, leaders, and citizens. While administrators and teachers are busy negotiating this tension, they are also occupied with a more fundamental challenge: finding means within limited budgets for novel learning opportunities, differentiated instruction for diverse groups of learners, and public engagement to increase support for public schools. Enter *service-learning*.

Service-learning is a teaching method that encourages students to employ the values, skills, and knowledge learned in the classroom in real-life experiences through engagement within their schools and communities. In public school settings, service-learning provides both the pedagogical framework and the educational practice necessary for novice practitioners, while assisting schools to achieve designated goals. The intent of service-learning, ultimately, is that the activity is useful to both the recipient and the provider; hence, everyone benefits.

As a superintendent of schools, I have seen firsthand the positive impact of service-learning. First, it is a great vehicle for expanding the capacity of schools to provide additional services and resources to students. Second, it provides support to K–12 teachers in the form of teaching assistants, while connecting teachers with faculty who supervise the college students and serve as conduits to best practices in teaching and learning. Third, it fosters the needed connection between theory and practice for newcomers to the teaching profession, providing essential opportunities for professional discourse, trial-and-error learning, and practical applications of learning theories. Finally, it encourages a spirit of community engagement that is critical to the well-being of our society.

As part of the Montclair Public School District's ongoing commitment to serving students from diverse backgrounds with a wide range of educational needs, since 1995 the district has provided service-learning activities in a variety of settings. These have included several in-school intervention efforts, such as middle-school level mentorship programs and coaching opportunities in a writers' room at the high school level. There are also school, community, and university partnerships related to the arts, women's studies, life skills, and youth engagement projects.

The most extensive service-learning effort, however, is an after-school program that supports academically struggling students with help in math and language arts. This program is instituted at various venues on an after-school basis throughout the academic year. In partnership with Montclair State University, the Montclair Public Schools pairs students in grades one through five with college students who are enrolled in service-learning courses spanning a wide range of academic disciplines. These college students work with the elementary school children individually and in small groups at various schools and at five community sites in town. Each site hosts two-hour sessions two days per week, providing the elementary school students with homework help, reading assistance, and educational activities designed to supplement their classroom lessons. The undergraduates who participate in service-learning are supervised jointly by Montclair Public Schools and Montclair State University staff and faculty.

Although it is difficult to attribute student achievement results in our schools exclusively to service-learning interventions, district staff members acknowledge that the university-level assistance contributes to the district's success. As the latest assessments indicate, the minority student achievement gap has been reduced at every grade level, and the number of students attaining proficiency on state-mandated standardized tests has increased.

The service-learning stories shared in this volume reflect a broad array of programs across diverse school districts. They tell stories about schools, communities, and higher education institutions and their efforts to connect theory and practice and, ultimately, to positively affect student learning and achievement. The stories are informative in a practical way. Administrators will see themselves and their communities represented in the pages that follow. Teachers and other school personnel will learn about relevant solutions or approaches for solving existing challenges, as well as useful strategies for expanding social capital in a school setting. In the end, it is about students gaining access to significant adults who can bridge divides, encourage learning, and inspire excellence.

Preface

Todd Kelshaw, Freyda Lazarus, and
Judy Minier

Recent years have seen an incredible expansion of service-learning initiatives throughout American higher education. As exciting as this boom may be, it is accompanied by the risk of idealistic and exuberant experimentation, which if conducted recklessly may in turn endanger service-learning partners in social, cultural, economic, and ethical ways. In creating this book, we are motivated by a great need for conscientiousness in the invention and execution of service-learning partnerships—care that must come in the forms of explicit theoretical grounding, reflective and strategic application, and sound empirical assessment.

This book is a collection of important and enlightening case studies, at once readably anecdotal, substantively rigorous, and critically reflective. All of these cases address actual service-learning projects in various educational and community contexts. When we initially conceived this project, we sought accounts of cases that we could categorize tidily—as in, "these three are about service-learning theory, these next three concern strategic practices, and the final three portray assessment methods and findings." The intriguing and diverse accounts assembled in this book certainly do portray and discuss important matters of theory, practice, and research in contexts of inventive and consequential service-learning applications. What we found, though, is that there is no clean way to demarcate considerations of service-learning's theoretical, practical, and empirical dimensions; their overlaps are inevitable and even necessary if one is to explore, reflect on, and derive useful lessons and ideas from case studies.

As we were realizing the richness of the case-discussions and the inappropriateness of our initial organizational plan, something else was becoming evident—an issue that not only tied the otherwise diverse chapters together but also gave each its particular basis. It is both intrinsic and dynamic, serving in each case as a funda-mental process, product, and—yes—problem of service-learning. This issue is *partnership*. Just as it is impossible (and counterproduc-tive) to cleanly delineate discussions of service-learning's concepts, techniques, and observations as presumably distinct modes of the service-learning experience, it is unfeasible to tease out partner-ship as a secondary or accessory phenomenon. Partnership, as these chapters illustrate, is *essential* to the invention, implementation, and outgrowth of the service-learning experience.

The partnering process is characterized by the develop-ment and maintenance of mutuality in all facets of a given service-learning project: beliefs, values, goals, modes of interac-tion, responsibilities, and beneficial outcomes. This reciprocal essence of partnership—an entirely relational mode of civic engagement—does away with any idea that service-learning is simply about volunteerism, service-provision, or similar notions that are tied to assumptions of unilateral action. As the authors in this collection of service-learning partnership cases testify, the process and outcomes are done not *for*, but rather *with*. To describe, reflect on, and assess our techniques of learning and engaging *with* is this book's basic purpose.

Partnership plays out in service-learning in two intermingling ways: as a collaborative pedagogy and as a community-building enterprise. As such, service-learning has roots in and consequences for how we teach and learn (and not just in terms of explicit educational content) and how we strengthen our civic fabrics. With this in mind, we have structured the book with two major parts. The first part features case studies that emphasize processes and outcomes of community-based partnerships. The second part includes cases that pertain primarily to teaching and learning issues of pedagogical partnerships.

Service-Learning Partnerships in Community Contexts

A given community's resources are often fragmented, with school, work, the arts, politics, and so on maintained as distinct spheres that must compete for funding and participation. The community's "center" may be decentralized or decayed. Cultural rifts are widened along ethnic faults. Those institutions that do have adequate resources may be accessible to only a select few. How might service-learning alleviate or even remedy such community problems? The five case studies in this section address ways in which partnerships that emerge through service-learning initiatives may foster collaboration, innovation, and the creation and sharing of resources. Such partnerships' spans of involvement and benefit include not only higher and secondary education teachers and students; they also engage and affect broader arrays of community stakeholders. Through these partnerships, resources are integrated, community centers are established, intercultural understanding and cooperation are forged, and institutions are remodeled in inclusive ways.

This section's first case study is "The Student Coalition for Strengthening Communities: A Service-Learning Partnership Between P–12 Schools and a Preservice Teacher Education Program." Here, coauthors Jeffrey B. Anderson, Christopher Daikos, Jon Granados-Greenberg, and Audra Rutherford identify ways that three secondary schools deal with the sixty hours of community service required by the Seattle school system. In chronicling a P–12 pre-service teacher education service-learning partnership called the Student Coalition for Strengthening Communities (SCSC), the authors address matters of social justice, collaboration (defined as a "step above partnering"), resource development, and the assessment of teacher education attitudes as they pertain to service-learning principles.

The second chapter in this section is "Reflections on University-School Partnerships at Providence College's Feinstein Institute for Public Service," by Keith Morton and Jane Callahan. This account chronicles a relationship of over twelve years between a university and three public schools (an elementary school and two middle schools) in Providence, Rhode Island. In describing the partners' efforts and experiences, the authors reflect on the partnerships' overlapping pedagogical and civic dimensions, thus contributing to theoretical and practical understandings of what it means to jointly learn and do in community-based contexts. These understandings ultimately challenge simplistically linear conceptions of service-learning partnerships by celebrating "dynamic, joint creations in which all the people involved create knowledge, transact power, mix personal and institutional interests, and make meaning."

Next, coauthors Robert Shumer, Susan Shumer, Rebecca Ryan, Joanna Brookes, M. Alejandra Reyes Cejudo, and Karin DuPaul provide "Metropolitan State University: Connecting with Community Through a University-Public Library Partnership." Jointly written in a way that highlights some of the various voices of this complex community-wide partnership, this chapter describes and analyzes the establishment of a library that conjoins and mutually benefits a public university in St. Paul, Minnesota, and its area residents and community groups. The case, in its enabling of vital community-based projects (English literacy education, for instance) and fruitful interpersonal, cultural, and institutional relationships, illustrates how "universities that live in communities, especially communities that are poor and underserved, can benefit their academic and social needs when they partner with the community for academic and civic outcomes."

The fourth chapter in this section is "Advancing Service-Learning Through Program Evaluation," by Nancy Nisbett, Sally Cahill Tannenbaum, and Brent Smither. They describe a partnership between the Recreation Administration and Leisure Studies program at California State University-Fresno and the Fresno County Office of Education's Department of Safe and Healthy Kids. In addition to detailing the conception and implementation of this service-learning partnership, the authors provide assessment of its strengths and weaknesses, its relevance to children's health, and its contribution to the service-learning field. This evaluation is enabled through the collection of both qualitative and quantitative data, which is presented in a detailed manner that may provide helpful ideas for others who are designing and executing assessment studies.

The final account in this series of chapters pertaining to service-learning's capacities for community-building is "Project ACtion for Equity: Service-Learning with a Gender Equity Focus on the U.S.-Mexico Border," by Judith H. Munter, Josefina V. Tinajero, Sylvia Peregrino, and Reynaldo Reyes III. Project ACtion for Equity (ACE) is a program for college students in teacher preparation coursework. It was developed and is sustained through collaborative efforts of partners at the University of Texas at El Paso, regional K–12 school districts, and the El Paso Chapter of the American Association for University Women. The program works with Hispanic mothers and daughters in border communities, integrates gender equity issues into academic coursework, and strives to increase minorities' and women's enrollment in graduate and professional schools. In their case study, the authors focus attention on the importance of addressing the root causes of social problems, and on the value of partners' interactive reflection and dialogue toward "merging the roles of service 'provider' and 'recipient.'"

Learning Processes and Outcomes of Service-Learning Partnerships

Essentially, service-learning is pedagogical. So, having explored ways in which service-learning partnerships affect relationships and resources in communities, it is important to home in on service-learning's processes and consequences as they pertain to teaching and learning. What problems and achievements do administrators, educators, and students experience as they conduct their partnerships? What kinds of learning may take place, in terms of substantive content, personal and cultural identity, and civic engagement? How can such learning be assessed, and how may it be maximized?

To launch this section, Linda C. Foote and Julie DiFilippo present "STEM Literacy, Civic Responsibility, and Future Vision: Examining the Effects of the Lawrence Math and Science Partnership." This case study makes effective use of somewhat traditional methods to determine the effectiveness of the program treatment. Using entry and exit surveys and focus groups, the project leaders assessed (1) the promotion of experiential and service-learning opportunities at Merrimack College; (2) the enhancement of undergraduate science, technology, engineering, and math (STEM) literacy, cultural awareness, civic responsibility, and leadership skills; (3) heightened academic success and interest in STEM for middle school youth; and (4) the provision of role models to enhance middle school youth's future vision and aspirations for postsecondary education. The project attempted to achieve these goals through instruction from university students, including education majors and others without any teaching background. The evaluation was designed to test undergraduate student participation and beliefs, the impact on the middle school student attitudes and their future in STEM subjects, and impressions made on partnership stakeholders.

Next, in "School-based Service Learning as Action Research," Deborah S. Yost and Elizabeth Soslau discuss Project Achieve, a model of urban professional development that aspires to heighten teaching effectiveness and student achievement. This program was created and implemented through the collaborative efforts of two LaSalle University professors and the principal of an urban middle school. In considering the question, "Are service and/or learning better because of the quality of the partnership?" the authors address the partnership's theoretical basis and practical outcomes, and they provide, through their explicitly acknowledged joint authorship, an effective meta-reflection on the value of self-aware collaboration.

The third chapter in this section is Douglas Prime and Donald Rhine's "Experiencing Engineering While Helping Others: UMass Lowell's Assistive Technology Design Fair." In this case study, the coauthors—collaborators in one particular university–high school partnership within the broader program—tell the story of the Assistive Technology Design Fair (ATDF), which "provides high school students with the opportunity to engage in real-world engineering design problems aimed at helping people with disabilities or special needs." The chapter describes an array of projects conducted by high school participants throughout the program and explains the logistics of ATDF's implementation. As well, the account provides empirical data that point to students' academic and civic growth.

Finally, as a methodological inroad for assessing service-learning's educational outcomes, we have Joannie Busillo Aguayo and Joyce Munsch's "Program Theory: A Framework for Collaborative Measurement of Service-Learning Outcomes." The authors posit that explicit links between program resources and outcomes must be identified in relational ways and then tested in order to determine program continuation and improvement. It is now well documented that assessment must feature a continuous feedback loop, through which ongoing activities may be evaluated in terms of a program's design, implementation, and effectiveness. Using an innovative "program theory" model, evaluators construct a plausible method for both program application and testing that responds to a given project's impact, process elements, or both. Because stakeholders identify such elements jointly, all participants in this model have buy-in when it comes to accepting and analyzing program achievements.

Hopeful Implications

Service-learning, as a practical pedagogy and conceptual ideal, is continuing to gain great popularity. At a recent conference panel session designed to introduce basic ideas of service-learning to higher education faculty, the discussion unfortunately avoided concrete techniques in favor of vague, albeit heartfelt, claims of service-learning's virtues, culminating in an exhortation to "just get out there and do it!" This book's editorial team is all for the doing of service-learning. However, we fear that there is much at stake; that "just doing it" without careful preparation and reflection may have harmful consequences in both community and educational contexts.

Conversely, the conscientious design, execution, and assessment of service-learning projects potentially offer great benefit to educators, students, and communities. Such success requires structured institutional support in universities, schools, and municipalities, as well as partners' careful consideration of their project's theoretical, applicative, reflective, and evaluative dimensions. We hope that this book's assorted case studies provide informative illustrations of how reflection can function across various kinds of service-learning projects.

Perhaps the greatest merit of these case studies, we believe, is in the chapters' diverse accounts of partnership. Especially when case-study coauthors are actual collaborators in service-learning partnerships, there are excellent openings for improved understandings and future innovations. Surely, case studies allow important opportunities for building, applying, and testing theories. These cases' qualitative dimensions—the narrative story lines and the authors' subjective reflections—offer compelling examples of service-learning partnerships in practice. Further, they provide an appropriately high degree of open-endedness, which enables readers to develop new, synthetic ideas for projects in other settings. Although contextual features of any given service-learning partnership make exact replication or transplantation impossible, the illustrated examples within these nine chapters will, we hope, spark others' ideas for novel, collaborative, and educational approaches to fostering substantive and civic learning as well as managing complex problems in their own communities.

Acknowledgments

This book has been made possible by the hard work and commitment of staff and faculty affiliated with the Service-Learning Program at Montclair State University, and—in the spirit of partnership—others throughout the Center's geographic, professional, and pedagogical communities. The editorial team wishes to acknowledge the outstanding support we received from Dr. Kenneth Brook, professor of anthropology; Dr. David Lee Keiser, associate professor of curriculum and teaching; Bryan Murdock, director of experiential education; Dana Natale, associate director of sponsored programs; and Jessica St. Clair, former MSU service-learning coordinator.

As well, we recognize the guidance and feedback provided by Dr. John Saltmarsh of the University of Massachusetts-Boston and Dr. Edward Zlotkowski of Bentley University. Their contributions to this book—from its inception to its completion—were invaluable.

Additionally, we express sincere appreciation to the five experienced educators and practitioners who served as the peer-review panel: Kevin Kecskes (director, Community-University Partnerships, Portland State University, Portland, Oregon), Lynn Montrose (academic internship program director, Regis University, Denver, Colorado), Robert Seidel (director, government resources, Communities in Schools National, Alexandria, Virginia), John

Spence (director, Texas Center for Service-Learning, Texas Education Agency, Austin, Texas), and Marshall Welch (director of the Lowell Bennion Community Service Center, University of Utah, Salt Lake City, Utah).

About the Editors

Todd Kelshaw, Ph.D., is Assistant Professor of Communication Studies at Montclair State University. His scholarship addresses communicative dimensions of democratic civic engagement. Along this line, he has particular concerns for the functions of dialogue and deliberation in community-based organizational partnerships, and for the civic potentials of service-learning pedagogies.

Freyda C. Lazarus, Ed.D., provided three decades of leadership to the Montclair State University campus to advance the civic and professional development of students through its service-learning, cooperative education, and community-based research projects and programs. She served as a project director for numerous state, federal, and foundation grants that supported innovative programming and faculty development initiatives to advance business and civic partnerships.

Judy Minier, Ed.D., has thirty-five years of public school and university experience as a teacher, professor, and administrator. She has worked at six American universities and in international educational settings in Central Asia, Southeast Asia, and the Middle East. Areas of scholarly interest include innovations in teacher preparation programs, diversity issues in schools and universities, assessment of learning, democracy in education, and curriculum redesign and development, as well as accreditation and program evaluation.

About the Contributors

Frank Alvarez is currently the superintendent of Montclair Public Schools, Montclair, New Jersey. He has spearheaded improvement projects to close the minority achievement gap and increase the infusion of technology throughout the curriculum. With prior experience as a high school teacher and principal, he provided leadership to the New Jersey Department of Education's Urban Initiative (Operation School Renewal) and continues to serve on the Middle States Association Board and the New Jersey Urban Superintendent Association's Executive Committee.

Jeffrey B. Anderson is professor of education at Seattle University, where he works in the Master in Teaching (MiT) program and directs the Academic Service-Learning Faculty Fellows program. He has written numerous articles and book chapters on service-learning and is coeditor of the book *Service-Learning in Teacher Education: Enhancing the Growth of New Teachers, Their Students, and Communities*. He also serves on the board of directors of the International Center for Service-Learning in Teacher Education and the International Association for Research on Service-Learning and Community Engagement.

Joanna Brookes has been a librarian with the St. Paul Public Library since 1998. Prior to serving as the Dayton's Bluff branch librarian, she served on the Bookmobile and at the Central Library. Joanna spent a year in 2001–2002 working in a public library in

Manchester, England. She holds a bachelor's degree from the University of Minnesota and a master of library and information science (MLIS) degree from the University of Wisconsin-Milwaukee.

Joannie Busillo Aguayo holds a master's degree in family and consumer sciences from California State University, Northridge, and is completing a doctorate in organizational leadership at Pepperdine University. Her research emphasis is on using theory-based evaluation approaches to document evidence-based family-centered practice in programs serving infants and toddlers with disabilities. As a trainer for the WestEd Center and the Department of Developmental Services, she trains early intervention practitioners in California on assessment and evaluation.

Jane Callahan is a professor of education at Providence College. She also teaches in the Public and Community Studies program. Her research interests combine education and service-learning development for pre- and in-service teachers.

M. Alejandra Reyes Cejudo serves as the manager of the Latino Learning Institute at Comunidades Latinas Unidas En Servicio (CLUES) in St. Paul, Minnesota. Her interests include adult ESL education, native language literacy, immigration and refugee issues, bilingual education, community service-learning, and the sociopolitical aspects of the ESL profession. Ms. Reyes Cejudo is originally from Mexico City, Mexico. She earned her master's degree from the University of Minnesota in Teaching English as a Second Language (TESL) with an emphasis in adult education.

Christopher Daikos is a graduate of the Seattle University MiT program and recently completed his administrative certification and an M.Ed. in educational leadership at the University of Washington. He is a house administrator at Meany Middle School in Seattle, Washington. Service-learning has been a key factor in many of his students' successes.

Julie E. DiFilippo serves as the executive director of Blessed Stephen Bellesini, O.S.A. Academy—a Nativity model and middle school of boys from limited income with the mission to graduate all students at or above grade level and place them in private high school.

Karin DuPaul is the community organizer for the Dayton's Bluff District Four Community Council.

Linda C. Foote is associate professor in the Department of Health Sciences at Merrimack College, North Andover, Massachusetts, and serves as director of the Lawrence Math and Science Partnership—a program that partners undergraduates with middle school youth in the city of Lawrence.

Jon Granados-Greenberg is a graduate of the Seattle University MiT program and has taught at the Center School in Seattle since 2001. Prior to this he taught in a private, residential treatment program in New Hampshire, a public middle school for special education students in Boston, and a Catholic school in Bogotá, Colombia. A Seattle native, Jon returned to Seattle in 1999 to dedicate himself to improving education in his home community.

Ira Harkavy is associate vice president and founding director of the Barbara and Edward Netter Center for Community Partnerships, University of Pennsylvania. As director of the Netter Center since 1992, Harkavy has helped to develop service-learning courses as well as participatory action research projects that involve creating university-assisted community schools in Penn's local community of West Philadelphia. Harkavy is a member of numerous boards, including the Advisory Committee for the Social, Behavioral and Economic Sciences (SBE) Directorate of the National Science Foundation; the International Consortium on Higher Education, Civic Responsibility, and Democracy (U.S. chair); and the Coalition for Community Schools (chair). In 2007, *Dewey's Dream: Universities and Democracy in an Age of Education Reform*, which Harkavy coauthored with Lee Benson and John Puckett, was published by Temple University Press.

Keith Morton is associate professor of public and community service at Providence College, Rhode Island. He also teaches in the American Studies program and is past director of the college's

Feinstein Institute for Public Service. His primary interests are in community history and sustainable community development.

Joyce Munsch holds a doctorate in human development and family studies from Cornell University and is a professor of child and adolescent development at the California State University, Northridge. Her implementation and support of a variety of community learning service programs on the CSUN campus were recognized in 2005 when she received the Faculty Senate Visionary Community Service Learning Award.

Judith H. Munter is associate professor and associate dean at the University of Texas at El Paso (UTEP). Her professional experience includes teaching, research, and program evaluation in Colombia, Brazil, and the United States. Her research focuses on teacher education, diversity, service-learning, and research methods.

Nancy Nisbett is an associate professor in the Recreation Administration and Leisure Studies program at California State University Fresno, coordinating the Community Recreation and Youth Services Specialization program.

Sylvia Peregrino is an assistant professor at UTEP, where she teaches courses in sociocultural foundations, multicultural education, and research methods. Her professional experience includes evaluating university and school partnerships participating in the Kellogg Foundations' Engaging Latino Communities for Education (ENLACE) grant.

Douglas Prime, director of the Future Engineers Center at the University of Massachusetts Lowell, is the founder of several innovative, informal science and engineering education programs for middle school and high school students, including DESIGN-CAMP summer programs, DESIGNLAB after-school workshops, and the Assistive Technology Design Fair. Mr. Prime has fifteen years of experience teaching middle school science and technology, developing hands-on science and design curricula, and offering professional development in technology and engineering for teachers. He holds a bachelor's degree in mechanical engineering and a master of education degree in curriculum and instruction, both from the University of Lowell.

Reynaldo Reyes III works as assistant professor of bilingual, ESL, and multicultural education in the College of Education at the University of Texas at El Paso. In almost all of his courses he integrates service-learning projects that focus on working with marginalized student populations and English language learners in high need schools and communities.

Donald Rhine has taught mathematics, physics, and engineering at Tyngsborough High School in Tyngsborough, Massachusetts, for seven years. He was one of the first teachers involved in the University of Massachusetts at Lowell's Assistive Technology Design Fair (ATDF) program. Prior to teaching, he worked in the finance industry and also served as an engineer and program manager for the United States Air Force. Mr. Rhine holds a bachelor of science in electrical engineering from Rensselaer Polytechnic Institute, a master of science in electrical engineering from the University of Massachusetts at Lowell, and an M.B.A. from the University of Rochester, New York.

Audra Rutherford completed her master's degree in education at Harvard University. In 2003 she served as a Service-Learning AmeriCorps VISTA member in a public middle school, then worked for four years as the community projects manager at Franklin High School's Public Service and Social Action Academy in Seattle, Washington. She now serves as the development officer for the Church Council of Greater Seattle.

Rebecca Ryan is the library-community outreach coordinator at Metropolitan State University. Her previous experience includes working in nonprofit arts organizations. She holds a bachelor's degree from St. Olaf College and is currently pursuing her MLIS at the College of Saint Catherine.

Robert Shumer is one of the pioneers of service-learning. He has contributed to the field in many arenas, including teaching in high school, developing an inner city community school, and serving as director for the Field Studies Development at UCLA and as founding director of the National Service-Learning Clearinghouse. Dr. Shumer currently teaches at the University of Minnesota and works as a national and international consultant for K–16 service-learning and evaluation and assessment.

Susan Shumer is the founding director of the Center for Community-Based Learning at Metropolitan State University, St. Paul, Minnesota. She received her bachelor's in English from St. Ambrose University in Davenport, Iowa, and her master of science in education with a focus on experiential and service-learning from Minnesota State University, Mankato. She currently acts as director of Community Outreach, Civic Engagement, and The Center for Community-based Learning at Metropolitan State. Ms. Shumer is a past recipient of the Pat Kowalski Leadership Award presented for exemplary leaders who share a vision and skills for strategically moving service-learning and campus community collaborations forward.

Brent Smither is the Leadership Academy Consultant with the Fresno County Office of Education Department of Safe and Healthy Kids and an alumnus of the Recreation Administration program.

Elizabeth Soslau is a doctoral candidate in the School of Education at the University of Delaware. She is a service-learning practitioner, researcher, and curriculum consultant and currently serves on the board of directors for Need in Deed, a service learning organization in Philadelphia, Pennsylvania.

Sally Cahill Tannenbaum is an associate professor in the Department of Communication at California State University Fresno and the CSU, Fresno, service-learning mentor. She is also a member of the Fresno County School Board.

Josefina V. Tinajero is professor and dean of the College of Education at UTEP and director of the nationally recognized Mother-Daughter/Father-Son programs. Her research includes biliteracy, two-way bilingual program development, and education of Latino students and parents.

Deborah S. Yost is a professor of education at La Salle University in Philadelphia, Pennsylvania. She has published numerous articles in teacher education journals and has presented papers at both the 2006 and 2007 American Educational Research Association (AERA) conferences. Her recent research highlights school-university partnerships and the results of a teacher leader model of professional development on urban middle school students' learning and achievement.

Partnerships for Service-Learning

Part I

Service-Learning Partnerships
in Community Contexts

1

The Student Coalition for Strengthening Communities

A Service-Learning Partnership Between P–12 Schools and a Preservice Teacher Education Program

Jeffrey B. Anderson, Christopher Daikos, Jon Granados-Greenberg, and Audra Rutherford

This chapter describes one successful P–12 pre-service teacher education service-learning partnership, the Student Coalition for Strengthening Communities (SCSC), which involves high school students, teachers, and administrators, working alongside pre-service teachers, teacher education faculty, and other community members. This collaborative service-learning initiative is designed to strengthen communities by helping high school students enhance their commitment to working for social justice while gaining the knowledge and skills needed to do this successfully. At the same time, pre-service teachers involved with this project gain the expertise and experience needed to implement service-learning with their future P–12 students.

Since 2001 this partnership has been working to develop, implement, and assess service-learning activities that benefit P–12 students, their communities, and their pre-service teacher partners.

A shared commitment to working for social justice is one of the dominant themes of this partnership.

Following a review of the literature regarding service-learning partnerships, an overview of the partnership is presented. Detailed descriptions are provided of four partnership members, including three public high schools in Seattle, Washington—The Center School, The John Stanford Public Service and Political Science Academy at Franklin High School, and the John Marshall Transition Center—and the Seattle University Master in Teaching (MiT) program. The chapter concludes with recommendations for building P–12 pre-service teacher education partnerships, followed by a discussion of ongoing challenges and future plans.

Review of the Literature: Service-Learning in Preservice Teacher Education

Research results and the experiences of teacher educators and pre-service teachers indicate that participation in service-learning activities can be a powerful learning experience for teacher candidates, and it can simultaneously support the learning of P–12 students while strengthening the communities in which they live (Anderson, Swick, & Yff, 2001). An increasing number of teacher education programs across the nation are addressing the challenges of integrating service-learning into their curricula. Anderson and Erickson (2003) identified 312 pre-service teacher education programs that included a service-learning component. Many teacher educators are becoming aware that successful service-learning activities in pre-service teacher education can contribute to effective practice in P–12 schools when graduates enter the profession with preparation in and commitment to implementing service-learning with their students (Wade, Anderson, Yarbrough, Pickeral, Erickson, & Kromer, 1999).

Many of the skills and dispositions needed for successful teaching are enhanced in pre-service teachers who participate in service-learning activities. These include sensitivity to diversity issues (Boyle-Baise, 1998); development of an ethic of care, including increased compassion and concern, willingness to serve others, and increased complexity of thinking regarding problems of childhood (Potthoff, Dinsmore, Stirtz, Walsh, Ziebarth, and Eifler, 2000); an increased belief in the ability of all children to learn; and enhanced awareness of individual differences (Root, Callahan, & Sepanski, 2002).

Root and Callahan (2000) examined mediating variables—characteristics of the pre-service teachers' service-learning experience—and how those characteristics related to outcomes. They found that the quality of the service-learning experience predicted positive outcomes from service-learning participation. Quality factors included pre-service teachers' having a voice in determining important aspects of the service-learning; the perceived challenge of the service-learning experience, with a greater challenge resulting in more positive outcomes; the project's perceived relevance to teaching; and the opportunity to work with culturally diverse individuals. They also found that perceived support—including adequate training to perform their tasks, and help from the instructor to adjust to the experience—predicted greater gains in teaching efficacy. The final mediating variable found to predict positive outcomes for pre-service teachers' service-learning experiences was implementation of service-learning in a P–12 setting. Pre-service teachers who had collaborated with a P–12 teacher and students in planning and carrying out a service-learning project made greater gains than others in acceptance of diversity and in their intent to use service-learning in their own teaching.

There is a lack of research regarding the impact of pre-service teachers' service-learning efforts both on P–12 students and on other members of the community. In one of the few published studies in either of these areas, Al Otaiba (2005) found that both pre-service teachers and P–12 students learning English benefited from engaging in service-learning projects that involved the pre-service teachers providing tutoring in reading.

P–12 Pre-Service Teacher Education Partnerships

Although teacher education programs are ideally positioned to develop and support P–12 schools as they create service-learning experiences for their students, the number of these types of partnerships has been limited and the number of studies examining these partnerships is even smaller. Some of the partnerships that do exist are partnerships in name only and do not involve true collaboration (Pickeral, 2003). A wide variety of explanations have been offered for this situation, ranging from different cultural norms in P–12 and teacher education related to the importance of research and publication, to the lack of time both groups have available to engage in the communication essential to developing trusting relationships (Zeichner, 2006). Educators in P–12 settings are under enormous pressure to increase test scores; as a result, they have less time or inclination to work with teacher education students and faculty. Thus the number of collaborative service-learning partnerships has not grown as rapidly as it potentially could.

Given the fact that teacher education programs must work with P–12 schools in order to give their students the opportunity to apply their developing instructional skills, and the need of P–12 schools for assistance in the time-intensive processes of planning and conducting service-learning experiences, it is natural that some successful partnerships would emerge. In addition, the principles of good practice for service-learning—including mutuality, reciprocity, and democratic participation—make it a potent connector of these two educational systems (Pickeral, 2003).

Much of the literature on P–12 teacher education partnerships consists of program descriptions. Wade (1997) presented a collaborative partnership she initiated involving students in her elementary social studies methods course, senior citizens, elementary school students, and the Big Brother/Big Sister organization. She concluded that it is essential to listen to and respect the interests of all collaborators; that one should start slowly, perhaps with a small initial project, in order to work out the challenges; and that collaborative partnerships can be highly enjoyable, efficient, and successful.

Pickeral (2003) provides a detailed description of Project Connect—a service-learning partnership involving pre-service teachers from Western Washington University, local middle school students and teachers, and community agencies. The results of this collaboration indicated that participating middle school students felt more attached to their community; developed greater understanding of local, national, and international issues; and enhanced their critical thinking and self-efficacy. The teacher education students obtained practical knowledge of how to work with middle school students and teachers and how to develop and maintain a successful service-learning partnership. Project Connect benefited initially from external grant funds and subsequently from support from the university and school district.

Although designed to guide the development of campus-community partnerships, including potentially all disciplines, the Campus Compact Benchmarks for Campus/Community Partnerships (Torres, 2000, pp. 5–7) provide valuable insights for teacher educators engaged in creating service-learning partnerships with P–12 schools. These eight benchmarks are organized into three stages and offer helpful developmental insights.

Harwood and Lawson (2001) drew on their experience with Project Connect and examined the literature on collaboration to develop ten elements essential for successful P–12 teacher education partnerships. These elements include the following:

- Clear communication

- Shared goals and goal clarity

- Strengths-based practice

- Clear role expectations

- Sensitivity to community partners

Three Stages of Creating Service-Learning Partnerships with P–12 Schools

Stage I: Designing the Partnership

Genuine democratic partnerships are:

- Founded on a shared vision and clearly articulated values
- Beneficial to partnering institutions

Stage II: Building Collaborative Relationships

Genuine democratic partnerships that build strong collaborative relationships are:

- Composed of interpersonal relationships based on trust and mutual respect
- Multidimensional; they involve the participation of multiple sectors that act in service of a complex problem
- Clearly organized and led with dynamism

Stage III: Sustaining Partnerships Over Time

Genuine democratic partnerships that will be sustained over time are:

- Integrated into the mission and support systems of the partnering institutions
- Sustained by a "partnering process" for communication, decision making, and the initiation of change
- Evaluated regularly with a focus on both methods and outcomes

- Liability and regulatory issues

- Preparation for service

- Reflection

- Celebration

- Project evaluation

They report that when these elements are applied, the results for all partners can be "tremendously rewarding and revitalizing" (p. 246).

Overview of the SCSC Partnership

The Student Coalition for Strengthening Communities (SCSC) was established to provide opportunities for P–12 students, P–12 teachers, pre-service teachers, and teacher education faculty to work together to develop, implement, and assess service-learning activities that address social injustices in their communities. The partnership includes students and teachers from over a dozen middle and high schools in the metropolitan area of Seattle, Washington, and pre-service teachers (called *teacher candidates*) in the Master in Teaching (MiT) program at Seattle University, who move through the four-quarter program in cohorts of fifty. Four of the partners—three high schools and the MiT program—are described in more detail further along in this chapter. Seattle University is a Jesuit institution and strongly supports the 465-year Jesuit commitment to employing education as a force to work for a more just society. This commitment is advanced by a centerpiece of the MiT program: a three-credit, required course titled *Service*

Leadership for Social Justice (TEED 520). The course uses the definition of social justice developed by Adams, Bell, and Griffin (1997):

> [A] socially just society is one in which all members have their basic needs met. In addition, in a just society all individuals are physically and psychologically safe and secure, able to develop their full capacities and capable of interacting democratically with others. (p. 3)

The course extends over all four quarters of the MiT program, although teacher candidates register for the course and receive a grade only in the fourth quarter. A primary goal of this course is preparing new teachers to be willing and able to implement service-learning with their future P–12 students. To accomplish this goal, a major component of this course involves teacher candidates' working in small groups of two to four to collaborate with a P–12 school to design and implement a service-learning project that addresses a social justice issue. The teacher candidates choose a P–12 school to work with from a dozen schools that desire to engage in service-learning with the MiT program. Many schools want to partner with the MiT program because the teacher candidates provide much-needed support for their service-learning efforts; the candidates address a genuine need of the P–12 schools. The teacher candidates also draw on the assets of each P–12 partner as they collaborate with the students and teachers at that school to carry out a service-learning project. Teachers and students from each prospective P–12 school come to the university to present their school and service-learning possibilities. Teacher candidates question them, begin brainstorming possible activities, and then choose which of the schools they wish to partner with. Allowing the teacher candidates to choose their service-learning partner has resulted in increased motivation among the pre-service teachers and a commitment to doing the high-quality, intense work over an extended period that is usually needed to make service-learning a success. In a like manner, the high school students and teachers interview the teacher candidates who have expressed an interest in collaborating and then determine whether those individuals would likely work well in their school setting.

The teacher candidates report that they are attracted to the three SCSC schools that will be described here because the teachers from these schools are graduates of the Seattle University MiT program and therefore have a strong understanding of both service-learning and the structure of the MiT program. They also note that the three schools demonstrate a clear commitment to using service-learning to address social justice issues, and they present themselves as well-organized and successful. In addition, teacher candidates find these schools easy to work with because they are all located within a few miles of the Seattle University campus. Approximately half of the dozen partnership schools express an interest in service-learning focused on a social justice concern, and roughly 75 percent of the teachers involved are graduates of the MiT program. These teachers are clearly informed that there is no guarantee that teacher candidates will help them with their service-learning, so they must present themselves, their students, and their service-learning program in a way that will attract these prospective teachers. MiT faculty give preference for inclusion in the program to those schools with high numbers of low-income and minority students, although there are participating schools from wealthier suburban communities as well as parochial and other private schools.

Roles and Responsibilities

After establishing the partnership relationship, the P–12 teachers, teacher candidates, and the MiT faculty meet to brainstorm possible approaches to developing a service-learning project. These approaches all involve the high school students' playing an important role in deciding what will be done and how the process will unfold. The process differs at each school based on the student interests, skills, curricular focus for that semester, and number of students involved. Service-learning projects at all these schools involve joint ownership; that is, the P–12 students, teachers, and teacher candidates share the decision making, work, successes, and challenges of carrying out their project.

The teacher candidates, P–12 students, and teachers also clarify the roles and responsibilities that each will take on to ensure the success of the project. This is facilitated by having each group of teacher candidates develop a service-learning action plan—an in-depth plan that details how all phases of the service-learning will be conducted. The middle and high school students and the experienced P–12 teachers also provide input into the content of these plans and offer suggestions to the teacher candidates. Once the initial partnering relationship is established, the MiT faculty members play a lesser role, engaging the teacher candidates in reflection activities and occasionally problem solving when difficult issues arise.

The teacher candidates each spend an average of thirty-seven hours working on the service-learning over the course of three to four months. They often introduce service-learning to the high school students, design and lead reflection sessions, do the back-ground preparation work with the broader community to set the stage for successful service-learning, accompany high school students as they engage the community, transport the high school students, teach academic content that integrates with the service and social justice action, and assess high school students' learn-ing and service performance. As a result, they learn how to plan and implement a service-learning project while providing service and support to busy high school teachers and students. The high school teachers provide oversight and guidance to the teacher candidates and step in where needed to keep the project mov-ing forward. This may involve any phase of the service-learning, especially if the teacher candidates are not available on a day when it is necessary to accomplish a specific task. The teacher candidates are also taking other teacher preparation coursework concurrently with their service-learning course. The high school students make most of the key decisions regarding the focus and logistics of their projects, and they collaborate as equals with the teacher candidates.

The Partnership Capstone Conference

The SCSC partnership for each cohort of teacher candidates concludes with the Seattle University Master in Teaching Service Leadership Conference. This professional conference gives the partners who worked on the various projects an opportunity to come together to reflect critically on their successes and challenges, and in so doing to begin the process of planning the next year's service-learning. This two-day conference typically draws 175 to 200 people, including P–12 students, teachers, community partners, the parents of younger P–12 students, the teacher candidates, and Seattle University faculty and staff. Teacher candidates from the next cohort often attend to gain an understanding of what has been done with service-learning by those ahead of them in the program. The conference serves to homogenize the learning and experiences of all parties involved. The conference also gives the P–12 students an opportunity to present their projects to an audience composed of many adults who are knowledgeable regarding service-learning and many social justice issues.

Partner Descriptions

The MiT program works with educational partners that include The Center School, The John Stanford Public Service and Political Science Academy at Franklin High School, and the John Marshall Transition Center. Here, these schools and the MiT program are described along with accounts of the particular partnership's outcomes.

The Center School

The Center School, opened in 2001, is a small (three hundred students) public school located in the heart of Seattle. The school has worked hard to build its arts reputation, and there is another element of the Center School that sets it apart from many other schools: a strong emphasis on civic engagement. The school has recently revised its mission to capture this emphasis: "The Center School will empower and inspire all students to positively impact the world." Civic engagement has become a core value of the Center School, largely because of the powerful presence of service-learning.

Service-learning occurs primarily in the eleventh grade humanities class, Citizenship and Social Justice. This class is the Center School's nontraditional answer to a traditional government, law, and society class, with American literature integrated with the social studies. The class is centered on social justice issues, primarily poverty, labor history, racism, and feminism. The fall service-learning project is a great example of how the integration of social studies, literature, and social justice works. Each fall, students are immersed in the topic of poverty. Students read Barbara Ehrenreich's Nickel and Dimed, visit health and human service organizations, and take part in lessons designed to give students a broad understanding of the gravity of poverty in their community. Thus, students assess the community need for human services, an important part of service-learning. Next, the Health and Human Services Project begins, the heart of service-learning at the Center School. Each fall students are confronted with the following guiding question during the Seattle City Council's budget process: How should the city council act in response to the mayor's proposed funding of health and human services? Students then learn how city government works, as well as the details of the mayor's budget. They hear a number of perspectives on the budget, including the viewpoints of the mayor, a conservative economist, and a human services provider. After considering these multiple viewpoints, students, in small groups, take a position on the guiding question and develop a detailed plan justifying their position. The final phase of the Health and Human Services Project is the most engaging: advocacy. Individually, students write and send letters to their city council members. In small groups, students advocate by choosing one of the following group advocacy options: spearheading a public education campaign through flyer distribution, writing and publishing editorials, creating and airing public service announcements, initiating a postcard campaign, or testifying at a public hearing. In short, students learn about the democratic process by participating in it. The culmination of this project is required attendance at the public hearing on the city budget, at which students testify to council members and enthusiastically support each other. Through this project, multiple course learning targets are met: students learn extensively about poverty, the city council, the city budget, advocacy tools, and the power of participation in the democratic process—especially because so far every year the city council has agreed with the students' positions.

Partnering with Seattle University's MiT program has been critical to the success of the Health and Human Services Project. The project is immense, consuming much of the curriculum in October. Furthermore, students work in small groups for much of the project, each group working on a different aspect. The teacher candidates ensure that each group receives sufficient supervision and guidance to successfully accomplish its task. Partnering is also important because it further demonstrates that the work done in class has an impact beyond the classroom walls, making the work more relevant to the students. Finally, because teacher candidates will soon have their own classrooms, the hope is that they will internalize how effective service-learning can be so that they too will incorporate it into their own classrooms.

Outcomes. There is copious evidence demonstrating that this project should be replicated. During the second year of the project, the new principal was nervous about the students getting so involved politically. However, students' post-project reflections indicated that the project had an overwhelmingly positive impact.

I learned a lot about city government and the budget process because of this project.

- Strongly Disagree: 0
- Disagree: 0
- Agree: 14
- Strongly Agree: 17

I believe learning about the government through active participation is an effective and great way to learn about it.

- Strongly Disagree: 0
- Disagree: 1
- Agree: 12
- Strongly Agree: 18

Because of this project, I am more likely to participate in the future in the democratic process.

- Strongly Disagree: 1
- Disagree: 7
- Agree: 14
- Strongly Agree: 9

This project has helped me become a more active citizen.

- Strongly Disagree: 0
- Disagree: 3
- Agree: 17
- Strongly Agree: 11

Individual reflections by students make an even stronger case. Here are a few excerpts from student reflections following the culminating public hearing:

"[The hearing] was, without a doubt, the best experience I have ever had at a school-related event."

"That was amazing! It was surreal, it was life changing . . . I must admit for most of the class, I was hesitant to believe that we, the kids, could make a difference, make a change. It was amazing!"

"I thought it was the most important thing I have ever done in my whole life."

"I knew that our group was made up of powerful people with extraordinary talent, but I had no idea we would leave the impact we did."

"CENTER SCHOOL ROCKED THE HOUSE! We were incredible. I have never felt so powerful in all my life. I actually feel that we made a difference, THROUGH SCHOOL!"

Further evidence of the project's success is the city council's agreement with the students' positions. Does that mean students are simply smart enough to pick the winning side? This is perhaps an overly simplistic explanation. One city council member wrote to the students, "I can honestly say your voices were heard." A powerful state legislator involved behind the scenes of the budget process said that he witnessed firsthand the students' tipping of the scales in the city council's decision.

Challenges. This success, however, did not come without challenges, the biggest being time. Organizing service-learning activities with five to ten different human service organizations is the most time-consuming task, but it has become successively easier as human service organizations have witnessed the quality testimony of students at the public hearings. It also takes a great deal of time to organize guest speakers, who have included economists, homeless people, city finance officials, and elected officials. Another challenge is making the project mesh with the schedule of the teacher candidates. Because the teacher candidates are completing other courses in the MiT program, they cannot be at the Center School on a daily basis; this can make it challenging to establish a rhythm for the project.

The John Stanford Public Service and Political Science Academy at Franklin High School

The John Stanford Public Service and Political Science Academy (JSPSA) at Franklin High School was created in 1999 by a small group of concerned government employees to address an aging and increasingly homogeneous public service sector. Based on the academic and social challenges faced by students at Franklin, particularly African American students, JSPSA was designed to provide a small-group, personalized education with the following goals:

1. To provide a challenging college preparatory curriculum;
2. To expose students to the public sector (government at all levels and the nonprofit world); and
3. To create and nurture a life-long ethic of service. (Franklin High School, 2009)

Franklin High School students elect to participate in one of six small learning communities prior to their sophomore year. Approximately fifty-five students are selected, based on individual preference and capacity to participate in the JSPSA for the last three years of their high school career. Currently, JSPSA serves approximately 150 students in the tenth, eleventh, and twelfth grades.

JSPSA strives to make its program rigorous, relevant, and based on personal relationships. To that end, JSPSA offers a challenging academic curriculum and complementary activities in two strands: service-learning and career-based learning. These activities help students find their passion, understand the interconnected nature of our world, connect with adult role models, and become more engaged in their schoolwork. Service-learning is integrated into all JSPSA core classes during all three years of the program.

Students are introduced to public service and service-learning at a required two-day retreat in the fall of their sophomore year. Students then take their language arts and social studies classes in conjunction, and their teachers work as a team to provide a rigorous and integrated academic experience for students. Throughout their sophomore year, students are encouraged to participate in a twenty-week cross-aged tutoring, service-learning project. Teacher candidates work with Franklin students and teachers to design the project, and it has grown in caliber and enthusiasm each year. The main focus of the project is on JSPSA students' tutoring of fourth graders from a nearby elementary school in writing and math.

In the eleventh grade, JSPSA juniors complete a legislative student voice project. This project is the result of collaboration between teacher candidates and language arts and social studies teachers in the academy. These groups work together to design and carry out an integrated service-learning experience during the legislative session each year. Students study the state legislative process in their history class, read legislation, and write legislative briefs and position papers in their language arts class. They then select pieces of legislation pending in the state legislature to advocate for or against. Next, the students write letters to the editor, prepare petitions, and hold community discussions around their chosen legislation. They "mock testify" before a panel of community members with extensive experience working with the Washington state legislature in support of or in opposition to proposed legislation. The students, staff, and teacher candidates then spend a day at the Washington state legislature, meeting with district legislators, attending public hearings, and advocating for or against proposed legislation.

Outcomes. More than half of the students in the junior and senior classes completed a survey on student attitudes by the Corporation for National and Community Service following their service-learning projects. As part of the service-learning survey, youth were asked questions to gauge their attitudes before and after service-learning activities. In all ten areas assessed, JSPSA students indicated that there was positive change in their awareness of community needs, communication, enjoyment of reading, and compassion. Two areas particularly stood out in terms of change. The greatest reported changes for students were their feeling that "I have plans to volunteer in the future" (28 percent) and "I understand other points of view about community issues" (23 percent).

Reflections gathered from sophomore students about their understanding of community needs and their role in creating community change were positive. Students expressed an increased understanding of community problems and a sense of empowerment as a result of their service. Staff members noticed the development of significant compassion and maturity among students as a result of their participation in service-learning activities at all grade levels.

The John Marshall Transition Center

The John Marshall Transition Center (MTC) is the most restrictive environment provided by the Seattle Public Schools for special education students whose Individualized Educational Plan (IEP) indicates that they have a learning disability related to an emotional behavior disorder. To be placed in the MTC program, students must have had an unsuccessful experience in another self-contained educational program in the district. The MTC program includes five classrooms and twelve staff. The majority of students spend the entire day at the MTC; a few are involved in other classes at an alternative high school. MTC students periodically become a danger to themselves or others; therefore, physical restraints and isolation cells are used, when needed. Approximately 80 percent of MTC enrollees are African-American males. During the 2005–06 school year, four of the students were shot, and most were arrested at least once. A majority of the students were on probation and assigned probation officers.

Service-learning empowers MTC students by giving them an opportunity to contribute to the community and successfully complete an area of study. Ideally, they become experts and share their expertise with the community. This is a scenario that none of the students had experienced prior to the MTC partnership with the MiT program. Service-learning is presented to students as a way to complete the sixty community service hours that are required by the Seattle School District for graduation. The guidelines are that service-learning will (1) address a genuine need in the community and (2) include an educational component for them.

Teacher candidates gain experience in working with adolescents who have special needs, and they learn how service-learning can be used to assist these students to transition back to mainstream high schools. The teacher candidates periodically visit MTC prior to the beginning of their service-learning experience to develop a positive relationship with the students. The teacher candidates introduce the concept of service-learning to the MTC students and guide them in a process of identifying a service-learning project that arouses their interest. The 2005–06 project involved cross-age tutoring with preschool children at the nearby First African Methodist Episcopal (AME) Head Start Program. Because the MTC students themselves came up with this project idea, they approached it with a high degree of buy-in.

Program Ideals and Teacher Candidate Responsibilities. A case that illustrates service-learning's potential impact is that of one student, M. Not every MTC student has such a positive experience, but M.'s case provides a valuable example of the program's hoped-for outcomes and the teacher candidates' roles in facilitating them.

M. had been incarcerated and remanded to psychiatric wards numerous times in the seven years prior to beginning tenth grade at MTC. He had been in highly restrictive special programs for the previous eight years without much progress. He was notorious for his emotional outbursts, violence toward staff, and highly sophisticated forms of vandalism. His IEP goals focused primarily on behavioral issues, including reducing his emotional outbursts. Early in the school year, MTC staff learned of M.'s passion for gardening and hiking. They decided to include M. in the service-learning program because they felt he could be more successful outside the restraints of the classroom walls and focused on the environment and community.

M. began a service-learning project that empowered him as a critical thinker. He directed his own studies of the environment and developed lesson plans for students at Head Start. M. was motivated to share his love of the environment with children who rarely get outside the city. M.'s lessons ranged from geology to gardening. He directed field trips to local parks, introducing students to the variety of plant life that surrounds them in the city. Before M. began this service-learning program, most staff had assumed he would never leave John Marshall's Transition Center; however, through his successful completion of this service-learning program, M. was able to transition to a regular high school. Service-learning provided a means for M. to demonstrate that he is capable of making a positive contribution to the community. He took ownership of the project and succeeded. MTC staff believe that had M. not participated in this service-learning project, he would still be at the MTC.

As a result of his participation in the cross-age tutoring service-learning project, M. achieved all his IEP goals and displayed no emotional outbursts once the service-learning project was under way. He continues to be successful at his new high school; he has joined the marching band and participated in homecoming activities. Service-learning was effective for M. because it provided him with a venue in which he could see himself being successful and contributing to the community. Each time M. arrived at First AME, staff were able to see his self-esteem grow, and he began exuding a newfound self-confidence.

The teacher candidates met with M. before, during, and after the service-learning experience to assist in making it successful. They developed a personal relationship with him, because there were enough teacher candidates to work one-to-one with the MTC students. M. asked many questions about college, and the teacher candidates provided him and other MTC students with a tour of the Seattle University campus. This was very valuable because no one in M.'s family had ever attended college. This exposure helped M. and other MTC students begin to see going to college as a tangible possibility for them.

Teacher candidates worked out the logistics of the service-learning experience, including transportation, scheduling, and liability issues. They also led reflection sessions and helped to emotionally and educationally prepare the MTC students for the cross-age tutoring experience by preparing and teaching lessons on how to be an effective tutor.

The Seattle University Master in Teaching (MiT) Program

As described earlier in this chapter, the Seattle University MiT program is a four-quarter, sixty-credit program designed to prepare new teachers for success in public and private P–12 schools. The program is structured around a cohort model, with two cohorts of fifty students each completing the program every academic year. Students are required to have a bachelor's degree prior to program admission. On completion of the program, approximately half the graduates are certified to teach at the elementary level while the other half focus on secondary schools. The average age of students is twenty-eight, and many come to the program with advanced degrees and/or considerable experience in other careers, including experience with service-learning as a learner in high school and/or as a college undergraduate.

The course, TEED 520, *Service Leadership for Social Justice*, serves as a fulcrum for relationships between MiT and its school partners. This service-learning topical course fits well with the mission and guiding beliefs and assumptions of the MiT program. The course, which was described in greater detail earlier, is rooted in this guiding belief:

> The social responsibilities of teaching are of fundamental importance to the program. These social responsibilities guide teachers to connect the classroom with the school and community to allow students to apply their learning to address real issues related to justice and global human rights. (Erickson & Anderson, 1997, p. 215)

This three-credit course extends over all four quarters of the MiT program. A primary course goal is to develop teacher candidates' commitment to incorporating service-learning into their future P–12 teaching. To achieve this outcome, all teacher candidates receive instruction regarding what service-learning is and how it can be used as a successful teaching method with their future P–12 students, including the completion of a service-learning lesson plan. They also participate in a service-learning project as learners, and they work closely with P–12 students, teachers, and other community members to design and conduct a service-learning project linked to the P–12 students academic curriculum. These three components of instruction—receiving instruction and completing a lesson plan, participating as learners, and conducting a project—have been identified as essential to preparing new teachers to implement service-learning with their future P–12 students (Wade et al., 1999). During the first quarter of Service Leadership for Social Justice, teacher candidates participate in a short-term group service-learning project designed to assist them in understanding how community service can be closely linked to the curriculum and used to achieve academic objectives. This is followed by detailed instruction regarding key principles of good practice for the use of service-learning with P–12 students (Anderson & Hill, 2001).

In the program's second quarter, teacher candidates partner with a P–12 school to design and implement a service-learning project such as those described earlier in this chapter. The MiT program has long-term, deep relationships with the majority of these schools. Each year several new schools are selected to work with current teacher candidates. The teachers at these schools are Seattle University MiT graduates who have been teaching for several years and have developed their service-learning skills to the point where they can effectively work with current teacher candidates to make a quantum leap forward in the quality and quantity of their service-learning. In this way, the current teacher candidates support the service-learning efforts of those who have come before them in the program and thereby enhance their understanding of the successful use of service-learning with P–12 students. The teacher candidates take other teacher-education courses during the time they engage in service-learning and meet regularly on campus to reflect on their service-learning experiences. During this quarter, the course helps teacher candidates develop their own understandings of what social justice entails. It also illustrates how service-learning can be an effective method for providing P–12 students with the knowledge and skills needed for standardized tests while helping them strengthen their communities by addressing unjust social conditions.

Before they implement their service-learning projects, teacher candidates collaborate with the P–12 teacher and students and with other community members to create a service-learning action plan. These plans, usually eight to ten pages long, address all key components of service-learning by applying the principles of high-quality service-learning studied in the first quarter of the MiT program.

During the third quarter of the MiT program, students engage in a full-time student teaching internship. Approximately half of them find a way to integrate a small service-learning project into a unit they teach during the internship, although this is not required. In the fourth and final quarter of the MiT program, all teacher candidates participate in the capstone Service Leadership Conference described earlier.

Outcomes. Research and program assessment data collected regarding teacher candidates' achievement of primary course goals indicate that the course is successfully fulfilling its purposes. George, Hunt, Nixon, Ortiz, and Anderson (1995) found that 86 percent of teacher candidates, surveyed anonymously at the time of their graduation, intended to use service-learning in their teaching, and Wade et al. (1999) found an even higher intent to incorporate service-learning (93 percent). More recently, Lyness (2006) reported a similar degree of desire to use service-learning (88 percent). It is clear from these data that a strong majority of MiT students leave the program fully intending to incorporate service-learning into their teaching.

The degree of actual service-learning implementation during teachers' first two years of full-time employment has also been measured on three separate occasions. George et al. (1995) found that 25 percent of MiT graduates did use service-learning as a teaching method with their P–12 students during their first two years of teaching. Wade et al. (1999) reported that 35 percent of the graduates surveyed had implemented service-learning, and Lyness (2006) found that 29 percent had done so. MiT graduates in all three studies cited lack of time to plan and lack of space in the curriculum as the main reasons why they did not use service-learning, despite their intention to do so. Given the challenges faced by beginning teachers, especially in an environment emphasizing high-stakes testing, a 30-percent implementation rate for service-learning can be seen as a successful outcome of participation in the MiT program.

MiT program assessment data indicate that most teacher candidates come to the program with a strong belief that an important component of schooling should include a focus on social justice. Eighty-four percent of students agreed or strongly agreed with the statement, "Schools should teach that good democratic citizenship goes beyond obeying the law. It means consideration for social justice rather than regard for selfish interests." Eighty-eight percent agreed or strongly agreed that "Schools should teach active participation in the community in order to help students learn a sense of responsibility and obligation to others." After completion of the MiT program, these percentages increased to 92 percent and 96 percent, respectively. After program completion, 90 percent of MiT graduates agreed or strongly agreed that "I am now more knowledgeable regarding specific methods I can use to teach for social justice than I was at the beginning of this program."

These comments from two teacher candidates who begin the MiT program without an understanding of service-learning or a commitment to social justice help demonstrate how an experience with service-learning can facilitate their growth:

> This course started out as a requirement, another thing to do. It ended up changing me. I have a deeper, more realistic understanding of social injustice and what schools can do to help. Very meaningful! I'm a good model for why service-learning will work with reluctant P–12 students as well.
>
> When I first heard about service-learning this year, I was interested only intellectually. I would have agreed with service-learning enthusiasts that it was the right thing to do, that a world in which service-learning was the norm both in and out of school would be a better place to live. I might have even agreed that it was my responsibility as a teacher to work toward that world,

but I wouldn't have done it. I was a service-learning fan, not an eager participant. But at some point the preaching about reflection in service-learning and the preaching about reflection in education from all of the MiT courses reached a critical mass in me. I understood that my service-learning project could be better, that it could have some goals, that it could be more than community service, and most importantly, that I could make it so. It was really no more than constant repetition finally being internalized, but to me it was an epiphany. Service-learning isn't beyond regular teaching; it is regular teaching, or it can be. It is a method I can use with regular teaching, as surely as I can use cooperative learning or discussions. So, I'm going to use it. And I now know it is worth using before I am completely comfortable with teaching, because the kind of teaching I want to become comfortable with is the kind that incorporates service-learning.

These two quotes provide support for the hypothesis that service-learning can be a successful pedagogy for teacher candidates. Many teacher candidates are more likely to *act* their way into new ways of thinking about teaching, schools, and social justice than they are to *think* their way into new ways of taking action in these areas. Jesuit Superior-General Peter-Hans Kolvenbach (2000) supported this proposition, and the use of service-learning as a pedagogy, stating, "[W]hen the heart is touched by direct experience, the mind may be challenged to change."

Reflection on the Program's Challenges and Potentials

The partnership described in this chapter demonstrates how two of the Benchmarks for Campus/Community Partnerships developed by Campus Compact (Torres, 2000, pp. 5–7) can be used to achieve success for all partners: first, genuine democratic partnerships are beneficial to partnering institutions; and second, genuine democratic partnerships that build strong collaborative relationships are composed of interpersonal relationships based on trust and mutual respect. In addition, all ten of the elements for successful collaboration identified by Harwood and Lawson (2001) are present to some extent in this partnership. However, the partnership is distinctive in regard to two of these elements: shared goals and goal clarity, and strengths-based practice. All four of these components needed for the creation of partnership success are discussed in this section.

The concrete benefits received by all of the high schools involved in this partnership and the Seattle University MiT program are practical and occur in every cycle of partnership interaction. Although these benefits alone are not sufficient for maintaining the partnership, without them the collaborative activities would soon fall by the wayside because the costs of partnering are too high in terms of time and effort. The benefits of partnering are not only concrete; they are essential to the success of the service-learning programs at each of the partnering institutions. Without the support of the teacher candidates, many of the high school service-learning projects would not happen at all, and those that would still take place would be smaller in scale and limited in quality. This is one reason why there is a waiting list of schools eager to partner with the MiT program. Without the partner high schools, the teacher candidates would not be able to have a hands-on experience of service-learning or learn from a teacher experienced in the use of service-learning with P–12 students. This would seriously diminish the quality of the service-learning preparation they receive.

Deep interpersonal relationships take time to develop and regular attention to maintain. The partners described in this chapter are able to short-circuit this process somewhat because the necessary relationships have already been established prior to the beginning of the partnerships. The university faculty and teacher candidates who relate well on a personal level and who share a similar educational philosophy are the only individuals considered for potential partners. Essentially, the MiT faculty cherry-pick the best of their graduates to partner with, and from this group they choose only those they relate well with on a personal level. This group is further narrowed to include only those graduates who take teaching positions within the greater Seattle metropolitan area and who are in a school that supports implementation of service-learning or at least allows it. Because one hundred students graduate each year and most of them gain employment in the Seattle area, even with these selective criteria there are still more MiT grads who want to partner with the MiT program than there are partners needed.

One issue that needs to be addressed at the beginning of each partner relationship is that of power dynamics. The MiT graduates have been used to deferring somewhat to their professor, but now they are equal partners in new roles. This requires an open discussion of the relationship and the decision-making roles of all parties. This has not been a difficult issue, partly because it is addressed early on and partly because the new teachers very quickly take the initiative to relate as equal partners. This is one reason they engage in service-learning and a reason they were selected as partners: they are assertive, risk-taking teachers who take the initiative to advocate for their students and institutions.

Because all of the high school teachers involved in the partnership have participated in the MiT program and have personally experienced the MiT service-learning course, they have a clear understanding of the goals of the program and what is needed to make the process a success. And because the MiT graduates are selected for inclusion in the partnership based, in part, on their commitment to using service-learning to address issues of social injustice, and the MiT teacher candidates are also studying this same use of service-learning, it is a fairly easy process to develop a deep understanding of the goals of service-learning for both the high school students and the teacher candidates.

Having an established relationship prior to beginning the partnership ensures that all parties have an understanding of each other's assets and limitations. This helps reduce the time and effort needed to conduct assets-and-needs assessments and quickly get to the point of designing plans that will build on the strengths of each party. For example, the teacher leader of the Center School service-learning project is highly politically astute and knowledgeable. Knowing this, the MiT faculty can encourage teacher candidates who have similar interests to collaborate with this teacher. Similarly, the MTC teacher is a highly motivating speaker and relates very well to teacher candidates, so he is often asked to present on service-learning and special education as a part of the on-campus portion of the MiT service-learning course.

The collaboration between the Seattle University MiT program and the schools involved in the partnership has proven to be very successful in achieving each partner's goals for student learning and community impact. These successes didn't come easily; earning them entailed dealing with several important challenges that remain as issues to be managed each year the partnership functions. These challenges are similar to those described by Pickeral (2003).

The first challenge relates to lack of time for all parties to prepare for and implement service-learning in their curriculum. All teachers and teacher education faculty report they are overloaded with work related to their normal job responsibilities. It is hard for them to find the additional time necessary to communicate, nurture the partnership relationship, and prepare students for successful service-learning. All report that once the partnership was established, this time requirement diminished somewhat but never disappeared completely. Having teacher candidates available to help facilitate preparation for service-learning activities also helped reduce the amount of teacher time required, but if a teacher candidate experienced a problem or had difficulty adjusting to the service-learning experience, more time was required from both P–12 teachers and university faculty to resolve these issues.

A related challenge is lack of space in the curriculum for service-learning activities. All partners have adjusted their courses to allow time for students to engage in service, reflect on service experiences, and demonstrate their learning. Despite these adjustments, pressure remains to condense service-learning in order to focus on other, often more traditional goals and classroom activities.

A third challenge has to do with logistics. Arranging schedules to allow time for teacher candidates to be at the schools on the dates essential for service-learning requires considerable flexibility and willingness to compromise from all parties involved. Because the teacher candidates are taking several other courses on campus at Seattle University at the same time they are working on service-learning, their schedules must be juggled and all of the MiT faculty need to give them some leeway in terms of assignment due dates and arranging the course schedule. This hasn't been a major problem, because these faculty do support the use of service-learning in the MiT program, but it is a continuous issue that must be constantly managed. It is essential that the service-learning faculty member maintain positive working relationships with colleagues. In addition, the high school teachers must adjust their class schedules to involve their students in service-learning at those times that the teacher candidates can be present. These teachers regularly request more dates to work with the teacher candidates than are available.

Another challenge involves the ownership and decision-making roles of the various parties in planning and carrying out the service-learning projects. The most successful projects provide the high school students, teachers, and teacher candidates with a meaningful role in deciding how key components of the project will be conducted. By giving all parties this type of voice, they all gain a sense of ownership in the project and are motivated to perform their best to make the project successful. When the high school teachers set up a project that is fully formed, with no room left for the teacher candidates to exercise their creativity, the teacher candidates experience frustration—and less professional growth. Similarly, if the teacher candidates are given carte blanche and told they can do whatever they want, frustration also results. They usually do not have the teaching experience or knowledge of the students, curriculum, or community needed to take complete responsibility for the success of a service-learning project. It's important that the high school teachers and MiT faculty give the teacher candidates a general framework for service-learning and guidance and support with crucial issues, while allowing the teacher candidates and high school students, along with community members, to plan and carry out the project details. This balance of structure and opportunity isn't easy to achieve, and it must be reestablished with each new group of teacher candidates.

We intend to build on the strengths and successes of the SCSC partnership by following the guidance provided by the Campus Compact Benchmarks and the elements developed by Harwood and Lawson (2001). Specifically, we need to develop structures and policies that will ensure the sustainability of the partnership over time. This will require finding ways to more deeply integrate a commitment to the mission of the partnership into the culture, policies, and practices of all the institutions involved. At present, institutional support consists of resources from Seattle University and verbal support from all the partnering institutions. However, more resources are needed—especially time to allow partners to go into greater depth in collaborative activities. Also, all the active partners at present are P–12 teachers, students, or university faculty; active involvement at higher levels (department, school, college, school district) would allow the formation of a formal partnership agreement between institutions rather than between individuals who happen to work at specific institutions. This may also help us to obtain external grant funds to build and sustain the partnership on all these levels.

We desire to put more effort into assessing partnership outcomes. Specifically, we want to more closely examine P–12 student learning outcomes and go much deeper into examining the processes we use to collaborate with community partners, such as the AME, legislators, and homeless shelters and other community-based organizations. There is also a need for much more assessment of the extent to which the organizations' desired outcomes are being achieved.

Implementing successful service-learning partnerships is an incredibly rewarding and revitalizing experience for P–12 teachers and students, teacher educators, and teacher candidates. Despite the hard work and messiness of all service-learning, the benefits far outweigh the costs. Collaboration among educators who know and respect each other, and who share similar beliefs and values, facilitates the partnership process. It is a win-win-win situation; teacher candidates and their faculty, P–12 teachers and students, and the larger community all benefit from the work inspired by these partnerships. All these collaborators learn with and from each other as they strengthen the roots of service-learning in their respective institutions and ensure that a greater number of service-learning opportunities will be available for P–12 students in the future.

References

Adams, M., Bell, L. A., & Griffin, P. (Eds.). (1997). *Teaching for diversity and social justice: A sourcebook*. New York: Routledge.

Al Otaiba, S. (2005). How effective is code-based reading tutoring in English for English learners and pre-service teacher-tutors? *Remedial and Special Education, 26*(4), 245–254. Retrieved October 4, 2006, from Education Abstracts database.

Anderson, J. B., & Erickson, J. A. (2003). Service-learning in pre-service teacher education. *Academic Exchange Quarterly, 7*(2), 111–115.

Anderson, J. B., & Hill, D. (2001). Principles of good practice for service-learning in preservice teacher education. In J. Anderson, K. Swick, & J. Yff (Eds.), *Service-learning in teacher education: Enhancing the growth of new teachers, their students, and communities* (pp. 69–84). Washington, DC: American Association of Colleges for Teacher Education.

Anderson, J. B., Swick, K. J., & Yff, J. (Eds.). (2001). *Service-learning in teacher education: Enhancing the growth of new teachers, their students, and communities.* Washington, DC: American Association of Colleges for Teacher Education.

Boyle-Baise, M. (1998). Community service learning for multicultural education: An exploratory study with pre-service teachers. *Equity and Excellence in Education, 31*(2), 52–60.

Erickson, J. A., & Anderson, J. B. (1997). Learning with the community: Concepts and models for service-learning in teacher education. Washington, DC: American Association for Higher Education.

Franklin High School (2009). Franklin Small Learning Communities: The John Stanford Public Service Academy. Online content available at: http://www.franklinquakers.org/program/academies.htm

George, N., Hunt, S., Nixon, D., Ortiz, R., & Anderson, J. (1995). Beginning teachers' perceptions and use of community service-learning as a teaching method. Paper presented at the National Service-Learning Conference, Philadelphia.

Harwood, A. M., & Lawson, R. (2001). Developing rich collaborations between schools, universities, and community partners. In J. B. Anderson, K. J. Swick, and J. Yff (Eds.), *Service-learning in teacher education: Enhancing the growth of new teachers, their students, and communities* (pp. 234–247). Washington, DC: American Association of Colleges for Teacher Education.

Kolvenbach, P.-H. (2000). The service of faith and the promotion of justice in American Jesuit higher education. Justice conferences: The commitment to justice in Jesuit higher education. Santa Clara, CA: Bannan Institute.

Lyness, L. (2006). Beginning teachers' experiences with service-learning. Paper presented at the International Service-Learning Research conference, Portland, OR.

Pickeral, T. (2003). Partnerships with elementary and secondary education. In B. Jacoby and Associates (Eds.), *Building partnerships for service-learning.* San Francisco: Jossey-Bass.

Potthoff, D., Dinsmore, J., Stirtz, G., Walsh, T., Ziebarth, J., & Eifler, K. (2000). Preparing for democracy and diversity: The impact of a community-based field experience on pre-service teachers' knowledge, skills, and attitudes. *Action in Teacher Education, 22*(1), 79–92.

Root, S., & Callahan, J. (2000). Service-learning in teacher education: A multisite study. Paper presented at the Fourth Annual Michigan Campus Compact Faculty Institute, East Lansing, MI.

Root, S., Callahan, J., & Sepanski, J. (2002). Service-learning in teacher education: A consideration of qualitative and quantitative outcomes. In A. Furco & S. Billig (Eds.), *Service-learning: The essence of pedagogy* (pp. 223–244). Greenwich, CT: Information Age Publishing.

Torres, J. (Ed.). (2000). Benchmarks for campus/community partnerships. Boston: Campus Compact, 5–7.

Wade, R. (1997). Collaborating with the community: A campus-based teacher educator's story. In J. A. Erickson and J. B. Anderson (Eds.), *Learning with the community: Concepts and models for service-learning in teacher education* (pp. 141–143). Washington, DC: American Association for Higher Education.

Wade, R. C., Anderson, J. B., Yarbrough, D. B., Pickeral, T., Erickson, J. A., & Kromer, T. (1999). Novice teachers' experiences of community service-learning. *Teaching and Teacher Education, 15,* 667–684.

Zeichner, K. (2006). Reflections of a university-based teacher educator on the future of college- and university-based teacher education. *Journal of Teacher Education, 57*(3), 326–340.

2

Reflections on University-School Partnerships at Providence College's Feinstein Institute for Public Service

Keith Morton and Jane Callahan

We early learned to know the children of hard-driven mothers who went out to work all day, sometimes leaving the little things in the casual care of a neighbor, but often locking them into their tenement rooms. The first three crippled children we encountered in the neighborhood had all been injured while their mothers were at work: one had fallen out of a third-story window, another had been burned, and the third had a curved spine due to the fact that for three years he had been tied all day long to the leg of the kitchen table, only released at noon by his older brother who hastily ran in from a neighboring factory to share his lunch with him.

(Addams, 1909, p. 127)

Contemporary approaches to youth work have their roots in the settlement house movement of the Progressive Era, fueled by experiences and observations like those made by Jane Addams, a cofounder in 1889 of Chicago's Hull House. The challenges, as Addams and her colleagues recognized them, were immediate: children unattended were at risk, adolescents were too-often truant and involved in a surprising amount of petty crime, too few youth either made it to or through eighth grade (as it existed in those days) or were taught a trade, and too many youth became child laborers in alienating factories and mills.

And, Addams argued, the problems were historic, abstract, and systemic. A new industrial economy produced poverty as predictably as it produced wealth. Support systems for youth and families in which all able-bodied adults had to work in order to get by were absent or inadequate. The culture sentimentalized children even as it treated them as invisible or as commodities, and contradictory, oppressive interpretations of women viewed them as homemakers even as they were pressed into factory work away from their children. In *The Spirit of Youth and City Streets*, Addams wrote,

> A certain number of the outrages upon the spirit of youth may be traced to degenerate or careless parents who totally neglect their responsibilities; a certain other large number of wrongs are due to sordid men and women who deliberately use the legitimate pleasure-seeking of young people as lures into vice. There remains, however, a third very large class of offenses . . . traceable to a dense ignorance on the part of the average citizen as to the requirements of youth, and to a persistent blindness on the part of educators as to youth's most obvious needs. (1909, p. 51)

Among her proposed solutions, not surprisingly, were the establishment of the Juvenile Protection Association, a juvenile court system, mandatory public schooling through high school, and child labor laws. At the heart of her efforts, though, were a range of community programs that connected youth with caring adults in a safe space, prepared children and youth for meaningful work, and challenged children and youth to prepare for lives as citizens and leaders in a democratic society. In short, Addams described what remain the objectives of today's youth development and after-school programs. She infused these direct service programs with her hope that children and youth educated in them would, as adult citizens, help resolve the cultural contradictions created by the harsh new realities of urban industrial capitalism.

Youth development and after-school programs today reflect these uneasy origins. As a response to contradictions in the economic and cultural systems of the United States, they are intended to provide a safe space in which children and school-age youth are nurtured, encouraged, and supported, as well as to support working parents. They help youth grow into responsible adults, preparing them to work in a system that makes after-school programs necessary. They have a measurable damping effect on local crime, but do little to remedy the age segregation of American culture that creates the opportunity for such crime (Halpern, 1999; National Institute for Out of School Time, 2006; White, 2005).

The Afterschool Alliance, for example, founded in 1999 as a national advocacy group at the instigation of the Charles Stewart Mott Foundation, makes a case for after-school programs by arguing that such programs "1. Keep kids safe. 2. Help working families. 3. Improve academic achievement" (Afterschool Alliance, 2006, 2007). The 21st Century Community Learning Centers initiative of the U.S. Department of Education was established in 2003 to support the creation of community learning centers that provide academic enrichment opportunities for children, particularly students who attend high-poverty and low-performing schools. The program helps students meet state and local student standards in core academic subjects, such as reading and math; offers students a broad array of enrichment activities that can complement their regular academic programs; and offers literacy and other educational services to the families of participating children (21st Century Community Learning Centers, 2006).

University-school partnerships are valuable precisely because they place everyone involved squarely in the cultural contradictions faced by children and youth, and they invite us to enter a cycle of reflection and action intended to work out these contradictions. William S. White, president and CEO of the Charles Stewart Mott Foundation—which played a key role in the creation of the 21st Century Community Learning Centers initiative—notes, "We know that afterschool programs provide a safe haven during nonschool hours. But we are also finding out that students who regularly participate in quality afterschool activities make better grades, complete more homework and have less absenteeism and tardiness" (White, 2005, p. 6).

Unspoken, but very near the surface, in the agenda moved so forcefully by the Charles Stewart Mott Foundation is the history that makes initiatives such as after-school programs necessary. Campus-school partnerships, we believe, are valuable precisely because they place everyone involved squarely in the cultural contradictions faced by children and youth, and they invite us to enter a cycle of reflection and action intended to work out these contradictions.

On its face, the simplest initiative in a college-based service-learning program should be working with K–8 tutoring and after-school programs, because of the following characteristics:

- Schools are fairly stable institutions, with long track records and clear lines of command.

- College students have been through school themselves, so they know the milieu and have previous experience on which they can draw.

- There is enough of an age difference between the K–8 and college students that at least one developmental stage separates them, making leadership (and classroom management) challenges easier.

The outcomes of the activities seem straightforward and tangible: help the K–8 students grow and learn in a safe and enjoyable environment. Success would seem fairly easy to measure as well. Do the program participants and college student volunteers keep returning? Do their experiences arouse their curiosity and motivate them to extend their learning beyond the scope of their present experience? Campus Compact has documented the community service initiatives of its member campuses every year since 1994 in a publication titled *Service Matters*. And in every year, as Campus Compact has grown from 305 to 975 member college campuses, programs serving children and youth have dominated service activities by a wide margin (Campus Compact, 1999–2005). A 1996 Rand Corporation study of the impact of federal Learn and Serve grants to higher education institutions found, among other things, that 75 percent of its 265 respondents were involved in programs that tried to "Improve the educational achievement of school age youth and adults," and 37 percent were working to "Further early childhood development and adult literacy" (Gray, Ondaatje, Geschwind, Robyn, & Klein, 1996, p. 15).

As straightforward as they seem, however, service-learning partnerships with K–8 schools are complicated. Since its inception in 1994, the Feinstein Institute for Public Service at Providence College has partnered with eight public and private elementary and middle schools for extended periods of time, and with three high schools on a more episodic basis. The goals of these partnerships have been to provide direct support to the schools' students, to help the schools increase their institutional capacity to accomplish their missions, and to provide Providence College's students with complex service experiences that entail questions of service, community, and democracy. This chapter describes some of our experiences with these partnerships as a way of establishing what John Dewey (1938) called the "situation" in which we are participating. We describe the work and context in which we have been involved; offer our reflections on this situation; and build on this experience and reflection to begin theorizing about campus-school partnerships.

Describing Our Experiences

For the purposes of this chapter, we draw primarily on our experiences at one public elementary and two public middle schools over a period of some twelve years. We draw, to a lesser extent, on our work with five other K–8 schools during the same period.[1] When the Feinstein Institute was starting at Providence College in 1994 and its service-based curriculum was being designed, its faculty (including us) made several decisions that shaped its direction. First, we would focus our service on supporting community institutions physically proximate to the college that promised our students a significant experience of service. We would, as well, focus disproportionately on institutions serving children and youth because doing so could tie us to the larger community's people, issues, and organizations, and because the required skills were within our students' reach. Third, we would, as much as possible, focus on community building rather than intervention and on asset identification and development. Additionally, we would concentrate on building sustainable partnerships that had a time horizon of roughly ten years.

An Elementary School

Harry Kizirian (HK) Elementary School, with so many of its students coming from the adjacent Smith Hill neighborhood, was a promising partner because it had the potential to fit all of these criteria (Morton, 1997). The school was originally designed for 450 students, but when we began working with HK in 1994, between 750 and 780 students attended each fall. More recently that number was cut to 596 students and, in 2006–2007, to 488 students. About half of HK's students are from the neighborhood, and about half are bused in. When we began our partnership, the school had two janitors, a principal, an assistant principal, and sixty teachers. At present, it has two janitors, a principal, an assistant principal, and forty-one teachers. HK has had a consistent student-teacher ratio of about twelve to one. It has relatively large populations of special needs and ESL students, however, which means that the "typical" classroom size is actually twenty-four students for one teacher and one aide—a ratio that is the district's official limit (Infoworks! 2006a). Each semester, between ten and thirty volunteers from Providence College help HK administrators and teachers with in-class tutoring and teacher assistance, and for nine years additional students, coordinated by a recent graduate, ran an after-school program two to four days per week for as many as four hundred participants.

We also hoped to work with the middle and high schools that the students from Smith Hill attended. We had initial institutional support and some resources to offer, as Providence College's vice president for external relations and planning wanted the Institute to play a role in youth development by collaborating with a newly formed Hospitals and Education Leadership for Providence Coalition (the HELP Coalition), made up of ten city-wide colleges and hospitals. This coalition, organized in large part to negotiate payment-in-lieu-of-taxes with the city, pooled financial resources that its members were then eligible to apply for. In our case, that meant an average of $12,000 per year for HK's after-school program. In addition, the Institute, working with the college's education department and HK, had secured a $250,000, three-year grant (1994–97) from the Corporation for National Service to bring service-learning into the elementary school and into the Education Department's teacher-training curriculum.

We began our work by talking with everyone who had a potential interest in the school: administrators, teachers, and officers of the teacher's union; elementary school students and parents; PTO members and other volunteers; people who lived around the school; staff of other youth-serving organizations, including the local community center and library; and Providence College students, faculty, and administrators. We talked with people at the middle and high schools. We hung out at the school a lot, and we spent a lot of time talking with the school's assistant principal, whom we respected a great deal, and with Tom Twitchell, a long-time neighborhood resident and a community organizer.

We—various iterations of all these stakeholders—put together a list of the resources we had to work with:

- Volunteers linked to college classes

- Faculty

- A CNS grant

- Off-campus work-study funds

- Youth workers from the community center

- Large numbers of children and youth willing to help start "something"

- HELP coalition funding

- A school building

- A several-acre lot adjacent to the school

A first-grade teacher who had grown up in the neighborhood and the assistant principal advocated effectively for an after-school program as the first priority of our partnership. Dialogues with people in the community also turned up issues and priorities: vacant and abandoned lots and houses, vandalism and graffiti, seniors afraid of young people, and an absence of jobs or programs for middle and high school youth.

Borrowing from the conceptual work of the West Philadelphia Improvement Corporation—a collaboration between that neighborhood and the University of Pennsylvania (Benson and Harkavy, 1997)—as well as concepts of asset-based community development drawn from various resources, a strategy emerged: to treat the school as a neighborhood hub and to design projects that drew together the greatest number of different groups while simultaneously addressing the greatest number of issues. We borrowed a set of fundamental questions from the YMCA's youth development philosophy (Jackson and Morton, 1990), the National Youth Leadership Council's leadership development training (Conrad & Hedin, 1982, 1987; Kraft & Kielsmeier, 1995), Harry Boyte's Public Achievement program (Boyte, 2001; Hildreth, 2000), and John McKnight's critiques of traditional service programs (McKnight, 1995a, 1995b; Kretzmann & McKnight, 1993). Like them, we needed to determine:

- How could we engage young people as a resource and not a problem

- How could we use vacant lots as a resource and not a problem

- How could we use the school's diversity and its learning goals (literacy and numeracy) as resources and not problems

And we recalled the conclusions Addams had reached some eighty-five years earlier:

> The old desire to achieve, to improve the world, seizes the ardent youth to-day with a stern command to bring about juster social conditions. Youth's divine impatience with the world's inheritance of wrong and injustice makes him scornful of "rose water for the plague" prescriptions, and he insists upon something strenuous and vital. (1909, p. 143)

We were committed to involving college students and school students as leaders in "something strenuous and vital."

We made off-campus work-study students, as well as volunteers drawn from our service-learning courses, available to the classroom teachers at HK. We established an after-school program and ended up creating a community garden that had several program elements. The largest, a ten-thousand-square-foot garden, was adjacent to the school on the edge of the open field that served as a sometime playground. The garden offered the benefit of being able to absorb as much work as people would invest in it and the capacity to survive some inattention.

Workshops and classes facilitated by Providence College faculty helped HK teachers tie the garden to the school's language, math, and science curricula. Because school was in session only from September through June, the garden also operated as a site for eight high school students to grow vegetables for market, from early spring through early fall, overlapping with the school year. These students received a guaranteed stipend and technical support. The service-learning initiative supported by CNS concentrated on garden-related activities. HELP Coalition resources supported the after-school program and a college student intern who worked with the high school students and their market garden.

Initially, the after-school program ran as a set of clubs that students could sign up for, six weeks at a time. Each club was supervised by two Providence College students who were in turn coached by a teacher from HK. Following the advice of the teacher's union, we paid teachers the going rate for after-school activities, the largest single expenditure in the program budget. Over time, driven first by the Providence School Department's desire to improve academic performance and then by the introduction of statewide evaluations of academic performance, the after-school program shifted its focus to literacy and numeracy, using fun activities as a draw for studying. The one unbreakable rule in all of this was "Do no harm." No one—child, college student, teacher, or community member—was to be put in a dangerous position; in our efforts to ensure this, we created systems such as background checks of volunteers, orientation sessions, training program, and requirements that no adult be left alone with an individual child. We strove to implement a quality principle for youth development programs that was developed by Kim Boyce during his time at the University of Minnesota YMCA: when working in youth development, you should create many opportunities for which short-term failure is possible, but do everything you can to guarantee long-term success.

It all worked, to a large extent: the HELP Coalition provided funding for teacher stipends to support the after-school program and for a summer intern to work with the gardens. Neighborhood residents watched and appreciated the after-school program. Teachers coached Providence College students on running clubs, and the clubs were always full—with three hundred to four hundred students turning up each week. Drawing on the example of micro-lending circles in Bangladesh (Grameen Bank, 2007), we organized $4,000 in investments from neighborhood residents as a start-up fund for the market garden, meaning that we did not have to look outside the community for grants and that the garden was literally community-owned. A local organic farmer donated a hundred cubic yards of compost (four tractor-trailer loads). City Year, a full-time community service corps for young adults, stepped up as a partner and made preparing the garden one of its key projects. The teachers were enormously creative in pointing their curricula toward the garden and integrating related projects such as in-class seed-planting and recess "rock dashes," in which students won awards for finding rocks "as big as their heads." Eight high school students were selected to work in the market garden, four of them gang members. Senior citizens—many of them Cambodian and Laotian, who lived on the ridge above the school—began to come down and offer advice to the gardeners. A teacher, retired from HK, worked with the college's education department to publish a curriculum guide based on service-learning, community gardening, and the district's academic goals (Manson, 1997). The activities at the school made it eligible to be designated a Child Opportunity Zone (COZ), which meant that federal funds were used to make the school a multiservice contact point for students and families as well as community police, social workers, and related service providers.

Although the in-class assistance and after-school program ran fairly smoothly, encountering only minor administrative glitches, the garden was vandalized seventeen times in its first fourteen days. People expressed concern that compost piles would attract rats. Rather than view these circumstances as failures or obstacles, we looked at them as opportunities to use the garden to address other community concerns: What were the roots of the vandalism? Why were there so many rats? Could composting be done differently? Youth workers and police officers from the juvenile division helped arrange several (ultimately successful) interventions with the middle school students responsible for the vandalism. It turned out that rats were a problem throughout the city, and the garden had no measurable effect on their presence; however, two environmental studies interns worked out an alternative composting system.

Providence College students came to the garden as volunteers on a weekly basis and worked there as off-campus work-study employees. They designed internships and attended countless meetings and informal discussions in the neighborhood.

From a teaching point of view, the partnership worked wonderfully. The after-school program gave Providence College students a low-stress way to initiate relationships with people in the neighborhood—children, their families, and neighbors. We told Providence College students repeatedly that the power of teachers, children, and families lay in their decisions about how much of themselves and their experiences they would share. As the service-learning volunteers got to know the people at the school and as they began to see with new eyes, they could begin to compare their experiential knowledge to their initial assumptions, to the statistics and history of the school, and to the broader context of public education in the United States. Comparing this rich experience with the statistical likelihood that half of HK's students would fail to finish high school, one volunteer eloquently summed it up: "The school *looks* fine—no holes in the walls, the teachers are nice, the kids are good kids. Why doesn't it work?"

Middle Schools

Our middle school partnerships had essentially the same intent as those for HK Elementary School, but they were implemented from the outset with a more narrow focus on tutoring and after-school programs. The focus on the academic institution, and the relative absence of focus on the community context, had a significant impact on how the partnerships evolved.

Esek Hopkins Middle School. In 1994, the Feinstein Institute also began working with two middle schools (grades sixth through eighth) located near the Providence College campus. We were first approached by the principal of Esek Hopkins (EH) Middle School, which was notorious for having one of the highest truancy rates in the state of Rhode Island. Like HK, it was an overcrowded, very diverse school with large numbers of Italian-American and African-American students, and many children from recently immigrated families, notably from Cambodia and Laos. We used a model similar to that at HK, if much less complex: a college student, supported through the Public Service curriculum at the Feinstein Institute, coordinated the program by recruiting college student volunteers, organizing orientation and training, developing a list of clubs based on student interests and volunteer skills, and serving on-site two afternoons a week. The principal recruited teachers, scheduled late buses, and coached the college student who was coordinating the program. As with HK, HELP funds were used to compensate teachers participating in the program at the going rate, in recognition that this was a part of their professional work. And also as at HK, many of the teachers spent most of their after-school compensation on program supplies. In the second year of the program at EH, the principal left, transferring to a local high school. Her departure dramatically affected the school's support for the program by complicating details such as afterschool buses and the recruitment of teachers. As well, it left our program coordinator with no one to go to for advice. This change demonstrated to us the importance of a strong principal (or an equivalent administrator) as an ally in the school, especially in a system that was unused to such partnerships.

Nathanael Greene Middle School. The second middle school with which we worked, Nathanael Greene (NG), located perhaps a half-mile south and west of Providence College, is the largest middle school in Providence (810 students); it inhabits a cavernous, gothic-style building with hallways that feel like tunnels. The school invited the Feinstein Institute to participate based on what its principal was observing at EH. Almost immediately, the principal and teachers called attention to the academic difficulties of its students; one-quarter of its students were flunking—or in immediate danger of flunking—one or more of the four core academic subjects. Within a short time, after-school clubs at NG shifted their focus to academic reinforcement, led first by a "Study Hard" club that assisted students with their homework and provided tutoring, then by a "Credit Recovery Program," the brainchild of one of the school's long-time teachers. In the latter program, NG students could redo failed work from courses they had flunked; if they completed the work, they could avoid summer school and pass to the next grade—better prepared, it was hoped, to succeed the next time around.

Where the Simple Becomes Challenging

Our partnerships with HK, EH, and NG proved challenging over time, and the challenges we faced collectively suggest both the predictable and the unpredictable difficulties facing such partnerships. Most important, our experiences suggest the profound ways in which circumstances external to particular schools—circumstances of policy change, politics, economics, and history—affect schools and partnerships. The challenges all point equally to the learning that is at the heart of such partnerships.

The Experience at HK Elementary School

At its best, the partnership with HK was a messy, fermenting compost of energy open to everyone who expressed interest. The garden spread toward the hillside, providing an eastern exposure perfect for fruit trees. Three hundred elementary school parents and students came to the first potluck celebration. The fluid coalition that formed around the garden—composed of people from Providence College, HK, City Year, the Smith Hill Community Development Corporation, the Smith Hill Center, the Smith Hill Library, and Keep Providence Beautiful—convinced the city's Park and Recreation department to rehabilitate the lot next to the school. Citing the garden, its volunteers, and the coalition as evidence of the community's worthiness, Park and Rec tore out the old playground, installed a new one, built stone walls, and put in a walking track and volleyball court.

At its worst, the project was complicated, confusing, and contradictory. There was too much going on at once. The leadership structure was flat to the point of invisibility, reforming each time a new problem was identified or someone new approached. Our tight focus on the neighborhood blinded us to the outside political pressures that were impinging on our work. For example, an important incentive behind Park and Rec's lot rehabilitation was to make soccer playing on the property impossible. This was in response to residents' complaints about enormous, unofficial soccer tournaments taking place in the school lot on weekends. We discovered this fact only after the park's rehabilitation was complete, and the politics around this got very rough for a while. Then Park and Rec officials wanted a new building, and they quietly used the growing energy around the garden and the renovated park to gain the necessary funding. They internally discussed control of programs at the new building with the community center director who, intent on moving to a fee-for-service model and seeing the potential for program dollars, agreed—again, without consultation—to the Park and Rec plan. The building was built—on top of the garden. Park and Rec adjusted its position and ran its own programs. We no longer had a garden.

Literacy and numeracy efforts at the school, built on service-learning and the garden, did not satisfy the demands of the Providence School Department for an explicit, test-oriented curriculum. The school's performance—contrary to teachers' anecdotal reports—did not appear to improve by objective measures; this undermined the service-learning effort. The school was noisy; the principal shouted all the time. Shortly after the CNS grant ended, the college's Department of Education decided to withdraw from the school, arguing that its students couldn't learn to teach effectively in such a dysfunctional environment.

The Experience at EH Middle School

Although it ran with some success for six years, the Institute decided to withdraw from the program at EH based on two recurring problems. First, two teachers involved in the program came to view working in it as an entitlement, meaning that they assumed their continued involvement and pay, even as they did a substandard job with the middle school students and the college students whom they were supposed to coach. They regularly missed program times, came unprepared, and berated college volunteers. The principal attempted, unsuccessfully, to deal with the problem; as the teachers threatened to file grievances against him, he was unwilling to press further. We chose to look at this as an opportunity to learn how to work with a problematic bureaucracy—and limped along for three years.

The second problem, and the one that ultimately proved the program's death knell, was busing. For three years running, procuring late buses for the after-school program was a constant challenge. In the second and third years, commitments came late and incomplete from the central school administration (late for a school that was fully Title One eligible and had been for years), and in the fourth year the buses simply were not granted. Unlike HK, where at worst a program could be run with the half of the student body who walked to and from school, buses at EH were a make-or-break resource. After pursuing every political avenue we could think of in this third year, we formally withdrew from the program.

The Experience at NG Middle School

At NG, the school's slightly different administrative structure, a better political relationship between the school and the central administration, and a dependable core of teachers allowed the program to survive three new principals in seven years. Another factor making a significant positive difference was the consistent presence of at least one, and sometimes two, Providence College faculty who saw the partnership with the school as an important part of their professional work, and who maintained an ongoing relationship with the school's administrators and teachers.

One of these faculty members, an untenured professor of political science, was interested primarily in studying public policy that affected children. A new principal at the school, in conversation with the Feinstein Institute's service-learning coordinator (the person who organized and maintained partnerships for the Institute's academic curriculum), asked that the after-school program give even more attention to remedial academic work. New to being a principal, and with strong support from central administration, this principal also created a new position—essentially an advocate for failing students—that was filled by an energetic, just-retired teacher who had come up with the concept of "credit recovery" and wanted to stick around and see it implemented.

While Institute students did direct service as tutors and after-school volunteers at NG, the faculty member agreed to figure out a way to track and measure the impact of the credit recovery program on NG's students and on the school. His research question was simple: were failing Greene students promoted at higher rates with this program than without this program?

General Challenges

In 2002, the HELP Coalition closed down, meaning that funds for the after-school programs would no longer be available. The schools discussed using Title One funds and funds that the city of Providence had received several years earlier from the Wallace Fund for youth development. Title One funds were difficult to redirect, and when they did become available they were not confirmed and released until late October or early November. A new coalition of schools and community agencies, known as the Providence After School Alliance (PASA), was created with a $5 million grant from the Wallace Foundation (Providence After School Alliance, 2006; Sylvester, 2006). (PASA was housed under a separate organization called the Education Partnership, itself a hybrid of two earlier education advocacy groups.) Working hard, PASA spent nearly three years in a planning phase, trying to bring together all the key players and build consensus on how best to develop an after-school system in Providence. Ultimately, the organization decided to concentrate its attention on the city's six thousand middle school students. Ironically, PASA's creation led many community agencies to wait and see who PASA would fund with pass-through grants before taking on more after-school programs, leading to a temporary slowdown in the development of such projects.

While PASA was involved in planning, small pockets of money remained available for continuing the after-school programs at HK and NG. The college declined to manage this money, however, as did several local community agencies and the schools themselves.

The bureaucratic problems of managing small grants in a moment of political transition meant that the after-school programs in which we had been involved, especially at the elementary school, were put on hold.

As we write this, relatively little remains from the initial ferment, symbolized by the garden, which lasted from 1994–1999; the long-running after-school program at the elementary school ended in spring of 2004; several publications on service-learning in elementary schools were written by teachers at the school (Callahan & Root, 2003; Manson, 1997); an education curriculum at the college has fully and authentically integrated service-learning into its methods courses; people continue to use the park; and there is a history worth knowing. The Providence After School Alliance, concentrating on middle schools, is attempting to resuscitate the program at EH, and to help expand the program at NG, which has survived.

Reflections: The Learning in Service-Learning

We hope that all these stories illustrate just how rich and complicated university-school partnerships can be and that they suggest the ways in which politics, economics, and history can come spilling in uninvited at any time. Two sorts of reflections emerge from this situation: the first concentrating on how and what individuals learn from their experiences, the other on how institutions learn from and are affected (or not) by their experiences.

Individual Learning

In these partnerships, Providence College volunteers, coming from courses located in the Public and Community Service program (which offers a major and a minor, and has its own curriculum) and the Education Department, struggle with the idea of service as a charitable act. As the school children extend their trust and friendship, the PC volunteers become increasingly conscious that they are doing their service as a class requirement, increasing the likelihood that they will break off the relationship at the semester's end. They come to realize, too, that the teachers and children have quite a bit of experience with volunteers like them—and, for the most part, have realistic and quite low expectations of the volunteers' staying power.

As they struggle to answer the question, "Why aren't these schools working well?" the PC students typically go through a predictable pattern of response:

1. *The community neglects its children, and that's why our help is needed. Parents don't, or can't, pay enough attention to their children. I am so fortunate to have what I have.*

2. After a short period of service, often as little as three or four weeks of one three-hour shift per week, the volunteer's focus shifts away from the presumed deficits of community members and toward consciousness-raising. *People outside the school don't realize that there's a problem; once they do, it will get fixed. Our/my volunteer effort will add enough extra energy to the school to help tip things in the right direction, and inspire others to pay attention.*

3. As the volunteers discover that much of the new insight they are gaining is familiar to teachers, administrators, and community members and is reflected in a voluminous literature on schools, they begin to wonder how it can be that this knowledge—that things are wrong and need fixing—is not acted on. *Someone in authority is at fault; we need to find out who this is and call them to task.* Initially, volunteers see the most likely culprits as those closest to the situation, people with whom they have direct experience: the principal and the teachers, who aren't from the neighborhood. They tend to view these educators as bureaucrats and union members who don't do any more than they have to, and point to the one or two heroic teachers who do care as examples of

what they mean. *The school needs caring, dynamic leadership.*

4. As the volunteers become familiar with the institutional systems framing education, they continue to believe that the problem is one of leadership; however, their gaze shifts to those who are more distant and who exercise power over the on-site leaders of a particular school: school boards, superintendents, the state's department of education, and federal authorities. *It's a political problem.* This shift brings some immediate relief; it allows the volunteers to delineate *us and them* in such a way that they can now feel allied with the principals, teachers, students, and families at their school. *The school board plays favorites and doesn't have enough funding to start with. People who don't know anything about the situation make too many decisions affecting the school. The principal has little or no real authority.* The volunteers' sympathy for the people they now perceive as allies causes them to reinterpret what they earlier perceived as apathy, and it brings a new worry: *What if our service makes no difference?*

5. The volunteers begin to believe that the problem is systemic and too complicated. *If you are poor you get ignored.* They recall their initial enthusiasm and ask, *Where do you start?* They are likely to confide, *I feel guilty about what I have.* And they wonder, *How do you overcome such institutionalized inertia?*

6. The volunteers either quit or find a way to accept that they are making a positive but limited contribution. *It's a long haul, and you can only do what you can do.* They become conscious of the social, economic, and political dimensions of the system in which they are working, but view their commitment to the relationships developed in the school as primary, sustaining, meaningful, and sometimes transformational. Their efforts toward institutional change

are informed and energized by this primary experience, but they are realistic, with success or failure determined by their commitment to the primary relationships rather than to political outcomes.

The problem, of course, is that although this pattern of response is—given enough time—fairly consistent in the aggregate, it does not fit comfortably in the space or time allocated to a college class or to the development of a particular student. Its timing is not predictable, often taking a year or two rather than a semester to work through, and it is an emotional and sometimes spiritual journey, as much as it is an intellectual one (Perry, 1970, 1981; Kohlberg, 1981; S. Parks, 1986, 2000). The consequences of quitting in mid-process are potentially grave, yet there are many pressures that make quitting seem like a good idea.

We interpret this process using a framework offered by Melvin Lerner, a psychiatrist responsible for the training of medical residents. Based on his observations, Lerner argues that it is a natural human impulse to help. And we think he is also correct in his conclusion that most of us, unless we can find some agency and success in our helping, will withdraw or, if we must stay on, begin to blame the victim as a way of protecting ourselves psychologically.

Lerner (1980) describes this process in his book, *The Belief in a Just World: A Fundamental Delusion*. After witnessing the affective changes in psychiatry residents whose patients did not improve despite the residents' best efforts, he sought to understand how we may (1) internalize the realization that the world is not just, (2) recognize that our agency may be limited, and—still— (3) continue to be present to others' sufferings and needs.

To be able to realize that the world is not just and to continue to care anyway is, we have come to think, what it means to give witness: to see what is true and to speak that truth to power. It is a rare experience in our society to give witness, and it places great stress on students who are called to do this. It is not an ideological witness, but rather, we think, a witness of trusting one's own experience and of embracing relationships that enrich one's life, even if they also bring some pain. In this sense, participants in our university-school partnerships come to participate in a form of witness.

As they make their way through this process of learning, volunteers also struggle with the ways in which these shifts in perspective cause subtle shifts in their prior relationships with family and friends. As the college students in the service-learning courses move from assumptions to knowledge grounded in experience, they discover that they are now different from their peers, who retain uninformed assumptions. Well-intentioned parents and friends ask them, "Why do you care about 'those people'?" (with the unspoken subtext, "more than you care about *us*"). Or their peers make offhand remarks that seem to diminish the children, parents, or teachers they have come to respect. Their answers to these and similar questions or remarks point out how much their thinking has changed, and how much their thoughts and feelings have come to differ from those of their friends. They are told that although it is a generous and good thing to help out, they can't make a career out of it or, if they do anyway, they are wasting their education and consigning themselves to a life of genteel poverty. The students in the service-learning courses understand that there is risk and possible loss if they continue to do what they do, and they rarely have experience or support to assure them that things will work out. They can find themselves in the midst of enormous doubt and inner turmoil. It is this developmental process that enriches and challenges everyone committed to learning from campus-school partnerships.

Institutional Learning

In much the same way as the college volunteers learn to interpret their experience in a new way, we have learned to interpret the cultural and institutional context framing the partnerships in new ways. The tendency of those watching the Providence School system during the last decade has been to concentrate on improving the quality of teaching or providing extra academic support to students. This tendency has been accelerated and compounded by the passage of the No Child Left Behind Act, and by an increasingly relentless focus on standardized academic testing as the primary tool for evaluating school performance (Meier and Wood, 2004; EdWeek, 2006).

Our experience suggests that, although in-class tutoring and after-school academic support may make some positive difference, the fundamental issues facing the Providence schools and their students lie outside that system, tied to a fundamental component of poverty in Rhode Island: housing. Or, to be more precise, it is tied to classroom turmoil created by what is called student "mobility": a measure of the percentage of students who move into and out of a school in a given year.

The students in Providence schools come from families with recent or generational ties to nearly forty countries, and in an average enrollment year the first languages spoken in their homes total more than twenty-five. In the last five years, the schools described herein have gone from a roughly equal mix of Anglo, Southeast Asian, African-American, and Hispanic students to more than 50 percent Hispanic, and many of the students' parents are recent immigrants. More than 90 percent of the students in the schools with which the Feinstein Institute collaborates qualify for free meals, despite the fact that most of these students have at least one parent who works full-time (Infoworks! 2006b; Providence Plan, 2006).

As we write, there is a six-year wait for subsidized housing in the city. In the preceding six years, gentrification in Providence has sharply reduced the availability of affordable housing. As of this writing, in Providence the families of the students at HK, EH, and NG often spend 80 percent of their monthly income on housing (National Low Income Housing Coalition, 2006; Rhode Island Poverty Institute, 2003). The schools' stability and mobility statistics—not maintained with dependable accuracy—suggest that at as much as 40 percent of the seats in the elementary school turn over at least once each year, and as much as 30 percent in the middle schools (Rhode Island Department of Education, 2006; InfoWorks!, 2006a). Our experience has led us to the conclusion that the biggest problem the schools face in Providence is housing. Our reasoning, helped immeasurably by Jessica Cigna—a public and community service major who volunteered at HK and did some careful statistical analysis while completing an urban planning internship (she graduated in 2001 and went on to work as a researcher for the Urban Institute)—goes something like this: The teachers report that their classes are too full of turmoil to become effective learning communities. More than class size, they say, the problem is that students come and go. Off the record, they say that standardized tests are worse than useless: the tests take away valuable teaching days, they emphasize things that don't fit with either the academic or the social needs of their students, and they aren't even administering pre- and post-tests to the same students, so the data are meaningless. The assistant principal for the first four years we were at HK used to argue eloquently that the real need was settling down the transience of students. "Give us a chance to build a safe, structured sense of community in the classroom," he would say, "and then let's see what happens." Teachers and staff feel that no one listens to what they have to say, and that it is easier to blame them for the problems than to address the problems.

Most of the jobsites where the students' parents or guardians work are in first-ring suburbs. Transportation by car or bus is an expensive and undependable proposition. Parents want to move into one of these suburbs—closer to work—as soon as they can. A broken-down car requires immediate fixing or a job will be lost. Fixing the car means holding back on rent. Buses take an hour or more each way. Few of the jobs have any health benefits. Even a brief illness of a parent, or the illness of a child, can mean days lost at work—loss of income, loss of job, rent unpaid. As their families make do, children in Providence schools move often—from apartment to apartment, from neighborhood to neighborhood, from relative to relative, and from relatives' homes to friends' homes and back again.

Even more suggestively, the mobility and stability indices statewide suggest that "successful" schools have a stability index of 92 percent or better, and a mobility index of 6 percent or less (these do not necessarily add up to 100 percent, as some "seats" can turn over multiple times, increasing mobility even as stability remains the same) (Rhode Island Department of Education, 2006; Infoworks!, 2006a).

From all of this, we conclude that stability in a classroom is a necessary—albeit insufficient—condition for effective learning and teaching. Test scores at these schools tend to improve when the students move less; when 96 percent of students (as is the case in the most successful schools across the state) begin and finish the school year in the same school. So the challenge for school improvement is fundamentally a housing problem. With better-quality, affordable housing available, families have an enormous incentive to stay put. If they stay put, competent teachers have a necessary condition for effective learning. If the schools improve—even according to measurements of what we have come to consider meaningless data—the families have a second huge incentive to stay put. And the desire to stay put translates, we think, into an economic transformation of the neighborhood as people make longer-term investments. The question remains, of course: how can affordable, quality housing be created and sustained? In our estimation, there is no credible evidence that this will come to pass in Providence in the foreseeable future.

All of this matters profoundly for our collaboration with schools. Children and youth are as transient in after-school programs as they are in schools. This being the case, how can we help more effectively, especially as the life experiences of our college students and the K–8 students so greatly differ? Given that the externally defined measures of success (higher scores on standardized tests that are mandated by state and federal statute) pretty much guarantee that failure (to improve test scores) is the likely outcome, how do we design collaborative projects with the schools that will authentically respond to the schools' and students' situations? How do we advocate for a more realistic understanding by school authorities of what we believe is the situation? And, perhaps most important, how do we teach this context in our classes?

This last question—how do we teach this?—concerns us especially, for a couple of reasons. First, there is a potential disconnect between the limited service experiences our college students have in the K–8 schools and the larger cultural context that shapes their experience. That is, they are experiencing the school first-hand, so they will base their interpretation of the systemic and cultural context on this narrower experience. How do we broaden the service experience of the students so that it includes some interaction with the families of K–8 students, with housing and related economic issues, when the pressure to focus on academic outcomes has resulted, in nearly every instance, on more attention to tutoring and less on the whole child or community involvement? Over time, our initial attention to the school as a "community hub," through which we work with a local community, has all but disappeared, having been replaced by an emphasis on increasingly narrow academic objectives.

This dilemma is summarized by Rick Battistoni, a Providence College faculty member who has been involved in these school collaborations from the start, in a 2006 interview:

> The first "lesson" college students will generally take away from their work in a school is "the family background of these kids doesn't allow them to succeed." When we started at HK, the parents' involvement made it possible to check this stereotype .... We need the right "prompt," additional pieces of experience, for these moments to occur .... The "problem of public education" is not a singular problem. You have to see

it as a challenge for each child—knowing them, their
backgrounds, their situations.

It is this context that is being lost. We might usefully think
of community as a dense web of relationships, and the breakdown of
community as the fragmentation of this web. In no small degree,
our experience with the schools is a witness to the unintended
but very real consequences of community fragmentation. As Carol
Merz and Gail Furman (1997, p. 6) optimistically argue, "Many
critics of schools say schools have become alienated from the
communities they serve, and rebuilding or restoring community
ties has become a major theme in educational reform." From our
point of view, No Child Left Behind and other policy changes
of the past decade have had the unintended result of dampening
this major theme and deepening this alienation. The result appears
to be two fundamental questions that frame university-school
partnerships: How can university-school partnerships help build
community? How and what do we teach and learn from the
fragmented experiences that we can offer our students?

Toward a Working Theory of Campus-School Partnerships

Effectively understanding and enacting partnerships between university campuses and P–12 schools requires grounding in explicit
principles. Here, we lay out a principle-based framework for conceiving, implementing, and reflecting on such service-learning
collaborations.

Basic Principles

Based on our experience and reflections, we suggest three questions
for grounding university-school partnerships:

1. With whom do we partner and why?
2. What are the interests of the key stakeholders, and are they
   fairly balanced?

3. Does our work together increase our capacity to act and strengthen our relationship?

Partnerships, especially those involving youth, require that the partners approach their joint effort thinking simultaneously about their institutional relationship and their individual relationships. In other words, what bureaucratic interests must be addressed, and what will we do with one another in the time and space created by our efforts? To manage this dynamic, we advocate the following tactics:

- Keep projects small in scale (and if one must scale up, keep the project a composite of small units, as decentralized as possible).

- Identify the mission and goals that will allow you to keep the basic elements of the partnership simple.

- As much as possible, build the mission, goal, and practices out from the articulated interests of the children and youth served, rather than in from bureaucratic priorities.

- Develop a cascading leadership model, in which everyone involved has a potential leadership role, and have as many decisions as possible made as far down the chain of command as possible, with the goals of increasing leadership capacity, retaining participants as their roles grow, creating space for everyone to contribute their gifts, blurring the boundaries that define who is serving and who is being served, and making the program resilient in the face of turnover or resource losses.

- Deliberately make the partnership and program dependent on volunteer leadership, as a way of balancing power with funders and bureaucratic administrators.

- Concentrate on expanding and deepening a web of relationships that embraces the children and youth; pay relatively less attention to academic outcomes.

The fundamental goal in all of this is to create a sense of place, a sense of belonging, and a sense of personal and communal agency in the children, youth, and college students participating in a program. Ideally, this emergent sensibility is articulated by each of them, on their terms. We agree with B. Mitchell (1990), who argues that the task we face is "repairing debilitating loss [of community], creating the right forms of belonging and creating an acceptable sense of becoming" (cited in Merz & Furman, 1997, p. 9).

Why This Framework and These Principles?

Underlying our analysis is the assumption that questions of university-school partnership are primarily questions about the relationship between representatives of a campus as an institution—people defined, at least initially, by their relationship to that institution as teacher or student or administrator—and people similarly defined by their relationship to a school as an institution—as staff, guests, students, or clients. It is less likely that a partnership has evolved out of personal relationships shared by people who understand themselves as being part of the same local, neighborhood-based community they wish to serve.

Partnerships developed out of institutional interests are inherently problematic; they form the basis of well-known critiques of service by John McKnight (1995), Ivan Illich (1990), and others. Most community service depends on a fairly simple algorithm: problem definition, intervention design and implementation, assessment of efficacy, redesign, and so on. At the heart of the critiques offered by McKnight and Illich is the deceptively simple observation that everything depends on who gets to identify and define the problem to be solved. From a slightly different vantage point, we can see that what is being contested in program design is *whose knowledge counts*: that of the people experiencing a situation or that of the people who observe it from a greater distance?

We do not understand this challenge to mean that we should follow Illich's demand that, as volunteers entering communities other than our own, we "Come to look ... Come to study. But do not come to help" (Illich, 1990, p. 320). And although we sympathize with Illich's concerns about socioeconomic and cultural gulfs between volunteers and service-recipients, we disagree with his observation that the only thing we can "legitimately volunteer ... might be voluntary powerlessness, voluntary presence as receivers, as such, as hopefully beloved or adopted ones without any way of returning the gift" (Illich, 1990, p. 314).

The basis for our rejection of this and similar arguments is that it stipulates opposing interests coming out of particular histories as the fundamental ground of the relationship between server and served. An alternative position, we would argue, is to understand that server and served are mirrors of one another and that in the United States, at this moment in history, our shared tragedy is the loss of community. The alternative position, then, is to set as a long-term objective in partner-building the integration of selves and institutions into a healthy community. As Paul Goodman suggests in his novel *Making Do*, "If there is no community for you, young man, young man, make it yourself" (quoted in Greenleaf, 1991, p. 8). An appropriate objective, and one with the potential to resolve the seemingly inherent contradiction described so eloquently by the critics of service, is the mutual creation of communities to which we can belong.

Too often, then, we think of university-school partnerships as linear, transactional relationships between or among representatives of institutional interests: community partners who serve their own mission and members, and—distinctly—higher education institutions that aim to educate their own students. From experience we know that the situation is much more complex than this: university-school partnerships are dynamic, joint creations in which all the people involved create knowledge, transact power, mix personal and institutional interests, and make meaning. We also know from experience and observation that partnerships are particular, and that it is difficult to predict that they will develop in any one particular way. There is no neat typology that allows one thing to lead, with any sense of inevitability, to another. The best we can do, we think, is to describe some of the various ways in which university-school partners most often work and to recognize the potential for those partnerships to develop over time in ways that challenge and deepen their collective work. As one Providence College faculty member put it,

> [The partnerships are] all about relationships—diversity, variety, thickness. We hoped and hope it will be a normal thing for PC folk to be in the [school] building enough that their presence is taken for granted. This is when reflection starts to become possible and allows for adjustments in what we are trying to do together. (Battistoni, 2006)

Further complicating matters, the deepening of partnerships is not a linear function in which one thing leads to another, with the new form replacing the old. Rather, partnerships accrete over time, gathering layers of experience much as sand and sediment settle on the ocean floor. Short-term or episodic community service events may create a context in which deep, mutually transformative partnerships can emerge over time. Or not. What matters is the willingness of the partners to listen deeply to one another and modify their behaviors as a result. This is important, we think, because it suggests that a partnership must be understood in its entirety, and that we ought not to mistake a part—a particular activity—for the potential of the whole.

Finally, we argue that what matters more than an activity the partners undertake is how they interpret and make meaning from their work together; how it is that they describe, interpret, care about, and give to what they are trying to do together. It is when this meaning is absent or lost that partnerships founder.

Conclusion

In this chapter we have attempted to weave together three strands: first, a strand of stories from our experience that serve as case studies; second, our reflections on that experience; and, finally, a description of the theoretical framework informing our efforts. We have described the ideas that serve as the basis for the Feinstein Institute's K–8 partnerships; asset-based community development; cascading leadership models for student development; positive effects of direct service on institutions, communities, and individuals; and how we learn and teach from service experiences. In short, we have tried to explain how we organized our efforts and why.

We would like to close with the following points:

- If a partnership between a school and a higher education service-learning program is to develop beyond an initial, mechanical relationship, the partners must share a philosophy and understanding of student development. This shared understanding comes only out of relationship and dialogue over an extended period of time, and the necessary trust is most often built on a series of small projects undertaken together.

- Sustainable partnerships entail relationships with numerous stakeholders inside and outside the school, and the learning opportunities produced by the experience are directly related to the depth of those relationships (among school administrators, teachers, teachers' unions, park and recreation staff, college

students, administrators and faculty, funders,
school students, and parents). Success is possible when
those stakeholders interpret their experience together
and come to share common goals. A number of factors
make it difficult to sustain these relationships.

- The depth of college student learning is dependent on
  the students' degree of involvement over time, ranging
  from students with a great deal of involvement in many
  dimensions of the school experience over an extended
  period of time, to students with a limited range of
  experience over a single semester. In turn, what
  students make of their experience is often affected by
  variables such as students' major field of study and
  vocational aspirations—variables that can inhibit their
  ability to try to see the whole.

- Successfully interpreting a school-based experience
  requires significant knowledge about social and cultural
  contexts of the K–12 students, both within and outside
  the school walls. Learning to see such systemic patterns
  is, we conclude, the essential link between working
  with individual students in a school setting and
  learning about the public and civic dimensions of
  education in the United States.

Note

1. Schools included in the composites:

- Harry Kizirian Elementary School (name changed from
  Camden Elementary in 2000; K–5, 488 students in 2005,
  down from 592 the previous year; 41 teachers, down from 42
  the previous year)

- Nathanael Greene Middle School (6–8, 810 students, 68
  teachers)

- Esek Hopkins Middle School (6–8, 592 students, 42 teachers)

- Paul Cuffee Middle School (K–8 Maritime Charter School, 400 students, 46 teachers)

- Veazie Street Elementary School (K–5, 548 students, 45 teachers)

- Sophia Academy (5–8 girls' school operated by Catholic nuns, 60 students, 4 teachers)

- St. Patrick School (K–8 Catholic school, 159 students, 11 teachers)

- San Miguel School (6–8 boys' Catholic school, 64 students, 4 teachers)

- Further information on each of these schools is available from Information Works! This is an annual publication produced through collaboration between the Rhode Island Department of Elementary and Secondary Education and the National Center on Public Education and Social Policy, at the University of Rhode Island: http://www.infoworks.ride.uri.edu/2006/default.asp

References

21st Century Community Learning Centers, U.S. Department of Education (2006). Purpose. Retrieved December 19, 2006, from http://www.ed.gov/programs/21stcclc/index.html

Addams, J. (1909). *The spirit of youth and the city streets*. New York: Macmillan.

Addams, J. (1960). *Twenty years at Hull-House*. New York: New American Library.

Afterschool Alliance (2006). About us. Retrieved January 2, 2007, from http://www.afterschoolalliance.org/about_us.cfm

Afterschool Alliance (2007). Afterschool action kit. Retrieved January 2, 2007, from http://www.afterschoolalliance.org/ACTIONKT.PDF

Battistoni, R. (2006). Interview notes of Keith Morton, October 2, 2006.

Benson, L., & Harkavy, I. (1997). School and community in the global society. *Universities and Community Schools*, 5(1-2), 16–71.

Boyte, H. (2001, September 1). A tale of two playgrounds: Young people and politics. Paper presented at the annual meeting of the American Political Science Association, San Francisco.

Callahan, J., & Root, S. (2003). The diffusion of academic service-learning in teacher education: A case study approach. In S. Billig & J. Eyler (Eds.), *Deconstructing service learning: Research exploring context, participation and impact* (pp. 77–101). Greenwich, CT: Information Age Publishing.

Campus Compact (1999–2005). *1993–94 National members' survey and resource guide.* Providence, RI. 1993; Service Matters, Education Commission of the States: Providence, RI, 1994; Service Counts, Lessons from the Field of Service and Higher Education, 1995. Campus Compact and Education Commission of the States, 1995. Published annually by Campus Compact since 1996 as Service Matters. 1999–2005 data retrieved from the website of Campus Compact as "Statistics" 1999–2005, http://www.compact.org/about/statistics/

Conrad, D., & Hedin, D. (1982). The impact of experiential education on adolescent development. In D. Conrad & D. Hedin (Eds.), *Youth participation and experiential education*, special edition of *Child and Youth Services*, (4) 3/4, 57–76.

Conrad, D., & Hedin, D. (1987). *Youth service: A guidebook for developing and operating effective programs.* Washington, D.C.: Independent Sector.

Dewey, J. (1938). *Experience and education.* New York: MacMillan.

EdWeek. (2006). Researchers ask whether NCLB's goals for proficiency are realistic. Retrieved November 29, 2006, from http://www.edweek.org/ew/news/no-child-left-behind/

Grameen Bank. (2007). Introduction. Retrieved January 2, 2007, from http://www.grameen-info.org/index.php?option=com_content&task=view&id=16&Itemid=112.html

Gray, M. J., Ondaatje, E. H., Geschwind, S., Robyn, A., & Klein, S. P. (1996). *Summary of major findings: Learn and Serve America, higher education.* Santa Monica, CA: Rand Corporation.

Greenleaf, R. (1991). *Servant as leader.* Indianapolis: Robert K. Greenleaf Center.

Halpern, R. (1999). After-school programs for low-income children: Promise and challenges. *The Future of Children*, 9(2), 81–95.

Hildreth, R. (2000). Theorizing citizenship and evaluating public achievement. *Political Science and Politics*, 33(3), 627–632.

Illich, I. (1990). To hell with good intentions. In J. Kendall (Ed.), *Combining service and learning: A resource book for community and public service* (Vol. 1, pp. 314–320). National Society for Experiential Education.

InfoWorks! (2006a). Measuring Rhode Island schools for change: School report cards. Retrieved September 26, 2006, from http://www.infoworks .ride.uri.edu/2006/reports/school.asp

InfoWorks! (2006b). Using information: Demographics, school performance, Providence District 2006. Retrieved January 2, 2007, from http://www .infoworks.ride.uri.edu/2006/pdf/DS-usinginfo/28d-info.pdf

Jackson, R., & Morton, K. (1990). Youth leadership development. In J. Kendall (Ed.), *Combining service and learning: A resource book for community and public service, vol. 1.* National Society for Experiential Education, (1), 359–374.

Kohlberg, L. (1981). *Essays on moral development, vol. 1: The philosophy of moral development.* New York: Harper & Row.

Kraft, R. J., & Kielsmeier, J. (1995). *Experiential learning in schools and higher education.* Boulder, CO: Association for Experiential Education.

Kretzmann, J., & McKnight, J. (1993). *Building communities from the inside out: A path toward finding and mobilizing a community's assets.* Evanston, IL: Center for Urban Affairs and Policy Research.

Lerner, M. (1980). *The belief in a just world: A fundamental delusion.* New York: Plenum Press.

Manson, R. (1997). *Partners in service.* Providence: Feinstein Institute for Public Service.

McKnight, J. (1995a). *The careless society: Community and its counterfeits.* New York: Basic Books.

McKnight, J. (1995b). Why servanthood is bad. *The Other Side, 31*(6).

Meier, D., & Wood, G. (Eds.). (2004). *Many children left behind: How the No Child Left Behind Act is damaging our children and our schools.* Boston: Beacon Press.

Merz, C., & Furman, G. (1997). *Community and schools: Promise and paradox.* New York: Teachers College Press.

Morton, K. (1997). What is it we are growing here? *NSEE Quarterly, 22*(3), 12–13, 20–22.

National Institute for Out-of-School Time (2006). Making the case: A fact sheet on children and youth in out-of-school time. Retrieved January 2, 2007, from http://www.niost.org/publications/Fact%20Sheet% 202006%20Feb9%20.pdf

National Low Income Housing Coalition Rhode Island (2006). Out of reach 2006. Retrieved January 2, 2007, from http://www.nlihc.org/oor/ oor2006/data.cfm?getstate=on&getmsa=on&msa=419&state=RI

Parks, S. (1986). *The critical years: The young adult search for a faith to live by.* San Francisco: Harper & Row.

Parks, S. (2000). *Big questions, worthy dreams: Mentoring young adults in their search for meaning, purpose, and faith.* San Francisco: Jossey-Bass.

Perry, W. (1970). *Forms of intellectual and ethical development in the college years: A scheme.* New York: Holt, Rinehart and Winston.

Perry, W. (1981). Cognitive and ethical growth: The making of meaning. In A. W. Chickering and Associates (Eds.), *The modern American college* (pp. 76–116). San Francisco: Jossey-Bass.

Providence After School Alliance (2006). Homepage. Retrieved January 2, 2007, from http://www.mypasa.org/

Providence Plan (2006). Providence neighborhood profiles: Smith Hill at a glance. Retrieved January 2, 2007, from http://204.17.79.244/profiles/smh_main.html

Rhode Island Department of Education (2006). Student mobility, stability rates 2004–05 by schools. Retrieved December, 19, 2006, from http://www.ride.ri.gov/Applications/fred.aspx

Rhode Island Poverty Institute (2003). The 2003 Rhode Island standard of need. Providence: Rhode Island College. Retrieved December 19, 2007, from http://www.povertyinstitute.org/matriarch/documents/RISN%202003.pdf

Sylvester, K. (2006). After school magnets, youth today. Retrieved November 7, 2006, from http://www.youthtoday.org/youthtoday/Nov06/front1.html, and http://www.wallacefoundation.org/NewsRoom/InTheNews/NewsClips/After-School+Magnets.htm

White, W. S. (2005). *Afterschool programs: Giving hope and help to all our children: Remarks by William S. White, President.* Flint, MI: Charles Stewart Mott Foundation.

3

Metropolitan State University

Connecting with Community Through a University-Public Library Partnership

Robert Shumer, Susan Shumer,
Rebecca Ryan, Joanna Brookes,
M. Alejandra Reyes Cejudo, and
Karin DuPaul

During the past century American universities have become increasingly connected with their local communities. From the Morrill Act and the creation of land grant institutions to the present service-learning and civic engagement movements, university-community partnerships have been important vehicles for student learning and for positive community development. During this period almost every conceivable form of partnership has been developed, from Jane Addams' early-twentieth-century settlement house in Chicago to the well-documented partnership between the University of Pennsylvania and its West Philadelphia neighborhood (Harkavy, 1999; Harkavy, 1997). In numerous ways—from tutoring, to mentoring, to delivering direct social services—university faculty, departments, and students have been addressing issues of the civil society.

Metropolitan State University (Metropolitan State), in Minneapolis-Saint Paul, Minnesota, is no stranger to community partnerships and service-learning. Originated as an urban university in 1971, its mission has been to develop educational and academic programs that engage students, faculty, and community members in programs and initiatives that bear mutual benefit: students learn from community experiences, faculty ground their teaching in real and constructive contexts, community members add important neighborhood knowledge to the education of university students, and communities receive real service and realize positive change. The result of this reciprocal relationship is one that integrates the learning and benefits for all involved in the collaborative process.

Over its thirty-five-year history, Metropolitan State has developed innovative approaches to educational programming that have garnered a national reputation for quality, accessibility, and civic engagement. The university's commitment to civic engagement is included in its vision statement:

> To be the premier, urban, public, comprehensive system university in the Twin Cities metropolitan area focusing on providing high-quality, affordable, educational programs and services in a student-centered environment. The faculty, staff and students will reflect the area's rich diversity and will demonstrate an unwavering commitment to civic engagement. (Metropolitan State University, 2006)

For an institution whose motto is "where life and learning meet" (Metropolitan State University, 2004), the importance of community connection and collaboration is not just a slogan; it is a fundamental component of the university's educational operation.

While many courses and programs have connected with the community throughout its history, the university formalized its partnerships when it created the Center for Community-Based Learning (CCBL) in 1996. Realizing there was a need for a central place on campus to coordinate the community-connected programs, the administration established a physical space and assembled a professional staff to oversee the community connections necessary to fulfill the university's commitment to civic engagement. Over the past decade, CCBL staff, working with faculty and community partners, has helped to create one of the better institutional affiliations in the state. Programs as varied as tutoring, mentoring, planning, and specialty initiatives such as the College for Kids project and the Achieving Higher Education and Dreams (AHEAD) program have brought the university into the neighborhood and the neighborhood into the university for mutual benefit. Given the fact that the surrounding community is economically disadvantaged, the university has worked hard to provide personnel and resources to address community issues.

This chapter describes Metropolitan State's unique relationship with the community and, particularly, a major community partner: the Saint Paul Public Library (SPPL). The SPPL—which consists of a central library, twelve branch libraries, a bookmobile, and a website—is an institution that provides both materials and services to the public. We analyze the development and impact of this unique partnership, exemplified through a joint library that has resulted in significant positive change in both the university and the community. Students, faculty, community members, and community institutions have all been affected by this unusual collaborative, and it has generated many service-learning opportunities. The goal of the chapter is to highlight the important outcomes of this partnership and explain how university-community collaborations can transform learning and the quality of life in a community.

A Unique Partnership

The library partnership is best understood through a description of its history, its cooperative staffing, and the features that intimately connect a community, a public library system, and a university. Focusing on these three dimensions helps to explain why it provides a model for service-learning practice that is both institutionally and community-based.

History and Background

Planning for a joint library system started in the 1980s and 1990s, when the District Community Council in the Dayton's Bluff neighborhood dreamed of having a local library. Although there is a library approximately three miles from the university, it was difficult to access, especially for families with small children. The Advisory Council pushed for a local branch, but none was forth-coming.

As a university without walls, prior to 1992 Metropolitan State did not have a library building. In 1993, Metropolitan State's newly seated president recognized the university's own library-related problems. She received a notice that her students were no longer going to have access to local private colleges' libraries. She also learned from MINITEX Library Information Network that Metropolitan State's lack of library services put it out of compli-ance for use of services. Last, several public libraries notified her that they objected to providing library services to Metropolitan State students. In other words, Metropolitan State had to address its own need for a library.

To deal with this concern, Metropolitan State's president engaged the City of Saint Paul and the Saint Paul Public Library system. From a shared need was born a commitment to develop a truly collaborative project, as revealed in the Statement of Intent (Metropolitan State University Community Library and Information Access Center, 2003):

> To accomplish this shared mission, the University col-laborated from the outset with the Saint Paul Public Library to ensure that this new facility would be a truly shared facility, and throughout the decade it took to develop the financial resources, plan and start constructing this remarkable facility, community col-laboration has been an integral feature every step of the way. (p. 2)

In 1995–1996, with funding from the Minnesota State Colleges and Universities (MnSCU) and a foundation gift, the university and its partners started the predesign process. A formal agreement was developed with the head of the Saint Paul Public Libraries, and a plan was put forward to develop a community-university library. Reflecting its concern for children, families, and community, the library would have a homework help center, celebrate multiculturalism, and strive for innovative approaches to addressing community concerns.

As plans moved forward, the university raised private funds for the facility. In 1998, with the guidance of a new president, it convinced the legislature to provide $1 million in planning grants. The funding and planning progressed, and on May 10, 2004, the $21-million, 86,000-square-foot library facility opened its doors to the community. Staff members were hired to develop the programs and materials, and the grand opening was celebrated on October 9, 2004.

The library building had two major components: a family-centered public library specializing in children's literature and including a teen homework center, and a university library that included an information commons, a fifty-thousand-volume collection, centers for math and writing, classrooms, a bookstore, an art gallery, and a center for teaching and learning. The entire facility was a partnership and collaborative effort that the university, the city, and the families in the community called their own. It was the first and only example in Minnesota of a public library and academic institution partnership providing cooperative library services out of a shared facility.

As the library was nearing completion, the university's Center for Community-Based Learning (CCBL), in partnership with the public library and other community entities, secured funding from the Bush Foundation to support programming, equipment needs, and a community outreach coordinator. This position was vital to the community's engagement in the library partnership.

This history demonstrates the incredible dedication necessary to make a community dream a reality. The tremendous commitment from the community, the Saint Paul Public Library system, the City of Saint Paul, private foundations and private donors, the Minnesota state legislature, and Metropolitan State were all necessary to create the facility. It took a decade to raise the money and provide the planning for the joint venture. It took the vision and commitment of two university presidents and a host of university staff to ensure its ultimate creation. As Metropolitan State's President Wilson Bradshaw stated,

> It is my belief that without this partnership there would not be a Saint Paul Public Library branch in the Dayton's Bluff neighborhood. It is also unlikely that our building plans would have met with such strong private and state support without our collaboration with the Saint Paul Public Library. Metropolitan State University long considered itself a "university without walls," but the walls built for this library have really brought the community and university together. (Metropolitan State University, 2004)

The project was an instant success. Recently, the Saint Paul Public Library Board, in a time of library service cutbacks, approved additional resources to increase the hours and staffing of the Dayton's Bluff branch library. Such increases were deemed necessary in response to the tremendous number of community and university patrons using the facility and services.

Unique Staffing

One of the unique features of the library collaboration was the actual sharing of personnel. Most prominent is the shared library-community outreach coordinator. Although the person filling this role is formally a Metropolitan State CCBL employee, she works as coordinator and communicator for both partners and as a liaison between the partnership and the East Side (Dayton's Bluff) community. The search and hiring committee for the coordinator included staff from the university and the public library, as well as community members. Both libraries are currently engaged in strategic planning, and the library-community outreach coordinator has been integral to these planning processes.

Her primary assignments connect the community with library programs and engage the library in outreach efforts toward expanded services and projects. Her annual evaluations indicate successes that include renewed alliances with community organizations (such as Comunidades Latinas Unidas en Servicio [CLUES]) and local schools, such as Dayton's Bluff Elementary and the Community of Peace Charter School. Her work builds on the long-standing relationships developed through the CCBL over the last decade.

Metropolitan State and SPPL librarians also work in tandem. They hold frequent joint meetings and plan events using shared staff. Continuous communication between the two systems facilitates an integration of university and public library programs and resources such as space and equipment. For example, public library patrons are able to use the computers and materials of the university library on a regular basis. Both university and SPPL staff monitor this use and discuss issues—such as whether to offer unfiltered access to the Internet and how to handle noisy youth—ensuring a smooth and efficient sharing of resources.

Unique Collaborations

Many community collaborations have emerged as a result of the joint library programs. Although it is impossible to describe all that has developed, the three-way relationship of the university, the library, and the community organization CLUES illustrates the unique programs and modes of partnership that have arisen.

CLUES moved within a few blocks of the Library and Learning Center shortly after it opened. This organization, ranked among the top twenty-five Latino non-profits in the nation, provides service in five core areas: mental health, chemical health, employment, education, and elder wellness. Its focus is on developing stronger and more successful families in the Latino community. It had a long history with the CCBL.

As the program became connected to the library, a personal and professional relationship developed between the CLUES Latino Learning Institute manager, Alejandra Reyes Cejudo, and the library-community outreach coordinator, Rebecca Ryan. As they shared information about programs and possibilities, each became involved with the other in program planning and program development. CLUES brought adult students from the ESL classes to the library for orientation and support. Students learned to navigate the library facility, use electronic and paper databases to locate Spanish-language resources, and acquire library cards. Starting with these initial field trips, families increasingly returned to the library, bringing their children and participating in the library's programs, such as Homework Help Center. Ms. Reyes Cejudo noted that the families were coming frequently enough to actually begin referring to the facility as "our library."

In its first two years, the CLUES collaboration grew tremendously. Adult involvement prompted the library staff to develop more computer instruction for adults and to embrace more language development support by purchasing more language-learning resources for the collection. Adults took classes through the Community Technology Empowerment Project (CTEP), an AmeriCorps program, and learned to search the Internet, write resumes, and set up email accounts. The library, with its public and university library computers available to everyone, challenged the digital divide by providing access to computers for an entire low-income community.

The year 2006 saw the library promote language learning using software programs, such as *Rosetta Stone*, to help community members learn and expand their knowledge of Spanish and English. The library became an institution that was perceived by the community members to be the safe, comfortable, and inviting place envisioned a decade before by the university presidents and advisory councils.

CLUES also became an active partner with the library to help in the acquisition of Spanish-language materials. Parents and youth brought in Spanish materials, and the CLUES organization was instrumental in working with the newly located Mexican consulate (in Saint Paul) to provide reading and multimedia material in Spanish.

These gains were not simply material; they included the development of community and interpersonal relationships. The Minnesota Children's Museum received a grant from the Houston Children's Museum to pilot a parent education and family literacy program for Spanish speakers called Para los Niños. The Children's Museum contacted libraries across the seven-county metropolitan area; all expressed interest. Because of the growing numbers of Latinos on the East Side of Saint Paul, and because of the connections with the university and support of the outreach coordinator, the Para los Niños pilot project was planned and established at the university-public branch library. The museum provided funding to hire a trainer for the program, which CLUES learned about from Ms. Ryan. Ms. Reyes Cejudo applied and was accepted. With her entry into the library, Ms. Reyes Cejudo facilitated an expanded network of personal and professional relationships and created new collaboration potentials among the library, the Children's Museum, and CLUES. Although the impacts of these overlapping connections defy quantification, it is certain that the connections between the library and the community bolstered the efficiency and effectiveness of Para los

Niños. As a result, the program was implemented in many of Saint Paul's community institutions, from the library to the museum. This was all the result of the university-community partnership.

Because of the university-community collaboration, the library was able to respond to community interest and continue to offer the Para los Niños program, even without the pilot grant support. Program staff members have made presentations about Para los Niños and its continuation to encourage other Minnesota libraries to pilot similar programs with community partners.

Impacts

The impact of the joint library facility can be tracked through several areas: *impact on learning*, which primarily focuses on university student learning; *impact on youth*, which focuses on youth participation in the homework help center and the Teens Know Best program; *impact on community*, which focuses on family literacy and adult community member learning; and *impact on the university*, which focuses on faculty learning, policy changes, and ways the university has benefited from the increased community involvement.

Impact on Learning

The ultimate goal of community collaborations was to have reciprocal impacts on all participants. College students, faculty, and educational institutions, as well as community organizations and individuals, were included in the planning, development, and implementation of programs to reap valuable mutual benefits. As Harkavy (2004) and others remind us, some of the primary measures of service-learning and civic engagement programs are registered in the intellectual, moral, and citizenship development of the participants and in the advancement of social institutions and democracy. As cited outcomes from the 1991 Wingspread conference on research (Giles, Porter-Honnet, & Migliore, 1998), the impact of university-community partnerships needed to manifest itself at all levels of participation. College students, children, families, community organizations, faculty, institutions of higher education, K–12 schools—in short, the community as a whole—had to show evidence of impact, change, and, ideally, improvement. Sigmon (1990) suggests that service-learning's major tenets include the following: (1) those being served must control the services provided, (2) those being served must become better able to serve themselves, and (3) those who serve are also learners and have significant control over what is expected to be learned. In the case of the library and its impact on all participants across the university-community partnership, these three criteria were all met.

In this section, the focus is on university students and the ways they fulfilled Sigmon's (1990) third major service-learning tenet through participation in various library programs. At its best, programming integrates the resources of the libraries, the university, and the community. Examples of this are demonstrated in the Teens Know Best Reading Group, the Third Floor Gallery, and the Homework Help Center.

Professor Adela Peskorz offered a group internship, Best Books for Young Adults: Publishing and Awards. In group internships (considered university courses), students engage in the study of a common issue. In this case, students implement the Teens Know Best (TKB) program, a reading group for twelve- to eighteen-year-olds that focuses on the selection processes for choosing young adult literature. The recommendations for approved books contributed to lists, such as the Best Books for Young Adults (BBYA). University students, having gone through an adolescent literature course, facilitate monthly discussions with teens, read ten books themselves on adolescent literature (reading, annotating, and defending the acceptance or rejection of the book), present three book talks about eligible titles at the monthly meetings, and complete a final paper summarizing their group experiences.

Evaluation of college student participation in TKB suggested that they obtained insights not normally acquired in a traditional adolescent literature program. First, they learned about the criteria used by the American Library Association (ALA) to evaluate young adult books, a framework not usually covered in a traditional course on the subject. Second, facilitating discussions with youth forced them to integrate the ALA evaluation process with the perceptions of real adolescents, so the content was not simply an abstraction, but an applied reality. Third, they learned group facilitation skills that helped them to get more substantive and accurate feedback about the literature from the books' target readers. Fourth, their service contribution was important to the growth of the youth they interacted with, and the recommendations for accepting or rejecting books actually helped libraries across the country select good choices for young adults. Many of the university students participating in the program did so with a career goal in mind, most often thinking of work as a high school English teacher or librarian. Therefore, university student participation helped them to learn about both fields as well as ways to integrate library activities into academic classes at the high school level. One important learning outcome was discovering this innovative framework in a service context, helping youth across the country to find interesting books at their local library.

Assistant professor Erica Rasmussen offered another group internship: Exhibition Practices. This internship was designed to teach university students about the basic functions and day-to-day operations of an educational art gallery. Students installed and dismantled three exhibitions that featured art by students, community members, and professional artists. In this process, students learned about handling art, lighting, publicity, working with artists, and event programming (such as receptions, artist's talks, and interdisciplinary presentations). The course was designed to prepare students for entry-level work in art museums and other exhibition environments that use these skills and knowledge sets.

This course was also important because it helped support the art gallery located on the library's third floor. This was a good example of how the facility itself enabled real service-learning. Without exhibitions that featured art by students, community members, and professional artists, there would be no gallery in the library. Without a gallery, there would be no faculty and student art displays, as the campus had no other secure and insured space. Rasmussen, as gallery director, was charged with maintaining a professional, community-responsive display that generated community interest and support. Students in her course helped with exhibitions and became very involved in the development of community art workshops. For example, her interns implemented workshops on book-binding and embroidery for Dayton's Bluff Elementary School. They have also developed art workshops.

Similar to the BBYA experience, the college students were engaged in real projects that benefited the region and gave them feedback and perspective from community members, such as the elementary school children who took the art workshops. True to Metropolitan State's motto, which celebrates the point where "life and learning meet" (Metropolitan State University, 2004), the course provided them with a context for their learning that was embedded in real community work. The nature of the course, and the community nature of the library, placed extra responsibility on the students to deliver goods and services that could be used by community members. Thus the existence of the library art gallery gave students real opportunities to apply knowledge and skill in gallery development, and at the same time provided a real place for art in a community that had few places where art could be viewed and appreciated.

The library offered other options for university students to fulfill service or service-learning requirements. These options centered on the Homework Help Center in the public library. Metropolitan State students were recruited to serve as homework center tutors and one-on-one mentors for the library's Read With Me literacy program (which focused attention on K–2 pupils). University students tutored in general subject areas for users whose ages ranged widely: kindergartners; adults returning to school; elementary, middle, and high school English-language learners; and community members who needed computer assistance and tutoring—all used the homework center. Tutors, many of whom came from the urban education program, learned of the specific educational needs of the community members and provided one-on-one assistance. They also learned about the library as a community resource, and they planned and participated in community activities taking place in the homework center.

Impact on Area Youth

A few programs illustrate the contributions the library made to young people. First, as noted in the yearly program evaluations (Shumer, 2006), the use of and support provided by the Homework Help Center showed growth as measured by the number of individuals served and the kinds of service provided. The first year saw an average of forty-five students per week use the Center; the second year saw that number more than double to ninety-three per week. The number of hours per month of tutoring provided by university students and staff in the first year was fourteen. Year two saw a fivefold increase, to eighty hours each month. There was a tremendous improvement in the amount of support provided to the youth who used the Center.

The groups of students served also increased in the two years of operation. In 2004–2005 there were youth from approximately fifteen area schools. By 2005–2006, youth from twenty-five different schools were represented, including elementary, middle, and high schools. Diversity of youth served also increased. Early on there were only youth who spoke English and Hmong at home; by the end of the second year six different home languages, including Amharic and Somali, were represented by the young people served.

This meant the library services were being extended to many new immigrants who populated the Dayton's Bluff neighborhood.

Perhaps most important, the nature of the support evolved. During the first year most youth who used the Homework Help Center were primarily interested in using the computers and working on their regular homework assignments. They didn't ask for much help from the tutoring staff. In the second year things changed: the Center became much more active in helping youth to improve their school work. As cited in the second year report:

> Perhaps one of the most important qualitative changes in the Homework Help Center was the actual services offered. Last year a majority of the youth who used the center completed their homework, but asked for relatively little help with their assignments. This year things have changed. More youth are actually using the services of the tutors and asking questions about their homework and assignments. Thus, more direct service is being provided to youth as they complete their homework assignments on time. It also suggests that more youth who need extra help are coming to the Homework Help Center .... This change reflects a more positive climate for homework help than in the first year. (Shumer, 2006, pp. 6–7)

Thus the services provided reached a different audience. No longer serving only youth who were doing well in school, the library began to affect the learning of youth with greater needs: those who required actual assistance in understanding and completing their homework assignments. The library was now reaching youth who tended to be poorer and have less proficiency in English and who needed adult guidance to understand topics and concepts taught in school.

The library had even gone beyond the personal services in the Center, launching a new opportunity for youth in 2006. Staff worked with a private online provider, *tutor.com*, so youth could gain additional support when the library was closed. The Homework Help Center was open only during the week; youth could use the online resources at the library after hours and on weekends. Since most youth did not have computers at home, this encouraged them to use the library facilities at hours that were not tracked by the Homework Help Center, yet were definitely the result of initial contact with that service.

The Homework Help Center, by serving as a gathering place for area youth, also helped them make a positive impact on the community. Through the youth advisory group, youth had a say in making the homework center a place that responded to their needs. Through the efforts of the advisory group and added mentorship by university students and other adults, the homework center served as a site for *manga* club, game night, sporadic performances, poetry slams, and informal learning activities. Many of the youth, as part of an option to pay off library fines, volunteered regularly in the library.

Youth were also affected by the library connections with the local schools. Because of work by the Outreach Coordinator and other CCBL staff assigned to school programs, more teachers and classes visited the library for orientation programs and opportunities to get library cards and use library facilities. As word has spread about the various programs available, the library has become one of the favorite entertainment spots for youth in the community (Shumer, 2005).

Youth have been impacted by regular and summer programming conducted through the University. Supported by CCBL staff, VISTA workers, student teachers, and other volunteers, College for Kids and Achieving Higher Education and Dreams (AHEAD) included library instruction in their curricular offerings. The College for Kids program served fourth, fifth, and sixth graders from three local elementary schools. In 2005–2006 more than 400 children participated in the program and 203 students attended a library class. The class started with a scavenger hunt that oriented students to the different parts of the library. Students then received instruction on how to use electronic databases and also how to find important resources. Feedback from the program staff indicated that students who participated were better able to discuss the library's purpose and activities and were better acquainted with using the online resources of the library. Minnesota school standards began addressing information literacy in the second grade, and these classes added to what was being taught in the elementary school connected to the library program.

In the summer of 2006 the university library, public library, and CCBL worked together to provide three apprentice positions for diverse high school students interested in library work. The three students hired responded to a job description sent out to local high schools. The apprentices worked in the public library, learning about daily library operations, and in the university library, where they worked with one of the reference librarians to help revise information literacy syllabi. They also worked with the CCBL to gain an understanding of various library and youth-related programming. One participant evaluated her experience this way:

> Yes, I am considering a career in the library. I can picture myself doing it because I love to read and I know that my career interest is in community service and helping others. A career in the library fascinates me because so many people come there and I know the library is able to provide them with learning resources. (D. Lee)

One of the premier collaborative programs that affected youth was the Teens Know Best Reading Group. This program, started at Metropolitan State by faculty member Adela Peskorz, who taught courses on library use and young adult literature, engaged high school students in the ongoing American

Library Association/Young Adult Library Services Association (ALA)/YALSA) Best Books for Young Adults program. In this program students reviewed actual adolescent literature and then made recommendations regarding the popularity, interest, and appropriateness of the material for libraries across the country. As a member of the national committee, Professor Peskorz provided an opportunity for the high school students to review and discuss the books and showcase their feedback about the books at a national conference. Five students, along with Peskorz, presented their thoughts to a committee at the national conference for the ALA in Chicago in June 2006. It was a major opportunity for the students, who had never done anything like this before, to build self-confidence and critical analysis skills and to share their perceptions of books designated for adolescent youth.

Ten to fifteen youth met each month with library staff and university students from Ms. Perkorz's group internship to discuss books and make recommendations to the national committee. By the third year, the program, now known simply as Teens Know Best (TKB), changed to a new focus, with youth actually reading publisher proofs of books before they were published. As many as thirty to forty youth participated regularly in discussions and reviews. This program was one of only fifteen nationally sponsored by the ALA; as such, it lifted the Dayton's Bluff initiative to a true leadership position in the nation. Youth were now providing direct feedback to publishers and authors before books were produced. It raised the power of their voice incredibly.

As a result of these levels of involvement, youth reported that participation in BBYA and TKB made them feel that they had a strong voice in the selection of library books and, in return, were making a contribution to others. L., one of the teen participants, enjoyed giving good recommendations to friends. She looked for books with "a good plot line, strong and deep characters—people who felt real: good first chapter and just something so it's not the same as all the others. A twist, or anything unique that draws you in" (Harvey, 2006).

Collaboration among the university, the public library staff, and the local youth met an important element of Sigmon's (1990) principles of service-learning: allowing the community to share power and control over their own library system. In the process, the BBYA/TKB initiative helped produce youth with critically minded understandings of what constituted good young adult literature. The initiative also provided a clearer sense of the libraries' and local participants' roles in the development and maintenance of democratic communities. It was a true reciprocal relationship: the community benefited from the position and influence of Ms. Peskorz in the ALA, the support and input of the college students improved the education of young people, and the power sharing of the public and university library system allowed youth to have a voice in the book selection process. The university side of the equation benefited from the input and perspectives of the local youth and the interest that the initiative generated in terms of community support. Although as of this writing no one is conducting research on the topic, it would be interesting to determine just how much BBYA participation affected the adolescents in the program, especially regarding their desire and ability to go to college, whether they select Metropolitan State as their choice, and whether the development of critical thinking skills enabled them to go on to higher education. The BBYA program had the potential to affect all these areas. Time and additional data will help to answer some of these questions.

It is clear from these examples that the joint library programs systematically affected the learning and motivation of community, school-based youth. Regular programs were developed between the library and the schools, and efforts were directed at improving academic achievement and community scholarship. This impact should not go unnoticed, because it laid a foundation for future collaborations that connect the library as an established partner contributing to the education of youth through their schools and through supplemental programs that enrich, motivate, and inspire.

Impact on the Community

There have been unquantifiable impacts on individual community members, community organizations, and even the culture and atmosphere of the community. Because a point-by-point chronicle of these impacts is beyond this chapter's scope, a few examples must suffice to provide a sense and flavor of what the community impact looks like.

Perhaps the most significant impacts on the community were through the emergent relationships between the library-community outreach coordinator and various community agencies. In each case the coordinator brought resources, ideas, and networks that have changed the processes and the substance of community work.

As mentioned earlier, the relationship between the outreach coordinator, the library, and the Children's Museum eventually led to the hiring of the CLUES manager by the museum. This allowed the Children's Museum to have instant outreach and credibility in the Latino community, and to have access to Ms. Reyes Cejudo's experiential knowledge and social networks. Simply put, the connections brought by these interpersonal linkages allowed the Children's Museum to connect with the Latino community in ways that would otherwise have been difficult to achieve.

Reciprocally, the development of the CLUES program was greatly enhanced by the connections with library personnel. Access and programs were developed to meet the needs of CLUES constituents. Computer programming for adults was added to the library offerings. All the CLUES ESL classes had library field trips, in which they received orientations, library cards, and access to all resources in both Spanish and English. CLUES students went back to the CLUES building and talked about the library as a vital resource. As a result, many CLUES adults and their families now use the library on a regular basis; in fact, the CLUES programming is intimately connected to the library services. Thus the personnel and programming offered through the library have made the CLUES initiatives richer, more tapped into the library's available resources, and more directly connected to an active learning center in the community.

The outreach coordinator had a similar effect on local schools. In addition to programs such as College for Kids, Metropolitan State offered numerous programs that affected the quality of learning opportunities in the schools. Specifically, the coordinator made important connections with many area schools, arranging field trips to the library that introduced students and teachers to its resources and programs. The effort created a change whereby teachers and students used the library's resources regularly. For example, in December 2005, forty-five third graders from Dayton's Bluff Elementary School attended an art exhibit and a book-making workshop at the library. Other schools, such as Hope Community Academy, had forty fifth graders attend the Culture of Peace exhibit and conduct research projects. In both cases, the library was seen as a regular part of the local schools' curricular offerings. This was especially important in light of concurrent funding reductions for the school libraries' staffing and functions. This use of the library as a community resource transformed the schools and enabled them to offer enriched library services as part of their educational programs. This occurrence is ironic, but appropriate, because this is precisely what was denied to Metropolitan State students (access to public and other college libraries) that made them experience the need to have a library of their own.

Another facet of the community impact has been through the university library's community borrower card program. Few universities allow free access to computers and materials in the library, but Metropolitan State's library allowed any user over the age of thirteen, who had a public library card free of fines, to obtain a community borrower card. This card enabled community borrowers to access the university library's unfiltered computers for two hours a day, borrow materials, reserve study rooms, and request reference assistance. This program opened the knowledge of the university to the community and represented a real commitment on the part of the university to allowing community access. Initially, some faculty members, students, and library staff were unsure about sharing the university's resources in this way. Some worried that community borrowers in the university library would make noise, create distractions, and take resources away from university students. Policies were developed, with input from the public librarian, that sensitively dealt with delicate situations. Because of the collaborative spirit, these policies prevented conflict between the diverse user groups in the shared library and enabled sensitive responses to both sets of user needs.

In addition to changing the way community organizations and schools did business, the joint library became an extension of almost all the community programs in the local area. The library's third floor had a community room that was available to community and university groups for public discussions and presentations. Community organizations, especially those affiliated with university programs, used the room with no charge. The community room rapidly became the most sought-after space in the East Side neighborhood and a central space for community gatherings.

While serving as an extension of programs, schools, and community agencies, the community library served a unique role: it was a source of community identity. The Dayton's Bluff environment, which housed the university and the bulk of immediate community surroundings, had important historical significance for the area. The history included waves of immigrants, their relationships with the region's Native Americans, and the area's important role in Saint Paul's trade and manufacturing. As expressed in community focus groups, there was an expectation that the library would serve an important role in maintaining and advancing this history through the compilation, research, and display of stories and documents. The library staff, as well as the university faculty, have responded by conducting research on various dimensions of the history (labor relations, burial mounds, and the like) and conducted public presentations on important topics. The library began historical projects around housing, art, and architecture that has impacted the residents' pride and identity. The public presentations were well attended and archived for future generations.

Thus the community library affected the community in many ways. It became a constant and important ally and contributor to community agency programs, schools, social and personal networks, and community identity. This was the result of the early, genuine partnership of the university, the public library, and the community, in which community change and well-being were constant goals.

Impact on the University

Many dimensions of the university were affected by the community library. The most obvious was the actual existence of the library. As President Bradshaw stated early on, there probably would not have been the library without the strong public and community support (Metropolitan State University Community Library and Information Access Center, 2003). Metropolitan State students and faculty members gained access to a state-of-the-art facility that provided the library resources required of a first-class institution of higher education. As a joint university-community library serving a college population of adult learners, whose average age is thirty-four, the new library provided many resources for higher education needs and allowed students' families to enjoy the books, programs, and exhibits. Previously, this kind of gathering space had not been available to Metropolitan State students.

In addition to the expected resources of the library (books, computers, reference collections, and so on), the community library provided a learning laboratory that allowed for good service-learning and civic education practice. To encourage more faculty members to incorporate service-learning in the library, the CCBL cosponsored a teaching seminar, resulting in five faculty members' adding library-related service-learning components to their courses. Course components developed ranged from a capstone in public and nonprofit management to societal issues in computing to family and child psychology. University students tutored in the homework center to experience the effect of researching with internet filters; planned literacy activities for parents, caregivers, and children; and participated in system-wide strategic planning with the Saint Paul Public Library. These students had unique learning opportunities through the physical and virtual space of the library, community, and university. And the community was always enriched through the operation of programs that raise its level of culture, awareness, and power to control its own institutions.

Perhaps the greatest impact on the university occurred every day as the institution projected its image and its programmatic face in the community. The fact that the university-community library was growing as a true community center—with people and programs that were invested in the development of the educational, aesthetic, and social aspects of the community—was further evidence that Metropolitan State functioned as an engaged campus. As with the entire initiative's origins, it became clear that the public library and the community could not do their work without the university's support and resources. In turn, the university could not reach its potential and institutional goals and agenda without the active engagement of the community through people, programs, and resources.

Discussion and Conclusions

This story is an example of how a university partnered successfully with its community for genuine mutual benefit and empowerment. From ideas born almost two decades ago, the vision of a library in the Dayton's Bluff area of Saint Paul was a dream nurtured in the community and eventually brought into reality when the needs of the community coincided with those of the university. Both required library services, and, as the story unfolded, it became clear that neither could obtain the desired outcome without the other. The arrangement saw both sides helping with fundraising, increasing support, and eventually encouraging the legislative will to secure the funds and space for the facility.

The rest is history. The common goals of developing a library facility that focused on the community and families, served the needs of all, and built educational and artistic programs were realized throughout the model's development and execution. From courses on literacy and adult language learning, to a homework center that assisted youth with in-school and out-of-school work, to connections with CLUES and other organizations that addressed needs of underserved populations, the joint library developed programs and resources that met real community needs.

The university and public library also dealt with conflict throughout the building process and during operation. It was not always easy to integrate an open access public library into a university library building. Who owns the furniture? Who repairs the computers? These problems were addressed during building by a team of representatives from the university and public library.

In addition, user populations did not always coexist harmoniously. Faculty members did not always appreciate sharing a library with families and young children, and families did not always appreciate the more complex university bureaucracy they had to navigate to obtain a community borrower card. Yet these differences created a civic learning laboratory found only in public gathering spaces—one that forced all involved to understand and work together.

The learning derived from these programs not only built community culture and community pride but also connected academic content with civic engagement. Students saw the reasons for authentic connection because their academic program fed the needs of their community. Responding to criticism from Stanley

Fish (2003) that academics should not attempt to educate students for citizenship, Harkavy stated that such criticism serves an important function:

> It splendidly illustrates what might be called the disciplinary fallacy afflicting American universities; namely, the fallacy that professors are duty-bound only to serve the scholastic interests and preoccupations of their disciplines and have neither the responsibility nor capacity to help their universities keep their long-standing promise to prepare *America's Undergraduates for Lives of Moral and Civic Responsibility* (Colby, Ehrlich, Beaumont, & Stephens, 2003). In effect, Fish boldly asserted what most professors now believe and practice but strongly tend not to admit openly. (Harkavy, 2004, p. 13)

Metropolitan State–Saint Paul Community Library took this argument one step further: universities that live in communities—especially those that are poor and underserved—can fulfill their academic and social/civic needs by partnering with the community. Building literacy programs such as BBYA and offering courses that require art exhibitions for academic focus are actions not exclusive to academic institutions. Such institutions can use community contexts and resources to make them credible and effective. In so doing, universities model for students their roles as active citizens, inventing and implementing programs that enhance learning and benefit the civic and cultural life of the community.

Critics of university-community partnerships, such as Fish (2003), must understand that not every university is financially secure, elite, and walled-off. In the case of Metropolitan State, the university needed community support for a library as much as the community needed the university. It was a partnership born out of mutual necessity that has flourished because of presidential and community leadership, shared visions of purposeful collaborations, and integration of financial and human resources. The partnership has paid big dividends for learning at all levels: K–12, higher education, and community.

Not every university has the unique timing and vision for conditions that require truly collaborative ventures around an institution such as a library. But there is much to be learned from cases such as this. "Life and learning" can meet in reciprocally enriching ways. We hope that will be the story for many other universities and communities as they work together to foster true civic partnerships. By collaborating, they can positively affect all who live and learn in the community.

References

Colby, A., Ehrlich, T., Beaumont, E., & Stephens, J. (2003). *Educating citizens: Preparing America's undergraduates for lives of moral and civic responsibility.* San Francisco: Jossey-Bass.

Fish, S. (2003, May 16). Aim low. *The Chronicle of Higher Education.* Retrieved September 15, 2006, from http://www.chronicle.com

Giles, D., Porter-Honnet, E., & Migliore, S. (1998). Research agenda for combining service and learning in the 1990s. *Advances in Educational Research, 3,* 119–128.

Harkavy, I. (1997). The demands of the times and the American research university. *Journal of Planning Literature, 11*(3), 33–36.

Harkavy, I. (1999). School-community-university partnerships: Effectively integrating community building and educational reform. *Universities and Community Schools, 6*(1-2), 7–24.

Harkavy, I. (2004). Service-learning and the development of democratic universities, democratic schools, and democratic good societies in the 21st century. In S. Billig & M. Welch (Eds.), *New perspectives in service-learning: Research to advance the field* (pp. 3–22). Greenwich, CT: Information Age Publishing.

Harvey, K. (2006, October 16). Voicing an opinion. *Saint Paul Pioneer Press,* pp. 1D, 3D.

Metropolitan State University. (2004). Metropolitan State University Library and Learning Center. Saint Paul, MN: Metropolitan State University.

Metropolitan State University. (2006). Mission and goals statement. Retrieved November 21, 2006, from http://www.metrostate.edu/policies/pdf/missiongoals.pdf

Metropolitan State University Community Library and Information Access Center. (2003). Statement of Intent for Collaborative Relationship with the Saint Paul Public Library. Saint Paul, MN: Metropolitan State University Community Library and Information Access Center.

Shumer, R. (2005). Final report: Year I evaluation: Metropolitan State University/Saint Paul Public Library Community University-Library and Information Center. R. Shumer.

Shumer, R. (2006). Final report: Year II evaluation: Metropolitan State University/Saint Paul Public Library Community University-Library and Information Center. R. Shumer.

Sigmon, R. L. (1990). Service-learning: Three principles. In Jane C. Kendall and Associates (Eds.), *Combining service and learning: A resource book for community and public service* (pp. 56–64). Raleigh, NC: National Society for Internships and Experiential Education.

4

Advancing Service-Learning Through Program Evaluation

Nancy Nisbett, Sally Cahill Tannenbaum, and Brent Smither

Experiential learning is a cornerstone of recreation programs at universities across the United States. Volunteer work, service-learning assignments, and internships are standard, providing real-world learning as well as service to the community. Students commonly accumulate hundreds and even thousands of hours at multiple agencies during their college careers. At California State University, Fresno, for example, students completing a degree in recreation administration graduate with more than 1,500 hours of experience in a wide variety of recreation agencies.

In many cases the service-learning opportunities focus on assisting agencies to implement recreation programs. Although worthwhile, these opportunities are often limited in both depth and breadth. Students participate in the implementation of the program, but they are brought in after both assessment and planning have occurred, and they leave before the evaluation has taken place. For recreation majors, although implementation is important, these other areas are crucial to their professional success; they are major competencies in the curriculum.

Recognizing the need to provide students with a richer experience that more effectively ties course objectives to agency needs, faculty of the Recreation Administration and Leisure Studies (RLS) Program at California State University, Fresno (CSU Fresno), created a partnership with staff from the Fresno County Office of Education (FCOE). Specifically, this partnership was created with one FCOE department, the Department of Safe and Healthy Kids. This department sponsors a wide variety of cocurricular programs focusing on the serious health issues of students in Fresno County. This partnership was formed to jointly identify and investigate projects that attempt to mitigate the health problems of K–12 students through recreation and physical activity programs.

This chapter describes the resulting project—the evaluation of an adventure race—from both the RLS and the FCOE perspectives. We highlight the strengths and weaknesses of the project, its relationship to the health of children, and its contribution to service-learning literature. The chapter begins with a review of relevant service-learning literature, followed by an introduction to both the RLS program and the FCOE and an overview of student health in Fresno County.

Literature on Service-Learning

As explained in the preface, service-learning has become increasingly used by institutions of higher education; a 2001 report by Campus Compact, for instance, noted that at that time more than seven hundred thousand U.S. college students were participating in service-learning activities annually, and that trends suggested ongoing increases (Campus Compact, 2001). A high percentage of the service-learning activities that university students participate in take place in K–12 settings.

The impact of service-learning on university students has been well documented. One of these is in academic achievement. Research indicates that students participating in service-learning are more likely to understand and critically appreciate course content (Akujobi & Simmons, 1997; Astin & Sax, 1998; Astin, Vogelgesang, Ikeda, & Yee, 2000; Batchelder & Root, 1994; Katula & Threnhauser, 1999; Klute & Billig, 2002; Markus, Howard, &

King, 1993; Melchior, 1999; Melchior & Bailis, 2002; Strage, 2000, Vogelgesang & Alexander, 2000).

The literature also suggests that service-learning enhances the social skills of students. Melchior and Bailis (2002) analyzed the findings of three major national service-learning initiatives to determine the benefits of using service-learning. The review found that students who participated in service-learning felt more confident in their ability to identify issues, work with others, organize and take action, and build a commitment to participation over the long term. Other scholars have drawn similar conclusions (Astin, 1996; Myers-Lipton, 1996; Payne, 2000; Yates & Youniss, 1996).

A growing number of scholars also applaud the value of action-research. Action-research integrates research, teaching, and service, balancing the need to gather data about important social concerns in the local community with the need of students to gain knowledge about applied research (Bass & Silverstein, 1996). Action-research allows students to become involved in the design and implementation of research as a response to specific needs in a community. The goal of action-research is not only to gather information about a community issue but also to strengthen communities by effecting change to improve the community (Harkavy, Puckett, & Romer, 2000).

When individuals with mutual interests work together in teams to study those interests and identify solutions, they are engaging in a specific type of action-research known as *collaborative action-research* (Hironaka-Juteau, Hergenrader, & Kraft, 2006). This type of action-research, geared toward improving professional practice, is especially suited to the inclusion of university students. Students are supported by a team while gaining hands-on experience and exposure to current issues in the profession. Sagor (1993) offered one approach to collaborative action-research, based on a five-step process: (1) problem formation, (2) data collection, (3) data analysis, (4) reporting results, and (5) action planning. With this process the research team and sponsoring organization are the primary audience for the results. However, the results could potentially affect a much larger audience if the research team goes beyond reporting the results to the agency and chooses to present the results at a professional conference or publish in a professional journal (Hironaka-Juteau et al., 2006).

Reviewing the service-learning and action-research literature, we found several articles addressing the value of university students conducting action-research in K–12 settings (Catelli, Padovano, & Costello, 2000; Price, 2001). The review also found several articles that addressed the evaluation of service-learning activities in these settings; however, it did not reveal instances of evaluation of other types of K–12 programs as a service-learning or action-research activity. Program evaluation—the systematic process of collecting information about the activities and outcomes of a program in order to make judgments or inform decisions about future programs—is consistent with the collaborative action-research process and is an important area of skill development for many university students (Patton, 2002). Exploring the implementation of this process in a K–12 setting with university students would be a positive addition to the service-learning literature.

The RLS-FCOE Partnership

Having addressed some relevant service-learning literature, we now provide background about the two partner organizations and a collaborative project, the Scout Island Adventure Challenge. In this section we briefly describe the RLS and FCOE's Safe and Healthy Kids program and look at how their partnership responded to the problem of adolescent health.

The RLS Program

The RLS Program was established at CSU Fresno in 1959. The Program offers a bachelor of science degree in recreation administration founded on a competency-based curriculum. In this professional preparation program, students acquire specific competencies in leadership, program planning, goal identification, recreation activities, budgeting, evaluation, administration and supervision, understanding clientele and working with diverse populations, professional ethics and philosophy, research techniques, public relations and marketing, communication skills, organizational systems, legislation, and facility planning and management. Students also select and develop additional competencies in one of four specializations: community recreation and youth services, commercial recreation, sports and entertainment facility management, and adventure recreation and tourism.

Experiential education is fundamental to the delivery of the RLS curriculum. Faculty members integrate a wide variety of experiential activities in their courses. Although activities such as hands-on learning in the classroom and field trips are extremely useful, faculty are strongly committed to the benefits of applying course competencies to real-world experiences. As a result, volunteer work and service-learning are common in the curriculum. In addition, students achieve their degree by completing a semester-long, full-time internship (over five hundred hours). As noted earlier, students graduate from this program with at least 1,500 hours of paid or volunteer experience in the recreation industry.

FCOE Department of Safe and Healthy Kids

In California, county offices of education are regional K–12 educational consortia. They provide educational oversight to the school districts located in their respective counties. FCOE, in particular, oversees thirty-four separate school districts in Fresno County. FCOE provides oversight and coordinates services to court and community schools, curriculum and instruction, migrant education, special education, the regional occupation program, guidance services, and health services.

The FCOE's Department of Safe and Healthy Kids focuses on the development of personal and social responsibility in youth. The department does this through a number of programs, including over one hundred after-school programs; a leadership institute; supplemental services for Title One program improvement sites; wellness, nutrition, and fitness programs; and sponsorship of a number of special events. The wellness, nutrition, and fitness programs include two showcase fitness and nutrition competitions: the Pentathlon Adventure Challenge, aimed at elementary school children, and the Scout Island Adventure Challenge, designed to attract high school students.

The Scout Island Adventure Challenge was initiated in 2004 when the Fresno County Superintendent approached FCOE staff with a request to develop a showcase event for high school students to promote fitness. The target students for the adventure challenge event were to be students not currently participating in traditional athletics. The challenge for FCOE was to design a race that high school students would find "cool," while still giving less-active students the opportunity to be challenged, to exercise, and to be part of a team.

To accomplish these objectives, planners decided to design the event as a series of challenges, resembling activities from one of the many adventure-based reality television shows. Additionally, global positioning system (GPS) technology was used to increase the "wow" factor of the race. To ensure an educational focus, planners identified relevant standards from the state high school educational standards. The goal of the adventure challenge was to promote physical fitness, enhance leadership and teamwork, and reinforce academics through recreation and physical activity.

The first race was planned for April 2005. It took place at an outdoor education facility run by FCOE, on a three-mile course with ten different challenges. A small field of eight teams competed in this first event. Each team was composed of two girls and two boys and had one adult coach. Every team finished the race, with a one-hour difference between the first and last place teams.

Immediate feedback from the first race was overwhelmingly positive. Every team wanted to race again and wanted more challenge. Based on this feedback, FCOE planned the next event without delay. The second running of this challenge occurred in October 2005. Seventeen teams participated. The race, expanded to six miles, included both physical and cognitive challenges. Events included running, biking, a river swim, and a climbing wall, as well as events focused on communication and problem-solving skills such as math problems, navigating with a GPS, and a group puzzle. All events required teamwork for successful completion. This event is the focus of the evaluation project described in this chapter.

Student Health in Fresno County

Although obesity is a serious issue for youth throughout the nation, the problem is more pronounced in the San Joaquin Valley of California. A high percentage of youth in the San Joaquin Valley are designated obese, having a body mass index (BMI) of 30 or above (BMI is calculated by dividing the body weight in pounds by body height in inches). A BMI of 30 indicates that a person is about thirty pounds overweight. Lack of nutrition and physical exercise are the primary factors leading to child obesity issues. Ethnic background, poverty, and lack of routine medical care also appear to be contributing factors. The medical and psychosocial consequences for the individual child and for the community in which they live are significant (Centers for Disease Control and Prevention, 2005; Central California Children's Health Institute, 2005; Sutton, Hernandez, Perez, & Curtis, 2004).

Analysis of the 2004 physical fitness test of fifth, seventh, and ninth graders by the California Center for Public Health Advocacy (2005) found that 30.2 percent of children in Fresno County were defined as overweight (having a BMI of 25 and above) compared with 28.1 percent in the state of California and only 16 percent nationwide (Centers for Disease Control and Prevention, 2005). More troubling, perhaps, are reports indicating that childhood obesity is on the rise in the San Joaquin Valley. In 2001, forty-two thousand adolescents (12.8 percent) in the San Joaquin Valley were overweight or obese (Sutton et al., 2004). By 2003, it was estimated that the number had risen to fifty-eight thousand (15.2 percent). The issue is particularly serious for Latino students. From 2001 to 2003, the reported number of overweight or obese Latino youth in the San Joaquin Valley doubled, from sixteen thousand to thirty-two thousand (Central California Children's Health Institute, 2005).

Again, nutrition and lack of physical exercise contribute to the problem. The Central California Children's Institute reported that in 2003, 58 percent of children from birth to age eleven living in the San Joaquin Valley did not eat the daily recommended five servings of fruit or vegetables (Sutton et al., 2004). Data from the UCLA Center for Health Policy Research (2001) indicated that two-thirds of the children in the San Joaquin Valley did not participate in sufficient physical activity. In fact, sedentary behavior, such as watching more than two hours of television daily, was reported by more than one-third of adolescents age twelve to seventeen. Pinzon-Perez (2006) looked at the effect of television ads on foods selected by Latino farm-working mothers for their children age five and younger. Television advertising was found to have a major influence on food selection patterns and played a major role in changing cultural beliefs about nutrition.

Poverty also appears to be a factor. In 2003 it was estimated that two-thirds of San Joaquin Valley adolescents who were overweight or obese lived in poverty. In fact, one-third of overweight adolescents came from abject poverty—households with an income significantly below the federal poverty level (Children Count!, 2003).

The impact of childhood and adolescent obesity is significant. Overweight children face a higher risk of developing high blood pressure and Type 2 diabetes. Excessive weight also complicates asthma; leads to orthopedic problems, high blood lipids, sleep apnea, and gallstones; and contributes to low self-esteem, depression, discrimination, and poor body image. Research also indicates that overweight children are more likely to be obese as adults, which in turn puts them at a higher risk of developing heart disease, stroke, cancer, and diabetes (Greer, Hernandez, Sutton, & Curtis, 2004).

In addition to the individual medical and psychosocial consequences of obesity, the costs to society are significant. The condition of being overweight or obese and a lack of physical activity costs California taxpayers $28 billion annually for medical care, worker's compensation, and lost productivity (California Center for Public Health Advocacy, 2004).

Partnership Goals and Benefits

In the fall of 2005, discussions were held between FCOE staff and faculty of the RLS Program. Discussions focused on identifying current FCOE projects that might provide good service opportunities for RLS students. The adventure challenge was discussed as a potential project, based on the two major obstacles it posed for FCOE staff. The first obstacle was the lack of an evaluation plan. Anecdotal evidence was collected at the conclusion of each adventure challenge; however, no formal evaluation plan had been developed. Although the anecdotal evidence had been positive, the absence of an evaluation mechanism made it difficult to verify goal attainment and identify weaknesses. The second obstacle related to funding. Although currently funded by the FCOE, the high cost of the adventure challenge (nearly $250 per student participant) made the search for alternative funding sources a worthwhile endeavor.

Both obstacles appeared to be appropriate action-research projects for the Programming and Evaluation in Recreation, Parks, and Tourism course. This course focuses on developing, evaluating, and sustaining recreation programs at a wide variety of recreation agencies. The decision was made to incorporate these two projects into the course for the spring 2006 semester.

RLS and FCOE Goals

For the RLS Program faculty, this project provided an opportunity to teach the fundamentals of research from conception to presentation. It also provided an opportunity for students to discover firsthand the importance of evaluation. For the FCOE staff, the advantages to participating in this collaborative project were twofold. First, the project would provide FCOE with an objective program evaluation to determine whether or not the adventure challenge was successful in meeting its objectives and if there were any long-term health and fitness changes. Second, students would identify alternative funding sources to help create a self-sustaining program.

Importance of the Partnership from the RLS Perspective

Many community agencies are able to provide the real-world interaction that the Program seeks. However, there are additional benefits to the partnership with this specific agency. To begin with, the variety of programs offered by FCOE provides opportunities for projects in a variety of courses. Also, as both are on academic calendar years, scheduling is not as great a hurdle as with other community agencies.

The use of recreation and special events by FCOE to promote health is also consistent with the effort of the RLS Program to promote the positive value of recreation. Providing the opportunity for students to observe and contribute to these benefits reinforces this core value of the RLS Program.

Finally, as FCOE is providing programs for the K–12 students of Fresno County, the partnership provides increased opportunities for university students interested in working with youth. The growth of after-school programming nationwide makes the opportunity to work with an agency that administers so many after-school programs especially important.

Importance of the Partnership from the RLS Perspective

For the Department of Safe and Healthy Kids, partnering with the RLS Program is viewed as useful in meeting the mission of the department. Through this service-learning project, RLS students served as role models for the high school students, exemplifying how to be responsive to the needs of the community. Second, as FCOE is always looking for energetic, creative, and responsible programmers for the one-hundred-plus after-school and youth development programs, this partnership provided the opportunity to form relationships with potential colleagues. Finally, through this partnership the department was able to get an evaluation report that it otherwise would not have obtained.

Cooperative Relationship Between FCOE and CSU Fresno

CSU Fresno identifies itself as a premier regional interactive university. Both the institution and its faculty have been recognized for their involvement in the community and their contributions in resolving community challenges. In testament to this, the university received a Community Engagement Classification by the Carnegie Foundation for the Advancement of Teaching (2006).

CSU Fresno faculty and students focus service and research on local issues. Education, in particular, is an area in which the university has provided regional leadership. The university grants hundreds of teaching credentials each year (Commission on Teacher Credentialing, 2007) and is recognized as a significant teacher training institution in the San Joaquin Valley and as a regional leader in educational leadership, curricula, and research (National Council for Accreditation of Teacher Education, 2006).

Because of the respective educational leadership roles of both CSU Fresno and FCOE, they have a long history of collaboration. Grants, program evaluations, and research endeavors are common collaborations. Both educational institutions recognize the importance of sharing information and expertise. They realize that the challenges (high levels of poverty, large immigrant populations, and high numbers of second language learners) faced by the schools of Fresno County are daunting and that a cooperative approach is beneficial to both educational institutions and to the children they serve.

The Assignment

This action-research project was created with the goal of addressing two specific problems identified by FCOE: (1) determining whether the adventure challenge was meeting its goals and (2) determining how to achieve long-term sustainability. The assignment description and results identified in this section will focus on the first of these problems, determining the effectiveness of the race. This problem was addressed through program evaluation.

Connection to Course Objectives

As related to course objectives, the purpose of this action-research project was to collaboratively investigate a professional recreation service delivery concern. The FCOE adventure challenge served as a vehicle for students to use newly acquired research skills. Specifically, through the project students would meet the following course goals, each of which is tied to an accreditation competency:

- Demonstrate knowledge of the purpose, basic procedures and interpretation, and application of research and evaluation methodology related to leisure services

- Understand principles and procedures for evaluation of leisure programs and services

- Demonstrate the ability to formulate, plan for implementation, and evaluate the extent to which goals

and objectives for the leisure service and for groups
and individuals within the service have been met

- Understand contemporary professional issues and the
  trends impacting leisure and human service
  agencies

- Demonstrate the ability to apply computer and
  statistical techniques to assessment, planning, and
  evaluation processes

Although not all students in the course were interested in youth
or outdoor programs, the universal need for program evaluation
and the connection between health and recreation are common to
all areas of the recreation profession, ensuring that the project was
meaningful for all students.

Implementation

Sagor's five-step process was used to format the assignment, as
follows:

Step one: Problem formation. The responsibility of the RLS
students in this first step was to break down the race goals and
objectives into specific areas of investigation, creating a list of areas
to research in order to form a solution. Along with determining
the areas of investigation, the students also needed to determine
sources of information. The students determined that they needed
to collect information from the participants, the coaches, and the
race staff to capture a total picture of the race. Once these sources
were identified, students divided themselves into groups by source.

Step two: Data collection. Each group reexamined the problem
statement and the research list to identify the areas of research most
suitable to their source. Students then determined the type of data
collection tools needed and created questions. The importance of
triangulating data was stressed, so all groups elected to use both
qualitative and quantitative collection methods. Groups worked

on collection tools, question selection, and question content, going through a minimum of two revisions after instructor feedback.

At the same time, groups also developed a data collection schedule and negotiated entry to collect the needed data. This included receiving approval from the human subjects review panels of both the university and FCOE. The staff and coaches group were able to contact their samples directly, using contact information provided by FCOE. To protect the high school students, the participant group made contact through the high school principals via a letter from the instructor and a follow-up phone call. The principals arranged a time and place for the RLS students to meet with the high school students.

Step three: Data analysis. For the quantitative data, students began by creating codebooks; the data were then entered into a statistical software program (SPSS). Students were asked to identify which statistical tests would be run on each question and how those tests would relate back to the original areas of inquiry. The instructor provided feedback on the test choices, and after appropriate revisions were made, the tests were run.

Qualitative data, including interview transcripts and answers to open-ended questions, were entered into a word processing program for ease of review and analysis. Constant comparison methods were used to find emergent themes. Once all group members agreed on relevant themes, they identified specific pieces of data, including relevant results from statistical tests, to support each theme.

Step four: Reporting results. Three methods of reporting results were used in this project: written reports, poster presentations, and an in-service presentation. At this step the groups were reconfigured, primarily to ensure that members from all three prior groups (participants, coaches, and staff) were in each of the new groups (report, poster, and in-service). This was important to ensure that all three perspectives were represented in every report format, but there was an added benefit: this reconfiguration also created an opportunity to change group dynamics.

Regardless of the method of presentation, all groups had to create an abstract and include four sections (introduction or purpose, methods, results, and recommendations) in their reports. Each group was also required to include at least one graph and one table. Other format requirements were specific to the individual method of presentation. For instance, time and space were issues for the oral and poster groups, respectively; however, each group had the opportunity to answer questions and provide clarification during their presentations. The written report group, however, had no means of conveying information other than their report, so the report needed to be as inclusive as possible.

A draft of each report was submitted to the instructor. In the case of the in-service presentation, a written outline was required as well as a trial run. After making the suggested revisions, groups created their final reports. They presented the in-service and written reports to FCOE staff during the final week of the semester. The posters were presented during a university event that same week and then shared with FCOE staff.

Step five: Action planning. The final step in the action-research process is to effect change. In collaborative action-research, that occurs through the process of action planning. Once the reports were completed, FCOE staff reviewed the findings and considered the recommendations. Student recommendations were joined with staff ideas and a list was prioritized based on areas of greatest need and plausibility of implementation. Those recommendations were then incorporated into the planning for the next race.

Project Results

The project outcomes were viewed as beneficial by both the university and the educational agency. This section reviews the results across three areas: the connection between the project and health, and the outcomes from the perspectives of both the RLS program and the Fresno County Office of Education.

Link of Project to Health

The recognition of the value of the adventure challenge to the lifelong wellness of Fresno County students was apparent in the recommendations made by the RLS students. Students came to recognize discrepancies between the intended and actual outcomes of the race and were able to offer recommendations for improvement.

For instance, nutrition was stated as a significant aspect of the adventure challenge, with educational standards related to health and nutrition embedded in the race. The evaluation, however, revealed that participants did not internalize this information; coaches and staff both saw this as an area for improvement. The recommendation from the RLS students was to provide additional information to the participants about proper nutrition prior to the race, make nutrition a more prominent aspect of the race itself (that is, more questions related to nutrition on the course), and model healthy choices by providing nutritious food during the race.

Because the adventure challenge was intended to promote fitness, the level of physicality of the race and ongoing fitness activities after the race were also included in the evaluation. Results revealed that participants viewed the race as slightly less physically challenging than the staff and coaches did; however, the amount of time in between the race and the evaluation may have affected this result. Regardless, the RLS students found the results compelling enough to recommend that the level of physicality of each event in the adventure challenge be reviewed and additional events considered. They also recommended increased follow-up after the race to optimize participant interest and encourage lifelong wellness practices. The program evaluation revealed that some teams continued to participate in fitness activities after the race. One team, for example, organized a fitness club at their school. Immediate follow-up by FCOE staff would make this more consistent among all the participants.

RLS View

From an educational standpoint, the project was a successful learning process. Mistakes were made and key elements were neglected, but the reflection process transformed those mistakes into learning opportunities. Mistakes ranged from lack of leadership and poor division of labor among the groups to difficulty creating their first survey instruments and analyzing the results. Time management is often a challenge for college students, and lack of time management skills proved to be a challenge for several of the groups, as it compromised the quality of their work.

In the end, however, each aspect of the research and evaluation process was attempted throughout the course of the project. Students were exposed to a real-life situation and worked to find answers and solutions. Through trial, error, and reflection, they learned the importance of evaluation, including how to decide what questions to ask, how to create and format questions, how to analyze data, and how to report results. Most important for an action-research experience, they had the opportunity to see their recommendations implemented as FCOE staged the next adventure challenge.

FCOE View

From the standpoint of the educational agency, the partnership was also seen as a success. The department was able to gather important data about the content and structure of the event and made changes to the adventure challenge based on the recommendations. In particular, the recommendation to more strongly link the adventure challenge to health and nutrition and the suggestion to increase event physicality were cited as areas of focus for the next adventure challenge. FCOE staff also found the evaluation report to be useful evidence to support future grant applications.

The partnership gave FCOE an opportunity to build professional relationships with the RLS students and instructor that will continue into the future. The process did take more time and effort than originally anticipated, particularly when working with RLS student groups that did not coordinate or manage time well and approached staff with last-minute requests. However, the FCOE staff believe that the benefits far outweighed the time invested; they view the project as a win-win situation, and they look forward to future projects with the RLS Program.

Reflection

Reflecting on the project, it is important to look at the elements that worked as well as those areas in need of improvement. This section addresses both the strengths and the weaknesses of the project design and implementation.

Strengths of Design and Implementation

In looking back, it appears that the main strength of this project was the communication between the RLS instructor and FCOE partner. The two spoke regularly prior to and throughout the semester. The FCOE partner was also in class on the day the project was presented, to reinforce the partnership as well as the importance of the project as a needed product for the county office.

Other strengths include the openness of FCOE to allow the project to be designed to meet the educational objectives of the course. Additionally, designing each step of the project to correspond with when specific skills were introduced and reinforced in class was also beneficial. Finally, a huge strength of the project was the opportunity for students to see the impact of their work. Not only did students receive positive feedback from FCOE staff during their oral presentation of their results, but they also had the opportunity to see their recommendations put into practice during the next adventure challenge.

For FCOE, the main strengths of the project were the specific recommendations made and the energetic college students who served as role models for the high school students. In addition, the concise timeline for the project and the accessibility of the instructor were helpful to staff members who had to incorporate the project into a chaotic work schedule.

Weaknesses of Design and Implementation

Many areas for improvement can be identified from the initial project. One of the most difficult aspects of the project was that the evaluation was completed three months after the adventure challenge was held and only a few of the RLS students were familiar with the event. Although the FCOE partner came into class to explain the race and showed a video of the event, it was still difficult for many of the students to fully understand the scope of the event.

In terms of the assignment layout, after introducing the project, students were allowed to select the aspect of the project on which they wanted to work. Providing this choice created groups of different sizes, which made workload distribution more difficult and created challenges in managing the learning experiences of the students. Lack of appropriate leadership was also a weakness as students in some groups used inappropriate leadership techniques. Because leadership development is an important part of the RLS Program, this challenge became an important class discussion and reflection opportunity; however, prior identification of leadership roles would have alleviated some of the struggle.

Finally, from an instructional perspective, not enough group reflection occurred. Reflection *was* embedded in each step of the project, most prominently in the form of weekly reflection meetings. During these meetings groups met with the instructor to discuss progress and challenges. This was a good opportunity to remind students of the purpose of the project and to reinforce the goals of the adventure challenge. Students also completed a final reflection paper to summarize their personal learning experiences. What was missing, however, was the opportunity to share reflections with the class as a whole, to connect the various aspects of the project in the minds of the students.

From the perspective of the county office, the main weakness was that the evaluation occurred so long after the event. It is assumed that vital information was lost simply because participants were too far removed from the experience. Although not a weakness of the student project, it is certainly an important variable in the outcome. Second, in retrospect, FCOE staff members were not accessible enough to the RLS students, probably because of an initial underestimate of the amount of time students needed to gather and process relevant information. Finally, gaining entry into the high schools to meet with the high school students was difficult for the RLS students, and the high school participants were unprepared for the college students. Better communication with the high schools was needed to smooth this process.

Continuation

Maintaining and strengthening the relationship between FCOE and RLS is important to both parties. So, to prepare for future projects, it is important to reflect on the lessons learned and the implications of this initial experience.

Lessons Learned and Suggestions for Improvement

First, RLS students need to have a better understanding of the event being evaluated. In this instance, because the race occurs in the opposite semester of the course, the solution is to involve the RLS students in the implementation of the event through other courses and through the student recreation association. This would ensure that RLS students are familiar with the adventure challenge and can hit the ground running when they get to the programming and evaluation course. For other collaborative projects, factoring in time for university students to gain familiarity with the program or event will be an important consideration.

Just as it is important to familiarize the RLS students with the event, it is also important to prepare the participants and coaches for the evaluation. In the future, both will be informed of the evaluation so that it is an expected part of involvement in the race. This expectation should increase recall during the evaluation process and reduce delays experienced by RLS students in attempting to gain entry into the schools.

Third, because these are large class projects with many different components, it is important to ensure that the RLS students see the whole picture and have a clear understanding of all aspects of the project. Obstacles and solutions must be discussed and shared by the class as a whole, not just in small groups, so that all students benefit from the process. Two solutions were identified to meet this need. The first is an asynchronous discussion board that will be set up on the course's Blackboard website. Weekly participation in this discussion will be part of the assignment. The discussion board will be a place where students can share progress, post questions, and get feedback from students, the instructor, and the FCOE partner. A structured reflection will also be incorporated into class on a weekly basis to maintain accountability and reinforce the interconnectedness of all project components.

To reduce or eliminate the difficulties with differing group sizes and role confusion, the partners will determine the size limits for each group in advance. When they explain the project to the students, they will also explain each group's focus. Students will rank order their preferences, and the instructor will assign group membership based on those preferences.

Another aspect of the plan is to create preestablished roles (convener, recorder, and so on) for each group. Each role will have predetermined duties. However, although this should reduce confusion and potential conflict, it also reduces the opportunity for this project to assist with leadership development. To continue to foster leadership development, groups will be reconfigured during the semester. Students will be in one group for the data collection process and in a different group for analysis and result presentation. Reconfiguring of groups will be consistent with how the project was implemented during the initial year; the difference will be that in the first group, roles will be prescribed; in the second, students will be responsible for identifying and designing the structure of their groups.

From the perspective of the FCOE, including staff members on the discussion board will help to reinforce the collaborative nature of the project and provide an alternative method for RLS students to reach FCOE staff. Because FCOE staff members are often out of the office, connecting with the RLS students can be difficult. In addition to the discussion board, FCOE staff will make themselves more accessible to RLS students by identifying specific times of availability.

Implications and Conclusions

In addition to the lessons learned about the structure of the assignment, it is important to consider the broader implications of this project. This final section will address the impact of the project on health, both locally and globally, and consider its applicability to other universities.

Impact on health issues. For this particular assignment, the impact on health issues can be seen in the recommendations resulting from the program evaluation. The implementation of those recommendations, detailed previously, will increase the focus on health and nutrition and reinforce efforts to promote lifelong wellness. The project itself, however, also increased the RLS students' own awareness of the connection between recreation and health. Students were able to see the role of recreation in creating lifelong health and fitness patterns.

From a more global perspective, in addition to providing students with an opportunity to better understand the magnitude of the problems associated with overweight in young people, the service-learning project helped the students better appreciate the challenges recreation programmers and educators face in designing programs that have a positive effect on this serious issue. They came to realize that the first step toward encouraging young people to make healthy lifestyle choices is to provide relevant, engaging learning opportunities. By investigating the adventure challenge, RLS students learned the benefits of integrating reflection and evaluation in program design. They also recognized their own role, the role of their instructor, and the role of the county office of education staff in facilitating program improvement.

Application to other K–12 and university programs. For recreation programs, as well as many other professional programs, the suggestion to complete a program evaluation will not be new. The service-learning aspect may be new for some, and it is hoped the action-research approach will be viewed as a valuable addition, but the underlying assignment would be expected. However, there are many, both in recreation and in other fields, who could benefit from the lessons learned and suggestions for improvement. The lessons described and their solutions are applicable to a wide variety of service-learning and action-research assignments.

What may prove most beneficial is a partnership with the county office of education. Academic departments from all over the university—including recreation programs—form partnerships with a wide variety of community providers, including non-profit agencies, municipal departments, and government agencies. However, a cursory literature review did not reveal any instance of partnerships between recreation programs and county offices of education. This is a partnership we encourage academic departments, recreation or otherwise, to investigate. The variety of programs offered by a county office of education, the abundance of facilities, and access to youth all make these agencies an invaluable community partner.

References

Akujobi, C., & Simmons, R. (1997). An assessment of elementary school service-learning teaching methods: Using service-learning goals. *NSEE Quarterly, 23*(2), 19–28.

Astin, A. W. (1996). The role of service in higher education. *About Campus, 11*, 14–19.

Astin, A. W., & Sax, L. J. (1998). How undergraduates are affected by service participation. *Journal of College Student Development, 39*(3), 251–263.

Astin, A. W., Vogelgesang, L., Ikeda, E., & Yee, L. (2000). *How service learning affects students: Executive summary.* University of California, Los Angeles, Higher Education Research Institute.

Bass, S., & Silverstein, N. M. (1996). Action-research: A practical model to link teaching, research, and community service. *Metropolitan Universities, 7*(3), 85–94.

Batchelder, T. H., & Root, S. (1994). Effects of an undergraduate program to integrate academic learning and service: Cognitive, prosocial cognitive, and identity outcomes. *Journal of Adolescence, 17*, 341–355.

California Center for Public Health Advocacy. (2004). *Overweight children in California counties and communities.* Davis, CA: Author.

California Center for Public Health Advocacy. (2005, August). *The growing epidemic: Child overweight rates on the rise in California assembly districts.* Davis, CA: Author.

Campus Compact (2001). *Annual service statistics 2000.* Providence, Rhode Island: Brown University.

Carnegie Foundation for the Advancement of Teaching. (2006). Carnegie selects colleges and universities for new elective community engagement classification. Retrieved December 8, 2006, from http://www.carnegiefoundation.org/news/sub.asp?key=51&subkey=2126

Catelli, L. A., Padovano, K., & Costello, J. (2000). Action research in the context of a school-university partnership: Its value, problems, issues and benefits. *Educational Action Research, 8*(2), 225–242.

Centers for Disease Control and Prevention (2005). *Overweight and obesity.* Retrieved September 23, 2006, from http://www.cdc.gov/nccdphp/dnpa/obesity/

Central California Children's Health Institute (2005). Confronting childhood obesity: A community challenge. *Proceedings of the Central California Childhood obesity leadership summit.* Retrieved December 10, 2006, from http://www.csufresno.edu/ccchhs/documents/childrens_institute/proceedings_obesity.pdf

Children Count! (2003). *The well-being of children in Fresno county. 2002–2003 Report Card.* California State University, Fresno, Central California Children's Institute.

Commission on Teacher Credentialing (2007). *Teacher supply in California report to the Legislature annual report 2005–2006.* Retrieved May 30, 2007, from http://www.ctc.ca.gov/reports/TS_2005_2006

Greer, F., Hernandez, V., Sutton, P., & Curtis, K. (2004). *Obesity and physical inactivity among children and adolescents in the San Joaquin Valley.* California State University, Fresno: Central California Children's Institute.

Harkavy, I., Puckett, J., & Romer, D. (2000). Action research: Bridging service and research. *Michigan Journal of Community Service Learning Special Issue, 18,* 113–118.

Hironaka-Juteau, J. H., Hergenrader, D., & Kraft, J. A. (2006, winter). Collaborative action research as a useful tool in program evaluation: A case study. *California Parks & Recreation Magazine, 62*(1), 48–53.

Katula, R. A., & Threnhauser, E. (1999). Experiential education in the undergraduate curriculum. *Communication Education, 48*(3), 238–255.

Klute, M. M., & Billig, S. H. (2002). *The impact of service-learning on MEAP: A large-scale study of Michigan learn and serve grantees.* Denver, CO: RMC Research Corporation.

Markus, G. B., Howard, J. P., & King, D. C. (1993). Integrating community service and classroom instruction enhances learning: Results from an experiment. *Educational Evaluation and Policy Analysis, 15*(4), 410–419.

Melchior, A. (1999). *Summary report: National evaluation of learn and serve America.* Waltham, MA: Center for Human Resources, Brandeis University.

Melchior, A., & Bailis, L. (2002). Impact of service-learning on civic attitudes and behaviors of middle and high school youth. In A. Furco & S. H. Billig (Eds.), *Service-learning: The essence of the pedagogy* (pp. 201–222). Greenwich, CO: Information Age Publishing.

Myers-Lipton, S. (1996). Effect of a comprehensive service program on college students' level of modern racism. *Michigan Journal of Community Service Learning, 3,* 44–54.

National Council for Accreditation of Teacher Education. (2006, March 15). *Recommendations by the accreditation team and report of the accreditation visit for professional preparation programs at California State University, Fresno.* Washington, DC: National Council for Accreditation of Teacher Education.

Patton, M. Q. (2002). *Qualitative research and evaluation methods.* Thousand Oaks, CA: Sage.

Payne, C. (2000). Changes in involvement preferences as measured by the community service involvement preference inventory. *Michigan Journal of Community Service Learning, 7,* 41–45.

Pinzon-Perez, H. (2006). Mass media factors influencing childhood obesity among Latino farm workers. *Journal of the 27th Annual Central California Research Symposium,* 65.

Price, J. N. (2001). Action research, pedagogy and change: The transformative potential of action research in pre-service teacher education. *Journal of Curriculum Studies, 33*(1), 43–74.

Sagor, R. (1993). *How to conduct collaborative action research.* Alexandria, VA: Association for Supervision and Curriculum Development.

Strage, A. A. (2000). Service-learning: Enhancing student learning outcomes in a college-level lecture course. *Michigan Journal of Community Service Learning, 7,* 5–13.

Sutton, P., Hernandez, V., Perez, M., & Curtis, K. (2004). *Children in jeopardy: A sourcebook for community action child health and well-being indicators in the central California region.* California State University, Fresno: Central California Children's Institute.

UCLA Center for Health Policy Research. (2001). *California health interview survey.* Retrieved September 24, 2006, from http://www.chis.ucla.edu

Vogelgesang, L. J., & Alexander, W. (2000). Comparing the effects of community service and service-learning. *Michigan Journal of Community Service Learning, 7,* 25–34.

Yates, M., & Youniss, J. (1996). Perspective on community service in adolescence. *Social Development, 5,* 85–111.

5

Project ACtion for Equity

Service-Learning with a Gender Equity Focus on the U.S.-Mexico Border

Judith H. Munter, Joesefina V. Tinajero, Sylvia Peregrino, and Reynaldo Reyes III

> ... [A]lthough the modern research university must
> serve society by providing the educational and other
> programs in high demand, the university must also
> raise questions that society does not want to ask and
> generate new ideas that help invent the future, at
> times even "pushing" society toward it.
>
> (Shapiro, 2005, pp. 4–5)

Project ACtion for Equity (Project ACE) is a community service-learning project for college students in teacher preparation courses of study, driven by a long-term vision and plan of action developed collaboratively by school, university, and community partners located on the U.S.-Mexico border: the University of Texas El Paso (UTEP), eight K–12 school districts, and the El Paso Chapter of the American Association for University Women (AAUW). The project and its activities are designed to enhance educational and career opportunities for Hispanic girls and women who suffer multiple forms of oppression based on gender, race, ethnic origin, limited English proficiency, and socioeconomic status. ACE is also a critical component in UTEP's College of Education paradigm shift, focused on enhancing pre-service teachers' knowledge and understanding of inequities in the public school system through service-learning program design. This chapter examines the evolving vision and goals of UTEP's College of Education and Department of Teacher Education as the institution integrates Project ACE and its service-learning focus into program design and delivery. This new vision for teacher preparation includes integration of a service-learning component that addresses the gender and social inequities experienced by female students in the schools and communities of the border region between Texas and Chihuahua, Mexico.

The following sections examine the overall design and development of Project ACE, the context and setting, theoretical framework, examples of pedagogy and service-learning in action, and preliminary outcomes of the project. As of this writing, Project ACE had recently completed its first year of operation, but the program and its activities build on solid, sustained partnerships (going back twenty years or more) of committed community action and documented outcomes resulting from the combination of service and learning at UTEP.

ACtion for Equity = ACE

In 2005, UTEP was granted funding by the U.S. Department of Education to build on the successes of its long-term, successful work with Hispanic mothers and daughters in border communities, initiating Project ACE. This program targets future and current K–12 teachers by integrating teaching and learning about gender equity issues into academic coursework. Since its inception, ACE activities and practice have been implemented by UTEP faculty from diverse disciplines who help to prepare future teachers. ACE provides support to these faculty members as they integrate service-learning activities into the coursework and internship activities that are conducted in local schools and communities.

Project ACE educators also work with colleagues across diverse disciplines to develop policies that address continued dispari-ties affecting minorities in general (and females in particular) vis-à-vis college, graduate, and professional school enrollment. The project engages K–12 teachers from school districts located on the U.S.-Mexico border and university faculty members specialized in education, engineering, and public health to move forward an agenda that addresses four major barriers to Hispanic women's and girls' (grades K–20) participation in higher education, preparing for specialization in science, technology, engineering, and mathe-matics (STEM) programs of study, and entry into STEM careers. These barriers include (1) structural inequalities in educational systems that have affected girls' and family members' perceptions of school and career opportunities and outcomes; (2) limited access to culturally and linguistically relevant role models; (3) lack of knowl-edge about how to prepare for, finance, and succeed in college; and (4) school district and university personnel's limited knowledge about gender equity issues (Brown, 2004; National Coalition for Women and Girls in Education, 2002; Tornatzky, Macias, Jenkins, & Solis, 2006).

Combining Service with Learning: An Idea That Works in Teacher Education

Service-learning is a methodology well suited for teacher education programs of study; this is particularly true in communities such as El Paso, Texas, where there are pressing economic, social, and educational needs in the local community. Projects that connect students to real problems in the local community, such as ACE, offer powerful possibilities for future teachers to learn democratic skills. Service-learning (that is, combining service to the community with academic coursework) is not just about teaching college students to volunteer their time. It shows them that their lives are linked to the community around them. Moving outside of and beyond the traditional role of the student as a passive learner, many service-learning participants have learned to think critically and to enhance their ethical awareness (Honeycutt, 2002; Sedlak, Doheny, Panthofer, & Anaya, 2003).

Commonly used definitions of service-learning reveal that this method for teaching and learning is a credit-bearing, educational experience that (1) enables students to learn and develop through active participation in thoughtfully organized service experiences that meet actual community needs; (2) is most effective when integrated into the academic curriculum, providing structured time for students to reflect by thinking, discussing, and writing about what they did and saw during the activity; (3) provides students with opportunities to apply newly acquired skills and knowledge in real-life situations in their own communities; and (4) enhances what is taught in class by extending student learning beyond the classroom and into the community, helping to foster the development of a sense of civic responsibility and caring for others (Bringle & Hatcher, 1995; Harkavy & Romer, 1999; Vogelgesang & Astin, 2000; Yamauchi, Billig, Meyer, & Hofschire, 2006).

This chapter provides an overview of the background in which Project ACE has developed at UTEP: outlining the border community and cultural context, describing the project design, indicating preliminary outcomes (including voices of participating students), and pointing to future directions for the further development of service-learning in teacher education, particularly at minority-serving institutions like UTEP.

The Context and Setting

UTEP is an officially designated Hispanic-Serving Institution (HSI) of higher education. The U.S. Department of Education designates an institution as an HSI when the student body consists of at least 25 percent Hispanic students. In the 2005–06 academic year, UTEP's student body was 72 percent Hispanic and ranked third in the nation in awarding degrees to Hispanics (University of Texas at El Paso, 2006). Located in a binational and bicultural region, the university is committed to community development in the underserved border region of west Texas. Institutional resources have been committed to these ends, providing dramatically increased educational and economic opportunities for people from this region and for all people of Mexican descent. In the College of Education, the goal of achieving access and excellence for all translates into active support for school improvement plans in educationally underserved local districts. Project ACE focuses attention particularly on action plans that provide support for girls, highlighting the underrepresentation of females in STEM studies and careers.

Since the passage of Title IX in 1972, mandating equal education opportunity for girls and boys, there have been some encouraging signs in the struggle to eliminate gender inequality in American schools. Both males and females who graduated from high school in 2000 were generally more likely than their 1982 counterparts to have taken various mathematics and science courses while in high school. Furthermore, the number of females taking classes in high school algebra, geometry, and calculus has increased and is now similar to the percentage of males taking these courses, and gender differences in mathematics achievement in most areas have continued to decline (Peter & Horn, 2005).

However, many of the obstacles that have traditionally limited opportunities for women persist in U.S. schools, and there is significant evidence that the content and processes of American schooling have been much more conducive to high achievement for White, middle and upper-class male students (for example, Nieto, 2000; Oakes, 2005; Sadker & Sadker, 2000). A report by the National Center for Educational Statistics (NCES) found that in 2004 only 33.4 percent of all female undergraduates enrolled in degree-granting institutions of higher education were from minority backgrounds (11.6 percent of all students enrolled were

Hispanic females), and although this percentage represents an increase over previous years, the figure is less than half of the total percentage of White non-Hispanic males (68 percent) enrolled in degree-granting institutions in the same year (National Center for Education Statistics, 2005). Females are underrepresented in leadership positions in U.S. schools, in spite of equal levels of preparation; low levels of female participation in STEM careers (science, technology, engineering, and mathematics) indicate a persistent and ongoing inequity in expectations, opportunities, and long-term outcomes for girls and women in U.S. society today. This is a gender gap our nation can no longer afford to ignore (American Association for University Women, 1998, p. 16).

ACE helps future teachers examine the ways in which traditional educational systems have developed and sustained barriers that discourage daughters and mothers from participating in higher education and professional careers. A primary goal of the project is to prepare a cadre of future teachers with knowledge, skills, and commitment to creating equitable educational opportunities for Hispanic girls and women in El Paso as well as in all communities where inequities and barriers to educational success persist.

El Paso, Texas: Life on the U.S.-Mexico Border

The project and activities described in this chapter are conducted in an area on the U.S.-Mexico border. El Paso County is a rapidly growing binational, bicultural west Texas community of nearly seven hundred thousand people, more than 75 percent of whom are of Mexican origin. El Paso is the fifth largest city in Texas, and rural areas surrounding the urban center are growing at a rapid pace. Located in close proximity to Ciudad Juárez, a point of entry from Mexico's state of Chihuahua to the United States, El Paso and neighboring communities are also among the poorest in Texas and the nation. The unemployment rate is twice the state and national average, and per-capita income is just two-thirds of the national average. According to U.S. Census 2000 data, almost

24 percent of all El Paso County residents live below the federal poverty line; for children the figure is worse. About 32 percent of the children in El Paso County live in poverty, compared with 21 percent in Texas and 17 percent nationwide (Meritz, 2005; U.S. Census Bureau, 2000).

Foundations of Project ACE: The Mother-Daughter Program

ACE builds on a successful model—the UTEP Mother-Daughter (M-D) Program—that works closely with cohorts of sixth-grade Hispanic girls in forty-five elementary and middle schools, encouraging them to achieve success in middle school, complete high school, and cultivate aspirations to attend college. Developed within a culturally responsive framework (Maier & Tinajero, 1995), UTEP's Mother-Daughter Program has involved more than three thousand young girls, together with their mothers, in a wide variety of activities that prepare them for higher education and professional careers. The program provides an inspiring example of how young women from disadvantaged socioeconomic backgrounds, many of whom are recent immigrants and speakers of English as a second language, can break through educational and career barriers. Through over two decades of operation, the Mother-Daughter Program has served the border community, establishing a sustained, collaborative partnership among parents, university personnel, and K–12 teachers from low-income school districts in the El Paso metropolitan area. The program was developed in 1986 at the University of Texas at El Paso by concerned individuals from the university, with strong and active support from the community, local school districts, and the YWCA. The Mother-Daughter Program instills in these participants high aspirations for educational achievement and career success. The program consists of a series of activities designed to help the girls and their mothers maintain their interest in school and to raise their educational and career aspirations. The program prepares students for a successful university experience, using a team approach that involves mothers directly in the educational process, along with a support network of school coordinators and teachers, community leaders, and professionals who serve as role models. Mothers are equal participants with their daughters, learning how to help their daughters succeed and advance themselves academically and professionally (Tinajero, 2002; Tinajero, Gonzalez, & Dick, 1991).

Impacts of the Mother-Daughter Program: Over Two Decades of Commitment and Action

Measures of the Mother-Daughter Program's benefits to girls and women have been both qualitative and quantitative, providing evidence that this model is sustainable, with demonstrable positive impacts on the community and its participants. Findings to date indicate that Mother-Daughter Program activities make a dramatic difference in attitudes, school attendance, graduation, and achievement levels of young girls and their mothers. Early studies (Tinajero, 1992), for example, indicated that 98 percent of the sixth grade girls enrolled in this program had successfully graduated from high school and committed themselves to continuing their education at the postsecondary level. This represents a 1.5 percent dropout rate among Mother-Daughter Program participants, compared with a 7 percent dropout rate reported among Hispanic girls attending the same high schools who did not participate in the program during the same time period. Furthermore, forty-five participating elementary schools in eight border school districts have documented improvements in participants' school attendance rates (Tinajero & Spencer, 1999).

Focus groups with mothers provide further evidence that their participation in the program has given them higher expectations for their daughters as well as for their sons. They describe themselves as taking a more active role in their children's education after having participated in Mother-Daughter Program activities. An unanticipated outcome of the program has been the mothers' increased interest in improving their own education as a result of their participation in the program. Numerous participating mothers have returned to school to complete a high school equivalency program, to study English, or to work toward a college degree and professional career.

Continuing Opportunities and Persistent Needs

> *Latina girls living in the United States have unique challenges and strengths as a function of living in what Gloria Anzaldúa (1987) calls the borderlands … Latina girls have the opportunity to examine their cultural values and beliefs against the dominant mainstream U.S. culture and to create themselves as transcultural individuals …. The transcultural process is complex and is characterized by simultaneous behaviors, perceptions, and cognitions that could have different, even contradictory, manifestations as these young girls interact with the dominant U.S. mainstream culture. This process of transculturation presents both challenges and opportunities for Latina girls.*
> (Denner & Guzman, 2006, p. 3)

Even as the Mother-Daughter Program provides inspiring examples of college outreach, community response, and sustainable partnerships, the need for enhancing equitable opportunities for all in this educationally underserved region is persistent and ongoing. Project ACE builds on lessons learned from Mother-Daughter Program activities and outcomes, attempting to address root causes of educational inequities by working directly with current and future teachers, engaging them in processes of change.

Gender equity has received attention in K–12 education since at least 1972 (U.S. Department of Education, 1997), but there has been minimal focus on this topic in programs of teacher preparation. Although numerous studies (such as May, 2005; Mewborn, 2003; Rice, 2003) have provided conclusive evidence that teacher knowledge in academic content areas is inextricably linked to children's academic achievement, most experts also concur that children's personal and social development are critical components that need to be addressed in K–12 classrooms to enable learners' development of their fullest potential. The most effective K–12 teachers possess the skills to design inspiring learning experiences and model caring attitudes to help every child achieve her or his highest potential in every subject area (Irvine, 2001; Noddings, 1992; Valenzuela, 1999).

Developing young girls' self-confidence and awareness of their skills is a strategy essential to effective teaching in diverse class-rooms (Irvine, 2001; Padrón, Waxman, & Rivera, 2002). Gender has frequently operated as a major barrier to educational completion in Hispanic communities, due to a wide variety of socioeconomic, cultural, and attitudinal factors. In border communities like El Paso, where socioeconomic hardships further exacerbate inequities, girls and women continually face limited opportunities to complete schooling and unequal access to higher education.

The need for highly qualified K–12 teachers across all disciplines, with knowledge of diversity and skills to address it, has been well documented. Recent reports (such as AAUW Educational Foundation Commission, 2000) provide evidence that the "computer culture" has been developed to respond to a primarily male audience. This study points out that although earlier research reports (see, for example, Brumberg, 1997; Gilligan, 1982) described girls' disinterest in technology as a manifestation of "anxiety" or "incompetence," more recent research challenges assumptions about gender roles in technology education and careers, indicating that the very characteristics of educational software and computer games (for example, excessive violence and redundancy) that successfully capture the attention of many young boys point to deficits in the design and implementation of technology instruction.

Furthermore, administrative and instructional personnel in K–12 schools with large numbers of English language learners have concerns about the quality of educational software in diverse languages, the limited availability of professional development, and the dearth of technical assistance available to teachers (Butler-Pascoe & Wiburg, 2003; Tornatzky et al., 2006). There is clearly a need to expand the number and diversity of the participants in the pipeline, and Project ACE moves this agenda forward by engaging pre-service teachers in service-learning, exploring theory and investigating applications of gender equity in K–12 classrooms. A major contention of the project is that increasing the number of girls and women who are technologically literate is a major step towards increasing gender equity.

Theoretical Framework

Faculty must assume a primary responsibility for
giving scholarship a richer, more vital meaning.
(Boyer, 1990, p. 78)

Several bodies of literature give shape to Project ACE and the diverse modalities through which teacher education coursework is undergoing reform at UTEP. As college students learn how to integrate principles and practice of gender equity into their work as future teachers, these participants develop reflective skills, becoming more aware of the values and beliefs about teaching and learning that have shaped their own educational experiences. Although as of this writing ACE is still in early stages of implementation, our preliminary evidence indicates that many of these students have begun to ask new questions and develop new understandings about gender, language, and race, and the many ways in which equity in education often eludes even the best-intentioned schools, teachers, and communities.

Redefining Scholarship

Boyer's foundational work (1990) on new paradigms for scholarship provides the foundation for ACE's framework, creating possibilities for organizing scholarly work across diverse disciplines in new ways, redefining relationships among teaching, research, and service in the academy. The new directions for scholarly work include the following: (1) the scholarship of integration—the search for connections among discoveries obtained by different approaches or from varied disciplines, which often leads to novel insights, both interpretive and interdisciplinary; (2) the scholarship of application—building bridges between theory and practice, and encompassing the tremendous opportunities for service that academics are uniquely poised to provide in their local communities; and (3) the scholarship of teaching—that aspect of faculty work in which scholars communicate their knowledge to students and empower them to develop the skills that they will need as future professionals (Boyer, 1990; Huber, 2004; O'Meara & Rice, 2005). Like many universities across the nation, UTEP has begun to recognize and reward the vast array of faculty roles, including civic responsibilities and creative forms of scholarship through community service-learning and community-based research in initiatives like ACE (Diamond & Adams, 2000; Hutchings & Shulman, 1999; Strand, Marullo, Cutforth, Stoecker, & Donohue, 2003). For example, recent revisions to the criteria for faculty promotion in the College of Education refer to "materials detailing innovative practices and programs; coordination of clinical and lecture courses" (University of Texas at El Paso, 2005). This has directly affected ACE faculty, several of whom are engaged in developing scholarly publications about their work with students and community members through this project.

Experiential Learning Theory

Experiential learning is one of the conceptual bases for the project and its activities. Advocates of experiential education have long claimed that active modes of learning can enrich, broaden, and deepen the knowledge base gained from readings and class lectures (for example, Dewey, 1938; Kolb, 1984; Shulman, 2004; Weil & McGill, 1989). Each of the academic courses featured in this model program provides students with the tools and knowledge that they will need to guide them through the experiential learning cycle (Kolb, 1984). As described by participants, the classes do not begin and end with a finite set of facts and information bites to be learned; rather, they are an "experience [that] definitely makes you get out and . . . learn from the real world . . . "

Civic Learning Theory

In recent years there has been a growing realization that higher education is falling short in its efforts to prepare students for lives of social responsibility and civic and political engagement (Barber, 1992; Kezar, Chambers, & Burkhardt, 2005; Shapiro, 2005). The university experience of our nation's future teachers will influence their moral development and thus their ethical judgments and their behavior as leaders. Invoking Dewey's assertion (1966) that education is where democratic participation in society is best learned, advocates of service-learning have challenged colleges and universities to move beyond traditional courses to prepare students for democratic citizenship. Proponents of this innovation in higher education claim that service to the community is improved by finding its grounding in the curriculum, and learning is deepened by expanding the notion of the traditional classroom to include real people and actual situations in society. Service-learning projects arguably can help to broaden students' perspectives and appreciation of others, as they often involve working in culturally and socially diverse teams toward concrete shared goals (Munter, 2002).

Culturally Responsive Pedagogy

Growing numbers of children in American society today come to school from diverse cultural, social, and linguistic backgrounds.

These youngsters may be first- or second-generation immigrants, raised in families and communities with their own cultural traditions and orientations. The children frequently experience cultural clashes when what they are taught at home is in conflict with what they are learning at school. Culture shapes how we see the world and interpret experience, and appropriate review, revision, and refinement of academic programs and curricula to fit the needs of our rapidly changing society are pivotal steps that effective educators must take in the twenty-first century (Cochran-Smith, 2004; Nieto, 2002; Sleeter, 2007). When families and households are viewed in terms of assets (that is, cohesive social networks and systems of knowledge), preservice teachers learn to understand and value the dynamic processes and historical forces that have created the foundations of diverse systems of knowledge.

Pedagogy and Practice: Examples of Service-Learning Through Project ACE

Project ACE integrates gender equity into a number of courses in UTEP's Teacher Preparation Program by engaging college students with the El Paso community in service-learning activities as an integral part of pre-service teacher preparation. These prospective teachers have unique opportunities to work with parents (chiefly mothers), grandmothers, and other family members throughout their coursework as they learn how to address gender equity issues.

In year one, Project ACE piloted and documented these initiatives through teacher education courses taught at professional development school (PDS) sites in nearby border locations. These PDS sites provide unique opportunities for students to try out new practices, document outcomes, and reflect on lessons learned (Teitel, 2003).

UTEP faculty from five different teacher preparation courses engaged with their students in inquiry about gender equity issues in diverse components of the teacher education program of studies. Each of the courses engaged students in application of theory through direct action and reflective exercises. An overview of each of the ACE courses follows here, with discussion of the pedagogical practices that engaged pre-service teachers in study of gender equity and application through service-learning. (See Figure 5.1.)

Unequal opportunities in the educational system results in an underrepresentation of Hispanic girls in science, technology, engineering, and math careers

Increasing pre-service teachers' awareness of gender equity issues will result in more equitable opportunities for girls in the classroom

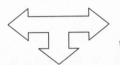

Pre-service teachers' learning is enhanced through service-learning praxis

Service-Learning Components

Pre-Service Teacher Preparation	Mother-Daughter Program
➢ Infusion of gender equity themes into the university curriculum in the following courses: science methods, math methods, multicultural education, and critical pedagogy ➢ Service-learning projects include: developing and implementing gender awareness lesson plans, career exploration activities, parental involvement activities, and oral histories or book talks at field placement schools with Mother-Daughter program activities ➢ Facilitation of workshops by pre-service teachers and faculty at the annual Mother-Daughter Leadership Conference and Career Day ➢ Pre-service teachers also serve as tutors at a feeder high school with a high percentage (99%) of Hispanic students, 93% of whom are considered economically disadvantaged	A college outreach program established in 1986 at the University of Texas-El Paso's College of Education focusing on sixth grade girls and their mothers at forty-five elementary schools representing all the districts in El Paso County

Figure 5.1. Project Action for Equity: Service-Learning with a Gender Equity Focus on the U.S.-Mexico Border

Science Education Methods

Professor A teaches a course titled "Teaching Science in the Middle Schools." This course is designed to help future teachers examine critically the perspectives, philosophies, materials, and strategies for effective learning in middle school science classrooms, to both reflect on the power of science in our society and participate in improving our society. Every aspect of this course is aligned with the goals of Project ACE. Students learn to understand the roles of women and underrepresented populations in science careers and science policy decisions and to engage in community outreach to learn from and with Hispanic families in the U.S.-Mexico border region. These future teachers interact with families, schools, and community members in the region, reflecting on the roles of culture, language, and gender in El Paso and its sister city, located in the border state of Chihuahua, Mexico. These hands-on activities have allowed students to rethink the ways in which they prepare lessons and interact with children and families and to reconceptualize their own roles as science teachers in border schools. In Professor A's course, for example, students learn about scientific principles that are key components of the middle school teacher's conceptual knowledge. Students in this course go out into the community, where they engage in experiences that focus on health and environmental issues affecting women and children. The students plan and implement service projects based on authentic local needs, designed to improve the quality of life on the U.S.-Mexico border. Examples of their service-learning projects have included family field trips to a local wetlands park and teaching science lessons to children and parents at a school in Mexico.

Schools and Communities: Applied Critical Pedagogy

Professor B's course examines the nature of the relationship between the school and the community in which it is embedded. On the U.S.-Mexico border, in a primarily low-socioeconomic-level community, pre-service teachers learn to become reflective practitioners, developing strategies to strengthen school-home relationships and focusing on the role of the schools in solving community problems to improve student achievement. In this field-based class (that is, taught in the schools), students work in groups to identify age-appropriate materials (lessons, books, websites, and so on) that promote the reduction of racial and gender gaps in education. Students use the findings from their classroom experiences as beginning teachers, writing reflective statements about their reasons for selecting diverse topics and describing how they will plan and implement lessons differently based on their new knowledge. Their practice lessons address three broad categories: book talks, female role models in STEM disciplines, and career exploration activities. The pre-service teachers search for developmentally appropriate materials on careers or books that question traditional gender roles. Through these exercises, future teachers become more aware of the gender bias in books for elementary school students and the scarcity of materials representing women in historically male occupations.

The pre-service teachers conduct lessons in local schools, engaging in collective reflection through discussion about their reflections on equity issues during class presentations with their colleagues. Pre-service teachers in kindergarten classrooms, for example, ask children to draw pictures of occupations of their choice. These drawings become the topic of a series of reflective dialogues with Professor B and classmates. The college students often find that the young children's career aspirations fall into traditional gender roles as early as kindergarten. Boys, for example, described themselves as future police officers, firemen, or military personnel, whereas girls visualized their future careers as cheerleaders, teachers, or nurses.

A similar assignment was implemented in seventh grade science classes. Pre-service teachers asked students to draw a "typical" scientist; all but one of them drew a male scientist. The college students noted that these children's notions about science indicate that their beliefs were based primarily on media representations and imagery (such as television shows and movies), portraying males as leaders, creators, and bosses, and women as followers. As a result, many of the pre-service teachers developed new lesson plans focusing on the contributions of female scientists, including women of color.

Multicultural Education for Secondary Teachers

An ACE course for pre-service high school teachers demonstrates complex ethical issues that often come into play when addressing gender equity with teachers and parents in diverse communities. Professor C teaches a course in the secondary education teacher preparation program that deals with issues of cultural, linguistic, and gender equity in secondary schools. His course uses a number of activities to spark discussion and debate, including film clips, news shows, chapters from literary works, and personal experience. During the semester, immigrant students who are English language learners at a low-income high school participate as speakers in the college classroom to talk about their experiences learning English in a U.S. public school. Intertwined through all of the discussion, activities, and coursework, controversial topics pique students' interest and lead them into in-depth conversations with Professor C's students. The politics of immigration, gender, race, economics, and ethnicity are frequent topics of debate from cultural perspectives unique to the immigrant student population. The class provides future teachers with unique opportunities to interact with high school students in the field component of their coursework.

The service-learning component of the course involves tutoring and mentoring in an after-school program at the same high school. For example, students in the course have tutored and mentored adolescent, Mexican-American female students, many of whom are English language learners, helping them to gain self-confidence through success in academics. The experiences and successes of working with culturally and linguistically diverse student populations are topics of discussion in subsequent class sessions, as well as through Internet-based, WebCT discussion boards. Reflective discussions throughout the entire course engage Professor C's students in identifying pressing issues that they have concluded must be remedied if Latina girls are to have better opportunities for advanced careers. A great deal of growth, learning, and understanding is derived from these discussions and contributes to their knowledge base on critical issues such as gender equity. Future service-learning projects for this course will include creating in-school and after-school "mentoring clubs" for adolescent boys and girls who will benefit from guidance by pre-service student teachers on issues of peer pressure, school participation, and attending college as a key to fulfilling goals and dreams.

Teaching Mathematics in the Elementary Classroom

Professor D's mathematics methods course provides yet another key example of the application of the ACE culturally relevant framework developed in collaboration with the local community. Her course works with a partner school in the development of "Parent Power Night" programs. These combination meeting-workshops include activities that (1) promote and support open communication between and among diverse family members and the school; (2) enable parents to learn new skills needed to assist their daughters and sons with mathematics and science assignments, and (3) highlight the unique skills and knowledge that diverse parents possess, focusing on ways family members can offer their own resources to promote student achievement. The sessions provide numerous opportunities for pre-service teachers to interact meaningfully with parents and families.

Communication skills are strengthened as pre-service teachers are paired with experienced educators who articulate the benefits to their schools from parent involvement. Working in teams with mentors and role models, pre-service teachers develop content-based teaching and learning strategies to help parents, grandparents, and other family members learn to support children's academic achievement goals at home. Concurrently, future teachers learn a great deal from parents as they carefully attend to the ideas and perspectives that these women and men share with them (Carger, 1997; Cooper, 2004; Munter, 2003).

Educational research and practice have indicated a clear linkage between parental engagement in schools and pupil achievement. Some of the documented outcomes are academic gains, enhanced self-esteem, improved motivation, and better school attendance (Delgado-Gaitan, 2004; Pérez Carreon, Drake, & Calabrese Barton, 2005). Yet despite this growing body of evidence, family and community involvement in schools throughout the United States remains minimal. Project ACE demonstrates the potential for expanding the scope of teacher preparation programs to meet the needs of the twenty-first century by incorporating context and integrating service to the community in the preparation of new teachers in culturally and linguistically diverse schools. The school-university-community partnership creates exciting opportunities for blending research and practice in the development of innovative approaches to preparing future teachers in today's increasingly diverse society.

Bilingual Education: Funds of Knowledge

In Professor E's course, students go outside of the school to interact with families and diverse community members. Her course, required of all pre-service teachers in UTEP's program of studies, focuses on school-community partnerships. Professor E teaches this course with a set of theoretical and applied learning activities that engage students in reflection about the roles of teachers in the struggle for equity. The service-learning component of the course engages students in presenting topics to young girls and their mothers during the Mother-Daughter Program Leadership Conference. As the UTEP students present themes and information to girls and their mothers, they are also engaged in learning about the roles of parents and families in public education. Furthermore, this course engages students in "funds of knowledge" (Gonzalez, Moll, & Amanti, 2005) projects, in which pre-service teachers get to know the families and their cultural practices, resources, and histories in order to understand or modify their teaching. Dyson and Genishi (1994) make a strong case for the "need for story" when they explain that "through stories, teachers learn of their children's cultures, of their diverse experiences, and of their connections to family and friends" (p. 2). Students develop their research skills as they collect data using diverse methods (such as participant observation and interviews) and use these ideas, concepts, and perspectives to interpret their findings.

Each of the five Action for Equity courses provides examples of the preliminary design of an evolving model. As pre-service teachers engage in study, reflection, and application of gender equity concepts within a service-learning framework, they encounter opportunities to bring about change in the local community, with education as the primary vehicle for promoting equity for all. The following section describes preliminary findings from the assessment practices that have been incorporated into the courses just described.

Assessing ACE's Outcomes: Preliminary Results

> *Service to the neighborhood and to the nation are not the gift of altruists but a duty of free men and women whose freedom is itself wholly dependent on the assumption of political responsibilities.*
>
> (Barber, 1992, p. 246)

Assessment activities in Project ACE take into account the history, culture, language, and context of the school and community partners. First- and second-generation immigrant families are not relegated to the role of "objects of inquiry"; rather, the knowledge that each family possesses is a primary resource used to shape project goals, processes, and outcomes. Through collaborative inquiry, pre- and in-service teachers develop new approaches to teaching and learning, creating new curricular frameworks that incorporate gender equity issues relative to local realities, engaging with school and community partners in active service and reflection on their experiences. Techniques such as focus group discussions and workshops enable future teachers, family members, and university faculty to reflect on their roles as agents of change, viewing home-school relationships through new lenses, with parents and community members as full partners in the decisions that affect schools and student achievement.

Pre-Service Teachers and ACE

Even at this early stage in the project's development, pre- and post-test outcomes indicate that future teachers engaged in this work are developing a greater awareness and knowledge base concerning gender equity. For example, more than one-third of Professor C's students' self-assessments indicate improved self-perceptions vis-à-vis their own knowledge about gender equity issues after one semester of experience in project activities (47 percent pre-test compared with 83 percent post-test). Overall, UTEP students enrolled in ACE courses demonstrated an average of 46.8 percent increase in their levels of knowledge and preparation concerning skills needed to achieve the goals of the project. (See Table 5.1.)

College students also provided significant input during discussion about project goals and outcomes. Students enrolled in ACE courses have engaged in reflective dialogue with their professors in organized focus group sessions, in which they reflected on their realization that socially constructed views about gender, race, and language have played a critical role in their own personal and professional development. These focus groups have served as assessment tools with self-selected ACE participants as they spend

Table 5.1. College Students' Responses to Gender Equity Knowledge Questionnaire: Percentage Rankings

	Professor A		Professor B		Professor C		Professor D	
	Pre (n=25)	Post (n=24)	Pre (n=29)	Post (n=28)	Pre (n=32)	Post (n=29)	Pre (n=26)	Post (n=32)
1. How knowledgeable are you about gender equity issues in the classroom?	56.0%	95.9%	79.4%	96.6%	46.9%	89.7%	65.2%	96.9%
2. How knowledgeable are you about creating gender-equitable lessons in your classroom?	32.0%	87.5%	69.0%	92.8%	56.3%	79.4%	44.4%	96.9%
3. How well prepared are you to develop STEM-related (science, technology, engineering, and mathematics) lessons in your classroom that are gender equitable?	20.0%	79.2%	44.8%	99.9%	25.1%	62.0%	23.1%	86.2%
4. How knowledgeable are you about incorporating a service-learning component into your classroom lessons?	24.0%	79.2%	51.7%	99.9%	31.3%	58.6%	15.3%	96.9%
5. How knowledgeable are you about evaluating materials you use in your classroom to ensure that they are gender equitable?	48.0%	91.6%	44.8%	89.2%	40.6%	82.7%	42.3%	96.9%
6. How prepared do you feel to advise students and their parents about STEM-related careers?	28.0%	79.2%	37.9%	89.2%	15.6%	58.6%	3.8%	86.2%
Totals	34.7%	85.4%	54.5%	94.5%	36.0%	71.8%	32.4%	93.3%

Note: Total average change from pre- to post-test results = 46.8% increase.

more time in study and discussion of the project and its impacts on scholars and practitioners dedicated to high-quality education for all. The purpose of the focus group interviews is to enable students to consider their own views in the context of the views of others (Fern, 2001; Madriz, 2000; Patton, 2002; Seidman, 2006). The group dialogue helps enhance data analysis and gives students a greater level of ownership in the research process. Emphasis in these group sessions is not on consensus but on the diversity and range of opinions of individuals within the group, as well as lived group experience (Krueger & Casey, 2000).

Focus group participants have been drawn from pre-service teachers enrolled in each of the ACE courses. Each one of the professors invited her or his students to participate in the focus group sessions. Ten students (two from each course) volunteered to participate, providing their own unique insights about the project processes and impacts. Findings to date indicate that there are valuable lessons to be learned from the common themes described by participants in programs that link pre-service teachers with Latino (and other recent immigrant) parents and communities in diverse settings.

The next section explores some of the deeper meanings behind the speakers' comments, to identify the themes that underlie them, linking them together to clarify the emerging themes and patterns more clearly. Many of the students reflected on their own upbringing and how gender had affected their experience. Student A recalled, "[L]iving in a border city, I was never introduced to any female engineers or doctors, so I thought that all those [professions like] engineers, astronauts .... [were] just for males." Similarly, Student B said, "[W]hen I was growing up, my elementary years, the more fortunate ones were favored, and if you were Anglo even more .... If you were Mexican, if you had money you were accepted but if you were not as well off they would put you to the side."

Many of the service-learning experiences resulted in greater awareness of equity issues in education. One student said: "I am going to give my students opportunities for working together and help make sure that all are engaged .... [E]ven after doing my lesson plans, I will reflect .... Were all the students engaged, both girls and boys?" Another student mentioned the need for going beyond traditional methods:

> I think you should "change it up"; I mean if math and science so far haven't really helped females to get up there, why don't we change it and try to make it interesting for everybody! Just try new and different things, like try to explain it two different ways instead of just one way, try to get everyone involved ... maybe role playing, or even just through advising ... talk to them like in a small group, because you know sometimes there's maybe a certain time in the day where it's reading time, maybe you want to show them, give them a lesson about different careers ... also maybe even giving them ownership to create their own guidelines, guiding them in a way that not just the boys but the girls can be whatever they want to become.

As a result of their service-learning experiences, students became more aware of the need to provide equitable role models. Student C stated: "It's going to be very important for me to bring good role models into my classroom, women role models, especially since we're living in a border city in a low socioeconomic community. It is very important ...." Another student mentioned, "What I would do would be to bring in a policeman and a poicewoman, a male nurse and a female nurse, a female firefighter and a male firefighter ... help my students think about different gender roles for careers."

Their service-learning experiences led these students to reflect on the importance of engaging families and community members. One student said,

> I think ... getting parents involved ... is one of the most important factors to try and break down this barrier of gender specific roles and stuff ... Most kids are with you for eight hours and they go home and their parents' influence is the most important to them. I don't care if those parents take no part in their children's lives at all, that's still influencing them, regardless of what anybody thinks. Even if those parents are not involved one bit, their not being involved is still influencing that child.

Another student stated, "I think primarily keeping communication open with parents about anything, not just gender equity lesson plans, no, just in general ... keep them up to date with what you are doing and why." Student H said,

> One way that we can help the parents to become engaged is showing them what opportunities their children have. It is really hard for us [as Hispanics] to let our girls go off to college, but maybe if we start at an early age, letting them know all the opportunities that they can have—you know, colleges, scholarships, and all that they can take advantage of—we can educate them at an early age. Then, once they are ready to go off to college they are going to be better off, they are going to be more informed, and ready to move on.

Open dialogues and discussions with students about equity issues invariably led to discussions about the implications for teachers in border communities; these conversations helped students to share their ideas about gender roles, as well as the roles of race, social class, culture, and language. As these future teachers became increasingly cognizant of the interrelationships among these components of their own unique identities, their discussion of the ways in which teachers relate to these characteristics of their students and communities highlighted new awareness of the teacher's role as an agent of change.

Preliminary findings from this project suggest that the service-learning curriculum is not simply a set of plans to be implemented, but rather is constituted through an active process in which planning, acting, and evaluating are all reciprocally related and integrated into the process. Project ACE allows for the learning encounter to be constructed within real situations, not hypothetical ones. Rather than taking cues from lecture notes and textbooks, students learn to "read the world" and view their own community and lived experiences as sources of legitimate knowledge.

UTEP Faculty Members and ACE

The team of ACE faculty described their work in this project as having transformative effects on the courses they teach in fundamental ways. Faculty noted that the pre-service teachers in their courses developed new insights and discovered new ways of describing their own experience as interns and student teachers in schools. For example, they described their students' abilities to express new understandings about the complex ways in which gender, language, discourse, and race interact with teaching and learning processes. Many of the students in Project ACE courses demonstrated that they had developed new perspectives on equity issues in general and gender roles in particular. Some of their perspectives and understandings relate to the importance of (1) the instructional materials that teachers choose to work with, (2) how resources are put together in curricula, (3) whose knowledge is represented as truth, (4) teachers' own personal perspectives on gender and race, and (5) how discourses are read from individual, socially defined perspectives.

At UTEP, engagement with school-community partners as full coequals in the service-learning project has been a shared vision and goal espoused by university faculty members. However, actual practice in the context of U.S.-Mexico border communities highlights the complexities of merging service and learning goals in balanced and reciprocal relationships. Faculty noted that many students recognized that life circumstances for children in poverty were difficult. Some of the UTEP students connected their own life stories to the children and families with whom they interacted. Yet rarely did those who started with a deficit perspective place poverty in a larger context of social inequities.

In the literature about immigrant families and communities, discourse concerning immigrant children and parents tends to center around the families' deficits (that is, parents' inability or unwillingness to support their children's school experience). Faculty must continue to find ways to promote students' ability to expose the shortcomings of deficit theories. If the goals of service-learning include helping students learn how to provide services to the community and how to address their needs, alternative voices must be present so that these projects can address root causes (as well as symptoms) of need. This approach suggests a focus on interactive reflection and continuing dialogue, accountability for the growth of all individuals, and merging of the roles of service provider and recipient (Maybach, 1996).

Community Members and ACE

Discussion of student and community voices in the service-learning component of Project ACE cannot be complete without mention of the need for further exploration of ethical dimensions of the service-learning project, including the need for greater reciprocity in the project's design and implementation. A severe limitation of programs like this one is the lack of time. One semester may be all the time that college students have available; this is particularly true in the case of working-class students who cannot continue to participate after the semester of the service-learning academic course. Critics of academic service-learning programs have highlighted the failure of some to make sure that the voice and needs of the community are included in the development of community service programs. When universities commit resources to inter-acting with communities in need, the relationships may lead to unintended outcomes—reinforcing boundaries and privileging the voice of the college students while devaluing the knowledge and experience of the community members. This top-down approach to community development ignores recipients' priorities and what they might have to offer. Community voice and active participa-tion are essential if we are to build bridges, make changes, and solve problems.

Although the project discussed in this chapter has yet, as of this writing, to collect and analyze further data from community members in the contexts we describe here, future components of this longitudinal study will also continue to explore impacts on service providers (that is, the college students) as well as recipients (children, families, and teachers) engaged in Project ACE.

Conclusion

Preliminary findings from this project point to the opportunity for service-learning to serve as a vehicle for colleges of education as they prepare future educators who will be committed agents of change in their own classrooms and communities. Working in the context of a predominately Hispanic community, with many low-income, high-need schools, Project ACE also illustrates the potential for universities to play key roles in developing educational pathways for underrepresented populations (such as Hispanic girls and women) to achieve their full educational potential. Over the next several years, ACE will continue to document the processes and outcomes of this sustainable partnership project, which has already demonstrated how communities and universities can work together to make a difference. More than twenty years of ser-vice through the Mother-Daughter Program have evolved into a multifaceted academic service-learning project, integrating gender equity and service-learning into coursework for pre-service teachers in a primarily Hispanic community. Lessons learned will provide valuable information for researchers and practitioners committed to working with diverse populations to bridge the gap between the "ivory tower" and the communities in which universities are embedded.

References

American Association for University Women (AAUW). (1998). *Gender gaps: Where schools still fail our children.* Washington, DC: AAUW Foundation.

AAUW Educational Foundation Commission on Technology, Gender, and Teacher Education. (2000). Tech-savvy: Educating girls in the new computer age. Washington, DC: AAUW Educational Foundation Commission on Technology, Gender, and Teacher Education.

Anzaldúa, G. (1987). *Borderlands: La frontera.* San Francisco: Aunt Lute Books. Cited in Denner, J., & Guzman, B. (Eds.). (2006). *Latina girls: Voices of adolescent strength in the United States.* New York: New York University Press.

Barber, B. (1992). *An aristocracy of everyone: The politics of education and the future of America.* New York: Ballantine Books.

Boyer, E. (1990). *Scholarship reconsidered: Priorities of the professoriate.* Princeton, NJ: The Carnegie Foundation for the Advancement of Teaching.

Bringle, R., & Hatcher, J. (1995). A service learning curriculum for faculty. *The Michigan Journal of Community Service Learning, 2,* 112–122.

Brown, K. (2004). A call for equity: Kicking the computer science door open for girls. *IDRA Newsletter,* Vol. XXXI, #7.

Brumberg, J. (1997). *The body project: An intimate history of American girls.* New York: Random House, 1997.

Butler-Pascoe, M., & Wiburg, K. (2003). *Technology and teaching English language learners.* Boston: Allyn & Bacon.

Carger, C. L. (1997, April). Attending to new voices. *Educational Leadership, 54*(7), 39–43.

Cochran-Smith, M. (2004). *Walking the road: Race, diversity, and social justice in teacher education.* New York: Teachers College Press.

Cooper, E. (2004). The pursuit of equity and excellence in educational opportunity. In D. Lapp, C. Block, E. Cooper, J. Flood, N. Roser, & J. Tinajero (Eds.), *Teaching all the children: Strategies for developing literacy in an urban setting* (pp. 12–30). New York: The Guilford Press.

Delgado-Gaitan, C. (2004). *Involving Latino families in schools: Raising student achievement through home-school partnerships.* Thousand Oaks, CA: Corwin Press.

Denner, J., & Guzman, B. (Eds.). (2006). *Latina girls: Voices of adolescent strength in the United States.* New York: New York University Press.

Dewey, J. (1938). *Experience and education.* New York: Macmillan.

Dewey, J. (1966). *Democracy and education: An introduction to the philosophy of education.* New York: Free Press. (Original work published 1916.)

Diamond, R., & Adams, B. (Eds.). (2000). *The disciplines speak II: More statements on rewarding the scholarly, professional, and creative work of faculty.* Washington, DC: American Association for Higher Education.

Dyson, A., & Genishi, C. (1994). *The need for story: Cultural diversity in classroom and community.* Urbana, IL: National Council of Teachers of English.

Fern, E. (2001). *Advanced focus group research.* Thousand Oaks, CA: Sage.

Gilligan, C. (1982). *In a different voice: Psychological theory and women's development.* Cambridge, MA: Harvard University Press.

Gonzalez, N., Moll, L., & Amanti, C. (2005). *Funds of knowledge: Theorizing practices in households, communities and classrooms.* Mahwah, NJ: Erlbaum.

Harkavy, I., & Romer, D. (1999). Service learning as an integrated strategy. *Liberal Education, 85*(3), 14–19.

Honeycutt, J. (2002). Outcomes of service-learning in a family communication course. *Academic Exchange Quarterly, 6*(4), 131–135.

Huber, M. (2004). *Balancing acts: The scholarship of teaching and learning in academic careers.* Washington, DC: American Association for Higher Education and The Carnegie Foundation for the Advancement of Teaching.

Hutchings, P., & Shulman, L. (1999). The scholarship of teaching: New elaborations, new developments. *Change, 31*(5), 11–15.

Irvine, J. (2001). Caring, competent teachers in complex classrooms. Charles W. Hunt Memorial Lecture, AACTE 53rd Annual Meeting, Dallas, TX.

Kezar, A., Chambers, T., & Burkhardt, J. (Eds.) (2005). *Higher education for the public good: Emerging voices from a national movement.* San Francisco: Jossey-Bass.

Kolb, D. (1984). *Experiential learning.* Englewood Cliffs, NJ: Prentice-Hall.

Krueger, R., & Casey, M. (2000). *Focus groups: A practical guide for applied research.* Thousand Oaks, CA: Sage.

Madriz, E. (2000). Focus groups in feminist research. In N. Denzin & Y. Lincoln (Eds.), *Handbook of qualitative research* (2nd ed., pp. 835–850). Thousand Oaks, CA: Sage.

Maier, M., & Tinajero, J. (1995). *Creating a hope and a future: The Mother-Daughter Program*. The University of Texas at El Paso: Office of News and Publications.

May, M. (2005). Improving teacher preparation. *Journal of Social Studies Research*. Retrieved September 15, 2005, from http://findarticles.com/p/articles/mi_qa3823/is_200510/ai_n15739596

Maybach, C. (1996). Investigating urban community needs: Service learning from a social justice perspective. *Education and Urban Society*, 28(2), 224–236.

Meritz, D. (2005, August). Poverty leaps in El Paso: Conditions show work hard to find. *El Paso Times*. http://www.elpasotimes.com/apps/pbcs.dll/article?AID =/20050831

Mewborn, D. S. (2003). Teaching, teachers' knowledge, and their professional development. In J. Kilpatrick, W. G. Martin, & D. Schifter (Eds.), *A research companion to the principles and standards for school mathematics* (pp. 45–52). Reston, VA: National Council of Teachers of Mathematics.

Munter, J. (2002, Winter). Linking community and classroom in higher education: Service-learning and student empowerment. *Journal of Nonprofit & Public Sector Marketing*, 10(2) [special issue on service-learning], 15–164.

Munter, J. (2003). The power of future teachers and parents learning together: A case study from the U.S./Mexico border. *TABE Journal*, 7, 27–34.

National Center for Education Statistics (NCES). (2005). Digest of education statistics tables and figures. Retrieved June 20, 2007, from http://nces.ed .gov/programs/digest/d05/tables/dt05_205.asp

National Coalition for Women and Girls in Education (NCWGE). (2002). *Title IX at 30: Report card on gender equity*. Washington, DC: American Association of University Women.

Nieto, S. (2000). *Affirming diversity: The sociopolitical context of multicultural education* (3rd ed.). New York: Longman.

Nieto, S. (2002). *Language, culture, and teaching: Critical perspectives for a new century*. Mahwah, NJ: Erlbaum.

Noddings, N. (1992). *The challenge to care in schools: An alternative approach to education*. Advances in Contemporary Educational Thought Series (Vol. 8). New York: Teachers College Press.

Oakes, J. (2005). *Keeping track: How schools structure inequality*. New Haven, CT: Yale University Press.

O'Meara, K., & Rice, E. (2005). *Faculty priorities reconsidered: Rewarding multiple forms of scholarship*. San Francisco: Jossey-Bass.

Padrón, Y., Waxman, H., & Rivera, H. (2002). Educating Hispanic students: Obstacles and avenues to improved academic achievement. Retrieved December 19, 2006, from www.coe.uh.edu/crede

Patton, M. (2002). *Qualitative research and evaluation methods.* Thousand Oaks, CA: Sage.

Pérez Carreon, G., Drake, C., & Calabrese Barton, A. (2005). The importance of presence: Immigrant parents' school engagement experiences. *American Educational Research Journal, 42*(3), 465–498.

Peter, K., & Horn, L. (2005). Gender differences in participation and completion of undergraduate education and how they have changed over time (NCES 2005–169). U.S. Department of Education, National Center for Education Statistics. Washington, DC: U.S. Government Printing Office.

Rice, J. (2003). *Teacher quality: Understanding the effectiveness of teacher attributes.* Washington, DC: Economic Policy Institute.

Sadker, M., & Sadker, D. (2000). *Teachers, schools, & society* (5th ed.). Boston: McGraw-Hill.

Sedlak, C., Doheny, O., Panthofer, N., & Anaya, E. (2003). Critical thinking in students' service-learning experiences. *College Teaching, 51*(3), 99–103.

Seidman, I. (2006). *Interviewing as qualitative research: A guide for researchers in education and the social sciences.* New York: Teachers College Press.

Shapiro, H. (2005). *A larger sense of purpose: Higher education and society.* Princeton, NJ: Princeton University Press.

Shulman, L. (2004). *The wisdom of practice: Essays on teaching, learning, and learning to teach.* San Francisco: Jossey-Bass.

Sleeter, C. (2007). *Making choices for multicultural education: Five approaches to race, class and gender.* Hoboken, NJ: Wiley.

Strand, K., Marullo, S., Cutforth, N., Stoecker, R., & Donohue, P. (2003). *Community-based research and higher education: Principles and practices.* San Francisco: Jossey-Bass.

Teitel, L. (2003). *The professional development schools handbook: Starting, sustaining and assessing partnerships that improve student learning.* Thousand Oaks, CA: Corwin Press.

Tinajero, J., & Spencer, D. (1999). Creating a future for Hispanic mothers and daughters on the U.S.-Mexico border. In M. Loustaunau & M. Sanchez-Bane (Eds.), *Life, death and in-between on the U.S.-Mexico border: Así es la vida* (pp. 95–112). Westport, CT: Bergin & Garvey.

Tinajero, J. V. (1992, Winter). Raising educational and career aspirations of Hispanic girls and their mothers. *The Journal of Educational Issues of Language Minority Students,* (11), 27–43.

Tinajero, J. V. (2002, October). Reflections on the law: The Mother-Daughter Program. *Equity Now Digest,* Equity Resource Center Publication, 8–9.

Tinajero, J. V., Gonzalez, J. L., & Dick, F. (1991). Raising career aspirations of Hispanic girls. *Fastback No. 320*. Bloomington, IN: Phi Delta Kappa Educational Foundation.

Tornatzky, L., Macias, E., Jenkins, D., & Solis, C. (2006). *Access and achievement: Building educational and career pathways, for Latinos in advanced technology.* Los Angeles, CA: The Tomas Rivera Policy Institute.

University of Texas at El Paso. (2005). College of Education Tenure and Promotion Guidelines. El Paso, TX: University of Texas at El Paso.

University of Texas at El Paso. (2006). *Facts 2005–06.* El Paso, TX: University of Texas at El Paso.

U.S. Census Bureau. (2000). Poverty status in 1999 of individuals. Washington, DC: U.S. Department of Commerce, Bureau of the Census [producer]. Washington, DC: U.S. Census Bureau. Retrieved September 15, 2006, from http://factfinder.census.gov/home/saff/main.html?_lang=en

U.S. Department of Education. (1997). *Title IX: 25 years of progress.* Washington, DC: Office of Educational Research and Improvement.

Valenzuela, A. (1999). *Subtractive schooling: U.S.-Mexican youth and the politics of caring.* Albany, NY: State University of New York Press.

Vogelgesang, L., & Astin, A. (2000). Comparing the effects of community service and service-learning. *Michigan Journal of Community Service Learning, 7,* 25–34.

Weil, S. W., & McGill, I. (Eds.). (1989). *Making sense of experiential learning: Diversity in theory and practice.* Berkshire, England: Open University Press.

Yamauchi, L., Billig, S., Meyer, S., & Hofschire, L. (2006). Student outcomes associated with service-learning in a culturally relevant high school program. *Journal of Prevention & Intervention in the Community, 32*(1/2), 149–164.

Part II

Learning Processes and Outcomes of Service-Learning Partnerships

6

STEM Literacy, Civic Responsibility, and Future Vision

Examining the Effects of the Lawrence Math and Science Partnership

Linda C. Foote and Julie E. DiFilippo

The Lawrence Math and Science Partnership (LMSP) provides a unique opportunity for Merrimack College faculty and students to collaborate with community partners. The program is designed to promote experiential and service-learning opportunities at Merrimack College; enhance undergraduate science, technology, engineering and mathematics (STEM) literacy, cultural awareness, and leadership skills; develop academic success and interest in STEM among middle school youth; and provide role models to enhance middle school students' future vision and aspirations for post-secondary education.

STEM Literacy

The need for science, technology, engineering, and mathematics (STEM) literacy in society keeps increasing, and of all citizenry, college graduates in particular should be prepared to respond to this need. An Association of American Colleges and Universities (AACU) report, *Greater Expectations: A New Vision for Learning as a Nation Goes to College*, recommends enabling students to become empowered, informed, and responsible learners ready to assume productive roles in society in both STEM- and non-STEM-related careers (Association of American Colleges and Universities, 2002).

The literature supports three compelling reasons why STEM education and its integration into the academic life beyond the classroom are important: (1) our future citizens must be *scientifically literate* if they are to contribute to today's interconnected, technologically dependent global community; (2) *active and experiential* settings in and outside the classroom enhance the learning process; and (3) there is a critical need to encourage *underrepresented groups* and training the trainer—paying particular attention to the STEM education of pre-service teachers.

To enhance *scientific literacy* and demonstrate a level of competency, students must acquire a certain breadth and depth of knowledge to use when formulating opinions and making personal and social decisions (Ahern-Rindell, 1999; Rutherford & Ahlgren, 1990). The National Research Council (NRC), in its 1996 "National Science Education Standards" report, states that scientific, literate individuals "identify scientific issues underlying national and local decisions and express positions that are scientifically and technologically informed" (National Research Council, 1996, p. 22). By applying those critical thinking skills, graduates become informed members of society (Accreditation Board for Engineering and Technology [ABET], 2005; Ahern-Rindell, 1999).

In its *Report on Reports*, Project Kaleidoscope (PKAL) focuses on how natural science communities flourish when the learning environment is "*active, investigative and experiential*, where the curriculum connects to the world beyond the campus and is steeped in the methods of research as practiced by professionals" (Narum, 2002, p. 5). STEM curriculum reform that extends beyond the traditional classroom is essential, and involving undergraduate students in an inquiry-based setting instills excitement, discovery, and an ability to construct a personal understanding of science and mathematics and a sense of ownership of the products at a critical stage of their academic career (Narum, 2002).

The American Association for the Advancement of Science (AAAS) and the NRC also support an education system that prepares a scientifically literate society, with reform focused on the following guiding principles: (1) all students, science majors, nonscience majors, and especially future educators, must be engaged in constructivist learning environments in which students build upon new understanding on an existing framework of knowledge; (2) active learning encourages a greater comprehension of the course content; and (3) the scientific method is best understood if it is carried out and applied to a situation as an inquiry approach to learning—engaging in the design and execution of the experiments and analysis of results, emphasizing science and the process as it is practiced by scientists rather than a series of predictable cookbook laboratory exercises that verify known information (American Association for the Advancement of Science, 1990; NRC, 1996, 1999).

In the 1991 report *Investing in Human Potential: Science and Engineering at the Crossroads*, AAAS editors suggest that not only will a person's scientific, technological, and quantitative literacy contribute to their career and productivity, but the failure to attract *underrepresented populations* to study STEM leads to a significant loss of such productivity and talent in the service of the nation (AAAS, 1991). Further, as a matter of meeting the anticipated demand for qualified scientists, engineers, and mathematics and science teachers, as well as national security requirements, there is a need for a strong STEM community to serve national interests (United States Commission for National Security, 2001). In a review of the AAAS report, PKAL editors insist that the job of STEM educators is to create not just science, but also *scientists*, in order to sustain an adequate pool of skilled professionals (Narum, 2002).

Both Project Kaleidoscope and the U.S. Department of Education (DOE) (Glenn Commission) focus on early intervention;

they also report that the single most important determinant of what elementary and secondary students learn in mathematics and science is contingent on how much their teachers know. Therefore, to produce exponential effects on society, teacher preparation must include content breadth and depth, and active learning must be central to its delivery (Narum, 1991; U.S. Department of Education, 2000). Moreover, the National Science and Technology Council's (NSTC) 2000 report suggests that precollege intervention projects support and promote interest in careers in mathematics and science-based disciplines through volunteer programs, workshops, and summer camps in which youth are partnered with undergraduate mentors and role models to "feed the pipeline" (National Science and Technology Council, 2000).

The National Climate: A Generation of Urban Poor at Risk

Nearly one-fifth of our nation's youth live in poverty (U.S. Bureau of the Census, 2004). Poverty rates are highest for families headed by single women, particularly if they are Black or Hispanic. Among all children under eighteen years old living in poverty (17.8 percent), race and ethnicity increases the risk: 33.2 percent of Black children and 28.9 percent Hispanic children live in poverty (U.S. Bureau of the Census, 2004). Many impoverished children who live in inner cities are confronted with crime, lack of supervision, substance abuse, inadequate health care, and poor high school retention rates. There are concerns with unsafe public streets and playgrounds, stress, unproductive use of unsupervised time, lack of academic support and homework assistance, and lack of enrichment opportunities and activities for these youth in economically disadvantaged situations (Afterschool Alliance, 2006). According to the 2006 Afterschool Alliance report *New England After 3 PM*, one in five New England children has no safe or supervised activity after the school day ends (Afterschool Alliance, 2006).

Equal access to education and retention is another societal concern associated with urban youth. Students from low socioeconomic status are eight times less likely to graduate from college than other students (Newman, Lohman, Newman, Myers, & Smith, 2000). Ainsworth-Darnell and Downey report that low-income minority youth are vulnerable to declines in academic motivation and performance during the transition to ninth grade, which may not be regained in the subsequent years of high school (Ainsworth-Darnell & Downey, 1998).

In response to a nationwide call for support, the number of after-school programs has increased in all major urban areas, and 14 percent of the nation's children who are between five and twelve years of age and whose mothers are employed outside the home are currently affiliated with an after-school program (Zhang, 2002). Numerous reports showed that the majority of after-school programs in urban communities share the common purpose of providing safe and positive environments for children. In a 2005 study by Darling, Caldwell, and Smith, safe and successful after-school programs are characterized by "highly structured activities, regular participation schedules, rule-guided engagement, direction by one or more adult leaders, an emphasis on skill development that increases in complexity and challenge, activity that requires sustained attention, and clear feedback on performance" (Darling, Caldwell, & Smith, 2005, p. 51). The earlier children participate in such programs, especially programs that provide enrichment in the academic areas, the greater the likelihood they will understand that higher education can improve their lives (Posner & Vandell, 1994). A 2003 report *Critical Hours: Afterschool Programs and Educational Success* by Dr. Beth M. Miller synthesizes current data from existing studies of after-school programs and concludes with several important findings. Dr. Miller notes a consensus in the research community that high-quality after-school programs—especially those that promoted active learning and consistent student participation—do increase student engagement, leading to positive, measurable academic outcomes (Miller, 2003). Enrichment programs, such as the Lawrence Math and Science Partnership described in this chapter, are vital to the success of low-income, minority students because they promote, during the middle school years, a vision for academic success and future careers. Notable programs also offer youth engaging academic and social role models, enhanced by training programs for pre-service educators or service-learning students involved in such programs.

The Local Climate and Community-Based Need

The city of Lawrence, Massachusetts, continues to face many challenges. Once a thriving industrial city, home to many of the nation's clothing and textile manufacturers, Lawrence's fortunes declined as the factories and mills along the Merrimack River closed. The middle class moved away along with these companies, and the population that replaced them was predominantly Hispanic and spoke English as a second language. At the time of this study Lawrence continues to struggle among the poorest communities in Massachusetts (349th for mean family income out of 351) and among the poorest cities in the nation (U.S. Bureau of the Census, 2004).

Lawrence public schools also reflect these economic hardships. In 2005 the district was 90-percent minority, 85 percent of whom were eligible for a free or reduced price lunch and 20 percent of whom spoke English as a second language. The district had one of the highest dropout rates in the Commonwealth at more than 12 percent (Lawrence Public Schools, 2005). There are, however, many agencies, colleges, and faith-based organizations working with the residents of Lawrence to rebuild and strengthen the city. In 2003 the Lawrence Math and Science Partnership (LMSP) was created to expand the opportunities for service-learning collaborative projects and to increase mathematics, science, and academic skills among middle school–aged youth.

The implementation of the LMSP came at a critical time. The 2003 U.S. Department of Education's National Center for Education Statistics (NCES) Third International Math and Science Study tested fourth grade students in twenty-five nations and eighth grade students in forty-five nations. Children in the United States were among the leaders in the fourth grade assessment, but by high school were among the last (National Center for Education Statistics [NCES], 2003). These same data, analyzed in the U.S. Department of Education report *International Outcomes of Learning in Mathematics Literacy and Problem Solving: PISA 2003 Results from the U.S. Perspective* (U.S. Department of Education, 2003), indicate that the U.S. performance in mathematics and science literacy and problem solving is lower than the average performance for most Organization for Economic Cooperation and Development (OECD) countries. From 2000 to 2003 there has been no measurable change in the below-average performance of U.S. students (U.S. Department of Education, 2003). These findings suggest a barrier and lack of improvement over time due to declining interest in STEM education and declining participation of American students in STEM careers.

Locally, public school students fared similarly to their national counterparts. In the Massachusetts Comprehensive Assessment System (MCAS) report from fall 2005, 61 percent of the Lawrence District eighth grade students were rated with "Warning" in math (equivalent to "Failing" in high school ratings) and another 25 percent were rated "Need improvement." The piloted MCAS Science and Technology Exam administered to eighth grade students revealed 66 percent with "Warning" scores and an additional 30 percent who "Need improvement." For two consecutive years Lawrence students were examined as a population aggregate and failed to meet or exceed the Commonwealth standards of Adequate Yearly Progress (AYP), and the District was "Identified for improvement" (Massachusetts Department of Education, 2001, 2004). The Commonwealth's high-stakes testing will continue in English and

mathematics, and Massachusetts' state-wide graduation requirements for the class of 2010 will be extended to include proficiency
in science and technology.

The Lawrence District's significant needs were well documented, and the Lawrence Math and Science Partnership was
launched to address such issues by expanding the number of youth
tracked in STEM subjects and promoting academic success and the
possibility of postsecondary education. The Partnership also created service-learning opportunities for students from Merrimack
College to collaborate and engage in building the capacity of
middle school students through the enrichment program.

College-Wide Mission and Academic Objectives

Merrimack College was founded in 1947 by the Friars of the Order
of Saint Augustine; it is a 2,500-student, comprehensive liberal
arts college located in North Andover, Massachusetts. The college offers a value-centered environment committed to integrating
liberal art studies with outside-the-classroom experiences including internships; regional, national, and international community
service; research with faculty; service-learning; study abroad; and
cooperative education programs. The intentional integration of
theory and practice with communication and critical thinking
skills applied in experiential learning settings and enriched by
reflection and assessment prepares students to make life choices that
are personally fulfilling, civically engaged, and socially responsible
(Merrimack College Experiential Learning Committee, 2005).

A review of national studies shows three positive effects on
experiential learning students in general and service-learning participants in particular. In such studies, undergraduate students
report a significant and positive effect on *interpersonal engagement*
and interaction and friendship with peers and others at the university (Eyler & Giles, 1999). Numerous studies indicate that
compared with nonparticipants, service-learning students report

engagement with the community outside the university as significantly enhanced. Students report a greater understanding of community problems and greater knowledge of diverse races and cultures (Astin & Sax, 1998; McKenna & Rizzo, 1999). They believe that they can make a difference, and they show a higher commitment to future community service beyond graduation (Eyler & Giles, 1994; Markus, Howard, & King, 1993; McKenna and Rizzo, 1999). Students' *academic engagement* is also enhanced by experiential learning opportunities. National studies show service-learning positively affects their acquisition and understanding of course concepts; they demonstrate a higher level of knowledge about the field of study, and they receive significantly higher grades than those for courses not linked to service-learning (Balazadeh, 1996; McKenna & Rizzo, 1999; Moely, McFarland, Miron, Mercer, & Ilustre, 2002; Sugar & Livosky, 1988).

Merrimack College offers a wide array of both on- and off-campus experiential learning activities for students; they are often specific to a program, department, and grant initiative or housed in the Division of Student Life. Service-learning is linked to the Augustinian devotion to community service and innovative teaching and learning pedagogies. Faculty members are reminded each semester to consider service-learning in their course design, and the Stevens Service Learning Center offers help with recruitment, agency placement, student database maintenance, and transportation. Despite the encouragement and logistical support, the practice of service-learning at Merrimack College is limited. Service-learning is incorporated into the curriculum by a modest 12 percent of the faculty, and there are few formal curriculum development workshops, incentives, or funds to further develop and pursue service-learning activities. However, student awareness and institutional aid at the level of coordination and staffing earn high marks. Taken together, institutionalization of service-learning at Merrimack College is generally assessed across all dimensions (Furco, 2003) as "Stage Two—Quality

Building"—midway in the three-stage developmental continuum.

In 2006 Merrimack College made a commitment to a college-wide academic strategic planning process. Having clearly defined its mission and vision, the college identified strategies to attain stated goals tied formally and purposefully to enhancing experiential learning and service-learning opportunities. It is widely understood that expanding and formalizing experiential learning and service-learning throughout the curriculum can be expected to revitalize current classroom pedagogies and cocurricular activities to deepen and enhance the academic climate of the campus.

LMSP Expectations and Initiatives

The specific goals of the Lawrence Math and Science Partnership were established in fall 2003 and continue to address the community-based needs by (1) promoting the institutionalization of service-learning as an experiential learning pedagogy and expanding the practitioner base, (2) increasing the number of service-learning opportunities, and (3) expanding the number of middle school youth served while tracking their academic success and their increased interest in STEM, post-secondary education, and future vision or career goals.

The Lawrence Math and Science Partnership initiatives are designed to serve 180 Lawrence middle school youth in grades five through eight. Each semester, service-learning undergraduates are recruited from courses across the curriculum and guided to varying degrees by their respective faculty to consider the elements of high-quality service-learning. Students are asked to research and consider the community-based need, collaborate with community members, find their student voice, implement meaningful service, reflect on and write about their experience, and discover how their service informs their learning and how their learning informs their service. Undergraduates are trained by the LMSP director during a hands-on STEM workshop and participate in a discussion about the middle school mind-set, led by diversity education professionals and administrators from the Partnership agencies. Based on their personal schedules and preferences, the service-learning students are matched with one of five community agencies and transported weekly to those partners after school to direct the inquiry-based STEM activities or experiments. The projects are chosen and developed to align with the Massachusetts Department of Education Curriculum Frameworks (Massachusetts Department of Education, 2001, 2004) in mathematics and the sciences for this age group. With the advent of high-stakes testing in Massachusetts and the recent addition of science competency to the MCAS determination, it is critical that the activities be guided by trained individuals and complement the curriculum in the schools.

Constructivism and active learning guide the work in the Lawrence Math and Science Partnership. Featuring this contemporary instructional process, the learning is student-centered, not instructor-dispensed. In this example of problem-based learning, youth and undergraduate mentors alike come prepared with a preexisting foundation of basic knowledge. They then build upon that as new content is delivered and explored. Studies indicate that students use critical thinking skills and perform better on outcome assessments when they are actively engaged in cooperative group activities and in problem-based learning settings (Hufford, 1991). Faculty and undergraduate mentors also adopted new roles in this environment, acting as facilitators and consultants, while supporting students' active learning.

With a service-learning mentor-to-youth ratio of better than one to three, the two-hour program features a weekly theme and includes one hour devoted to mentoring, discussions, puzzles, and word games to develop scientific literacy, mathematics, and problem-solving skills, and to offer homework help. The second hour focuses on the experiment or hands-on engineering or design problem, which is formatted to be consistent with the scientific method and challenges the participants to develop, execute, and manage data from their own experiments. To celebrate the completion of each academic year, a community-wide poster session is held in conjunction with the Division of Science and Engineering Capstone, Honors and Research Day. The youth and their families attend the event, and middle school students display posters describing their favorite experiments. Service-learning undergraduates connect their course content to the STEM enrichment program and display computer-generated posters describing those connections, their experiences, and personal reflections of their youth and program site. The combination of both undergraduate and middle school students presenting their work to each other in the same venue is a way to reinforce the continuum of STEM education and the value of service-learning.

The Merrimack College Lawrence Math and Science Partnership continues to directly respond to the national outcry for enhancing STEM literacy and teacher training and the community-based need for STEM enrichment and for youth skills and attitudes that help establish future academic and career goals. A Merrimack College study encompassing activities from 2003 through 2006 shows significant progress toward the measurable and specific goals of the Partnership, thereby (1) promoting experiential learning and, for a majority of participants, expanded service-learning opportunities; (2) enhancing service-learning while focusing on undergraduate STEM literacy, cultural awareness, civic responsibility, and leadership skills; (3) developing middle school youth's academic success and increasing interest in science, technology, engineering, and mathematics; and (4) providing role models to enhance the middle school youth's future vision and aspirations for postsecondary education.

Assessment Method

With an understanding of the Partnership and the social issues that it addresses, we turn to the means of program assessment. Here we describe the participants (subjects) and the assessment instruments.

Subject Group 1: Partnership Stakeholders

The Partnership drew on the expertise and dedication of seven community partners and five agencies that work with youth on a daily basis. The agencies included ¡Adelante!, Asian Center of Merrimack Valley, Bellesini Academy, Lawrence Boys and Girls Club, and the Girl Scouts of Spar and Spindle Council (now Girls Scouts of Eastern Massachusetts). Each of these agencies recruited middle school students for the program, provided a site for instruction, and assigned a site staff member to serve as the primary contact. Community agencies attended and contributed to the diversity training and educational psychology workshops for the mentors held each semester and before the Summer Campus Program. Sharing the agencies' expertise and best practices helped to inform and empower the undergraduate mentors.

Briefly, ¡Adelante! is a non-profit, community-based organization that serves more than four hundred urban Latino youth and their families from Greater Lawrence. The agency focuses on the preparation of eighth grade students to make a successful transition to high school and toward acceptance at rigorous private schools. Youth who participate are expected to give time to their community through service as tutors and mentors for the younger children. The Asian Center of Merrimack Valley is the only agency in the greater Lawrence area whose primary mission is to work with the Asian community. Founded in 1987 by the Sisters of Charity, the agency was formed in response to the critical unmet needs of the members of a new Asian immigrant and refugee population making their home in the greater Lawrence area. The agency has developed into a multiservice, family-oriented, intergenerational agency focusing on language education, citizenship preparation, social service strategies and advocacy, and youth after-school enrichment. The Bellesini Academy is a private, independent Catholic middle school, dedicated to providing a quality, free education to young men with limited financial means. The students are primarily Catholic and Buddhist, and 97 percent are members of a minority. The school opened in September 2002 with the sponsorship of Merrimack College and held its first graduation in spring 2005. The Lawrence Boys and Girls Club is a longstanding resource for the youth and families of Lawrence. The mission of the Lawrence Boys & Girls Club is to maintain a club for all youth without distinction of race, sex, color or creed; to provide behavior guidance; and to promote the health, social, educational, vocational, and character development of all its members. The Girl Scouts of Spar and Spindle Council serves more than 15,000 girls and 4,300 adult members in northeastern Massachusetts. The council provides after-school programs, sports, career exploration, and special interest programs to build character and success in young women.

Subject Group 2: Middle School Youth

The 273 middle school youth (generally grades five through eight, and filling approximately one thousand slots over the three years of the study) were selected through self-identification as well as through teacher and agency staff recommendation. Applications were completed to include demographic information and parent or guardian permission to photograph the students and access their academic records. A control population of middle school youth (N = 34), enrolled in the Lawrence Family Development Charter School and ¡Adelante! but not participating in the LMSP activities, were additionally identified and assessed.

Subject Group 3: Undergraduates

The study was undertaken by Merrimack College with logistical support provided by the Stevens Service Learning Center. The Center led the undergraduate recruitment phase, facilitated transportation, and tracked the human resource and service-learning documentation. The Center annually manages five hundred students, has more than sixty site placements, and supports more than twenty-five faculty members who incorporate service-learning in over fifty classes.

Assessment Instrument 1: Youth Surveys

Consultants from the University of Massachusetts Donahue Institute Research and Evaluation Group were retained to design a comprehensive assessment plan for the Partnership. Youth participant surveys that asked both formative and summative questions were administered annually and after the LMSP summer campus programs. The Middle School Youth Survey was developed to track individual middle school student responses over time. The instrument was administered a total of six times beginning in summer 2004 and ending in summer 2006. Cover sheets were used to identify the students for each survey administration. This technique for tracking students was developed to allow for confidentiality and manageable methodology. Researchers examined the responses and identified trends and significant changes in perceptions and attitudes about their experiences in learning math and science and their career aspirations. The Donahue Institute generated biannual technical reports that were informative resources and helped guide programmatic changes, and they concluded the study with a three-year final report.

In separate analysis, additional surveys were designed and administered by undergraduate pre-service teachers enrolled in Merrimack College education psychology courses. This field research experience was integrated into the curriculum content but was not designed or implemented as a service-learning course. The field research provided a resource of data that was managed and analyzed each semester, and the three-year, aggregated data were analyzed and compared, focusing on the perceptions of both LMSP youth participants and control populations.

Assessment Instrument 2: Undergraduate Participation Surveys

Undergraduate participants were assessed for both service and learning. Given equal weight, *service* was assessed using time sheets and site coordinator evaluations, while *learning* was assessed using in-house and Donahue Institute surveys that required students to purposefully link the program activities to their course content. Additional measured outcomes of learning were attendance at training sessions, frequency of accessing resources on the LMSP web-based Blackboard site, and completion of an additional four-foot-by-three-foot reflective poster formatted as a Microsoft PowerPoint slide. The University of Massachusetts Donahue Institute Merrimack College Service-Learning Student Surveys were anonymously administered to the mentors at the end of each semester (fall 2003 through spring 2006), and the aggregated findings were reported. In addition to soliciting program feedback, the consultant surveys evaluated what undergraduates gained from the program personally and why they chose to be involved.

Assessment Instrument 3: Stakeholder Interviews and Focus Groups

From December 2003 through January 2004 and June through July 2005, the Donahue Institute conducted phone interviews with the Partnership agency's executive directors to solicit comments and feedback. In March 2006 the executive directors met on campus to discuss the Partnership and the future of the LMSP. Summaries of those agency directors' comments are reported herein along with data gathered from the youth and undergraduate surveys.

Assessment Results

Assessment data provide some insights about the program's goals. Here we present study results pertaining to goals for undergraduate student participation, undergraduate student advances, academic impact on youth, youth and future vision, and stakeholders' impressions.

Evaluation and Outcome of Goal 1: Undergraduate Student Participation

Over the three-year study, Merrimack College undergraduates (n = 434) served in a variety of capacities in the Lawrence Math and Science Partnership. Anonymous surveys were collected from 207 respondents out of a possible 434 students who participated, for a 48-percent response rate over the six survey administrations. A majority of survey respondents (169, or 82 percent) served as mentors identified as service-learning students. They were trained to deliver the inquiry-based STEM activities and were expected to reflect on this opportunity that helped to develop their own scientific literacy and scientific method and data management skills taught in their biology and chemistry laboratory courses. Others extended their commitment and additionally served as site coordinators (38, or 18 percent), providing peer leadership by overseeing the program and evaluating the mentors each semester. Additional undergraduates overseen by faculty from the Education Department were recruited to develop and administer youth surveys, thus providing community service to the LMSP while actively learning the theory and techniques of education research in an authentic setting. The data generated from those assignments were analyzed and presented each semester in an education psychology course forum. Other undergraduates enrolled in management information system courses were selected to develop a Microsoft Access database for the collection of youth demographic data and scores, thereby practicing and reflecting on their MIS skills while contributing to a community-based need. Of those surveyed over the three years (six semesters), most served two to four hours per week (179, 87 percent) and a select group served more than four hours per week (27, 18 percent). Of those surveyed, 171 were female (83 percent) and 35 were male (17 percent); 185 were white (90 percent), 9 were Hispanic/Latino (4 percent), 7 were Asian (3 percent), and 5 were multiracial or "other" (3 percent). One hundred forty-three were first or second year students (70 percent) and sixty-three were members of the junior or senior classes (30 percent). The mean age for the respondents was 19.6 years old, with a range of 17 to 29 years old. In the first three years of the program, the number of undergraduates that participated in the LMSP grew appreciably (see Figure 6.1).

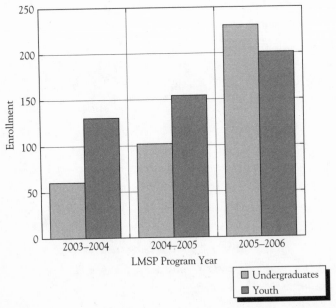

Figure 6.1. Lawrence Math and Science Partnership Participants, 2003–2006.

Note: Data developed from the youth and undergraduate LMSP surveys 2003–2006.

Of those respondents who reported academic majors and minors, 17 were majors and affiliated with the School of Business (8 percent), 71 (35 percent) had major academic programs affiliated with liberal arts (8 percent political science, 8 percent history, 6 percent English, 6 percent psychology, and 7 percent other); and 118 (57 percent) were majors and affiliated with the Division of Science and Engineering (15 percent biology, 15 percent health science, 13 percent sports medicine, 6 percent math, and 8 percent others). Of the 125 (61 percent) that reported an academic minor program, 60 (30 percent) were teachers in training for either elementary education or special education/education with moderate disabilities, and 15 (7 percent) declared Spanish as an academic minor. To illustrate the reported academic major division affiliation by gender, Table 6.1 shows that 91 (44 percent) of the respondents were women affiliated with the Division of Science and Engineering, 69 (33 percent) were women from Liberal Arts, and 27 (13 percent) were men from the Division of Science and Engineering.

When asked why they decided to became service-learning students in this program, 206 respondents chose all options that were applicable to them and indicated, as reasons for their participation, "satisfaction of helping others" (126, 61 percent), "for course

Table 6.1. Undergraduate Participants by Academic Division

Current College Division	Females			Males		
	Number	Females	Percentage of All Respondents	Number	Males	Percentage of All Respondents
Science and Engineering	91	53%	44%	27	77%	13%
Business	11	6%	5%	6	17%	3%
Liberal Arts	69	40%	33%	2	6%	1%
Totals	171	100%	83%	35	100%	17%

Source: Data developed from the undergraduate LMSP surveys 2003–2006.

credit" (118, 57 percent), "giving back to the community" (108, 52 percent), and "enjoy working with middle school students" (103, 50 percent). Notably, 85 respondents (41 percent) indicated "teaching experience" as a motivating force, and not all respondents who received service-learning course credit indicated that "credit" was the driving force in their decision to participate.

At Merrimack College, undergraduates pursue a teaching license by selecting a content area as a major and choosing education as a minor. Because 30 percent of the college mentor respondents indicated they were education minors, researchers analyzed their reasons for participation in this program, comparing those of education minors with those of the non-education minors. Items that were significantly different showed that education minors who enrolled in small teacher education classes as service-learning students were required to participate in the program, and significant numbers expressed interest in gaining teaching experience (see Table 6.2). Briefly, results of this analysis found that only 17 (8 percent) of all respondents who were education minors indicated that the program participation was not required of them, whereas a more significant number (115, 56 percent) of non-education minors chose to participate on their own. Also statistically significant was the number of education minors who participated for reasons other than for teaching experience (14, 7 percent) compared with 107 (52 percent) of other respondents who participated for reasons other than teaching experience.

Evaluation and Outcome of Goal 2: Undergraduate Student Advances

Integral to the "learning" assessment within the service-learning experience, 207 undergraduates completed learning gains evaluations and reflective surveys by indicating all attributes that apply. Each semester's data was collected and managed; as shown

Table 6.2.   Pre-Service Teachers Participate for Teaching Experience

Reasons for Participation	Education Minors		Non-Education Minors		
	Number	%	Number	%	p-value*
Class Requirement					
Yes	40	19%	34	17%	
No	17	8%	115	56%	<.001
Teaching Experience					
Yes	43	21%	42	20%	
No	14	7%	107	52%	<.001

Source: Data developed from the undergraduate LMSP surveys 2003–2006.

*The p-value of <.001 using Fisher's Exact Chi Square Test of Significance between the respondents who identified themselves as education minors and the remainder of the respondents.

in Table 6.3, 199 of the undergraduate mentors (97 percent) considered the program's "contribution to society" as aiding their own development and learning, rating it a "3" or "4—A lot." Also highly rated as a "3" or "4—A lot" were "personal development" (191, 93 percent), "making new college friends" (156, 77 percent), "scientific communication" (147, 77 percent), "the process of science" (91, 70 percent), "career development" (128, 62 percent), "academic achievement" (121, 59 percent), and "scientific literacy" (120, 58 percent). Not surprisingly, of those who selected "making new college friends," 37 percent were freshmen, 20 percent were sophomores, 14 percent were juniors, and 6 percent were seniors, for a total of 77 percent. Low-scoring attributes were "spiritual development" and "applying data management/computer skills."

The items in this section of Undergraduate Student Advances were also analyzed by respondents who indicated they were education minors versus other survey respondents. It was shown that the "program contributed to their personal development" choice

Table 6.3.   Reflections of Undergraduate Learning Gains

Rate How This Program Contributed to the Following Aspects of Your Development or Learning	3 or 4—A Lot		2 or 1—Not At All		Number	Percent
Contribution to Society	199	97%	6	3%	205	100%
Personal Development	191	93%	15	7%	206	100%
Making New College Friends	156	77%	47	23%	203	100%
Scientific Communication	147	71%	59	29%	206	100%
The Process of Science*	91	70%	39	30%	130	100%
Career Development	128	62%	77	38%	205	100%
Academic Achievement	121	59%	84	41%	205	100%
Scientific Literacy	120	58%	86	42%	206	100%
Spiritual Development	95	46%	110	54%	205	100%
Applying Data Management/Computer Skills	67	33%	138	67%	205	100%

Source: Data developed from the undergraduate LMSP surveys 2003–2006.

*This survey item not added until Spring 2005 administration; it was not asked of the participants in Fall 2003, Spring 2004, or Fall 2004.

showed a statistically significant difference between these groups when "career development" was considered. On a scale of "1—Not at all" to "4—A lot" of all who were education minors, 23 percent selected "4—A lot" or "3," and 4 percent selected "2" or "1—Not at all." In contrast, of the non-education minors, 34 percent indicated that "career development" enhancement by the program was "2" or "1—Not at all" (see Table 6.4).

Evaluation and Outcome of Goal 3: Academic Impact on Youth

Lawrence Math and Science Partnership middle school youth were recruited through efforts sponsored by the Partnership agencies. Anticipated enrollment of 180 youth per year was exceeded in year

Table 6.4.   Pre-Service Teachers' Participation Contributes to Career Development

Rate How This Program Contributed to the Following Aspect of Your Development or Learning:

Career Development

Education Minor	1—Not At All	2	3	4—A Lot	p-value*
Yes	4 (2%)	4 (2%)	23 (11%)	26 (13%)	<.001
No	21 (10%)	48 (24%)	55 (27%)	23 (11%)	

Source: Data developed from the undergraduate LMSP surveys 2003–2006.
*The p-value derived using Pearson's chi square test of significance.

three (see Figure 6.1). The Middle School Student Survey was first administered in the summer of 2004. It was then also distributed in fall 2004, spring 2005, summer 2005, spring 2006, and summer 2006, for a total of six administrations. Over the course of these administrations, 273 individual students responded to the survey. Of those students, 98 (36 percent) enrolled in the program for more than one semester or summer camp and as a consequence completed the survey more than once. Of those who participated more than once, 22 percent participated two or three times and 14 percent participated for four through six semesters or summers. Ultimately, 175 respondents (64 percent) participated in only one survey.

The majority (85 percent) of the 273 respondents attended grades five through eight, although there were 14 percent who attended grade four or below and 1 percent who attended grade nine or above. A majority of the youth participants were of Latino background (89 percent) and 11 percent were of Asian (Vietnamese or Cambodian) descent; 48 percent were males and 52 percent were females.

In the survey section that asked how much students agree with statements regarding how science should be taught, because of the sample size and for ease of reporting, the results were collapsed from a range of five responses (NO!!, no, Not Sure, yes, and YES!!) into three categories: No (NO!! and no), Not Sure, and Yes (yes and YES!!). A majority of youth indicated "Yes" that they "like experiments, measurements, and judging" (57 percent); they "prefer finding out why something happens by doing an experiment rather than being told" (69 percent); and they feel that "science is one of their favorite classes" (62 percent). At least three-quarters of the youth surveyed indicated that "science classes are mostly fun" (75 percent), they were "comfortable working with [their] classmates in small groups" (74 percent), they "prefer doing experiments rather than just watching them or reading about them" (83 percent), that "science classes and activities have taught [them] how to observe, question, get data, predict, test, conclude and share" (74 percent), and they "put a lot of effort into [their] science work" (75 percent).

In the case of youth participants who filled out surveys two or more times, the data derived from the first and last surveys that each participant completed were labeled as "entry" and "exit." The Pearson chi-square test of significance was run to determine whether there were any statistically significant changes in the responses to the statements from participants' entry into the program and their exit. The majority of items just mentioned showed no significant change over the life of the project, and youth perceptions of science classes and activities were stable. One item that did significantly change was the youths' perception of their "effort put into [their] science work." In this case the "effort" changed negatively and significantly from entry to exit (see Table 6.5).

To examine potential differences between male and female survey "repeaters," a Pearson chi-square analysis was run at entry and exit. Consistently throughout this section of the survey that reports change from entry to exit, boys answered more positively

Table 6.5.   Youth Perceptions of Learning Science and Future Vision

How Much Do You Agree with the Following Items:	No		Not Sure		Yes		Significance p-value*
I put a lot of effort into my science work	#	%	#	%	#	%	
Entry	4	4%	19	21%	68	75%	negative,
Exit	9	10%	22	24%	60	66%	p=.03
When I'm older, I would like a job experimenting and testing things	#	%	#	%	#	%	
Entry	27	31%	27	31%	34	39%	negative,
Exit	26	30%	37	42%	25	28%	p<.001

Source: Data developed from the middle school youth LMSP surveys 2003–2006.

*The p-value derived using Pearson's chi-square test of significance.

at entry than at exit. It is also consistent that the girls answered more negatively at entry than at exit. A few of these items showed this trend to be statistically significant. For the item "Science classes are mostly fun" there was a significant difference between male and female responses at entry ($p<.001$). Males were more positive than females were at entry. However, there was no significant difference at exit. The following items also had a significant difference between male and female responses at entry but not at exit: "I like figuring out problems and how things work" ($p=.002$), "I like building, testing and fixing things" ($p=.001$), and "Science classes and activities have taught me to: observe, question, get data, predict, test, conclude, and share" ($p=.047$) (see Table 6.6).

Table 6.6. Youth Attitudes and Future Vision by Gender

How Much Do You Agree With These Items?		No	Not Sure	Yes	N
Science classes are mostly fun	Entry-Female	6 (24%)	6 (24%)	13 (52%)	25
	Entry-Male	1 (1%)	11 (16%)	59 (83%)	71
	Exit-Female	3 (12%)	7 (28%)	15 (60%)	25
	Exit-Male	21 (29%)	19 (26%)	33 (45%)	73

Entry value, significant difference between genders (p<.001); exit values, no significant difference

I like figuring out problems and how things work	Entry-Female	8 (32%)	1 (4%)	16 (64%)	25
	Entry-Male	4 (6%)	10 (14%)	57 (80%)	71
	Exit-Female	5 (20%)	5 (20%)	15 (60%)	25
	Exit-Male	18 (25%)	18 (25%)	36 (50%)	71

Entry value, significant difference between genders (p<.002); exit values, no significant difference

I like building, testing and fixing things	Entry-Female	7 (28%)	6 (24%)	12 (48%)	25
	Entry-Male	3 (4%)	8 (12%)	57 (84%)	68
	Exit-Female	6 (24%)	6 (24%)	13 (52%)	25
	Exit-Male	16 (23%)	12 (17%)	42 (60%)	70

Entry value, significant difference between genders (p<.001); exit values, no significant difference

Science classes and activities have taught me how to: observe, question, get data, test, conclude, and share	Entry-Female	3 (12%)	7 (28%)	15 (60%)	25
	Entry-Male	1 (1%)	14 (20%)	54 (78%)	69
	Exit-Female	2 (8%)	6 (24%)	17 (68%)	25
	Exit-Male	16 (23%)	20 (29%)	34 (49%)	70

Entry value, significant difference between genders (p=.047); exit values, no significant difference

Table 6.6.   (Continued)

How Much Do You Agree With These Items?		No	Not Sure	Yes	N
When I'm in HS I will probably take extra science or technical classes	Entry-Female	10 (42%)	9 (38%)	5 (21%)	24
	Entry-Male	14 (21%)	22 (32%)	32 (47%)	68
	Exit-Female	12 (48%)	7 (28%)	6 (24%)	25
	Exit-Male	27 (39%)	21 (30%)	22 (31%)	70

Entry value, significant difference between genders (p=.045); exit values, no significant difference

When I'm older, I would like studying and discovering things no one else has ever found	Entry-Female	9 (36%)	5 (20%)	11 (44%)	25
	Entry-Male	6 (9%)	13 (19%)	51 (73%)	70
	Exit-Female	7 (28%)	11 (44%)	7 (28%)	25
	Exit-Male	15 (22%)	22 (32%)	31 (46%)	68

Entry value, significant difference between genders (p=.004); exit values, no significant difference

I would like to be a scientist or engineer	Entry-Female	14 (58%)	7 (29%)	3 (13%)	24
	Entry-Male	21 (30%)	21 (30%)	27 (39%)	69
	Exit-Female	12 (48%)	5 (20%)	8 (32%)	25
	Exit-Male	19 (27%)	27 (39%)	24 (34%)	70

Entry value, significant difference between genders (p=.022); exit values, no significant difference

Source: Data developed from the middle school youth LMSP surveys 2003–2006.

The p-value derived using Pearson's chi-square test of significance.

Evaluation and Outcome of Goal 4: Youth and Future Vision

In the youth survey section that asked how much students agreed with statements regarding future academic plans, pursuing science in college, and pursuing science as a career, the results were again collapsed from a range of five responses into three categories: No (NO!! and no), Not Sure, and Yes (yes and YES!!). A majority of youth indicated they "would like studying and discovering things no one else has ever found" (64 percent); 40 percent indicated they "would probably take extra science and technical classes," and 87 percent "expect to go to college."

Where entry and exit surveys were collected, Pearson chi-square testing was again run to determine whether there were any statistically significant changes in youth academic and career aspirations. The majority of items again showed no significant change over the life of the project. Items that did significantly change included "When I'm older, I would like a job experimenting and testing things" and "I would like to be a scientist or engineer." In these two cases, the opinion again changed negatively and significantly from entry to exit (see Table 6.6).

When these responses to future vision were broken out by male and female "repeaters" at entry and exit, again boys answered more positively at entry than at exit and the girls more negatively at entry than at exit. Males were significantly more positive than females were at entry for the items "When I'm in high school, I'll probably take extra science or technical classes" (p=0.45), "When I'm older, I would like studying and discovering things no one else has ever found" (p=.004), and "I would like to be a scientist or engineer" (p=.022) (see Table 6.6).

Partnership Stakeholders' Impressions

The results summarized in Exhibit 6.1 were compiled from data collected by the Donahue Institute during interviews with staff members or the directors of each of the five Partnership sites. The interviews were conducted in December 2003 and January 2004 and again in June and July 2005. The purpose of the interviews was to determine the directors' perspectives of the Lawrence Math and Science Partnership after-school program at their respective sites.

Exhibit 6.1. Partnership Stakeholders' Perspectives: Donahue Institute Interviews January 2004, July 2005

What were your expectations for the Lawrence Math and Science Partnership?

- To engage our youth in math and science activities

- To increase awareness about math and science and careers in those fields

- "To have additional meaningful programming for use at my center"

- To excite the youth about learning math and science

- To provide additional resources for youth in terms of staff, materials, and curriculum

Any unexpected benefits?

- The youth get to know and learn from college students.

- Merrimack College students have built strong relationships with youth.

- Merrimack College students have become involved in programs outside of math and science program.

- Youth actively revisit what they learned in school.

Any unexpected problems?

- Youth did not always complete written parts of the assignments.

- Fewer students enrolled than expected.

- Youth not committed and only attend sporadically.

- Sometimes the experiments are too easy for the youth.

What have you observed about the program that benefits students?

- Increased exposure to science.

- College students are passionate about science and are good role models for youth.

- Youth engage in positive interactions with adults.

- Youth enjoy the activities, especially when they create something they can take with them and show to other children not in the class.

- "It gets them excited about learning, especially in areas that they don't seem especially fond of in school."

- Youth are developing their writing skills.

- Youth are learning and having a great time.

- Youth display more creative thinking and positive relationships with Merrimack students.

- Youth show an appreciation for the subject matter — "it's creative and fun and hands-on."

Partnership agency directors expected the LMSP to engage their youth, increase their math and science skills, increase their awareness of higher education, and expose the youth to undergraduate mentors. An agency director reflected that the LMSP "provides the youth an opportunity to explore science and science related topics outside the normal classroom setting in a fun and innovative way taught by young men and women with whom they can instantly connect because they share the common bond of being students." Unexpected benefits included the following: (1) the Merrimack College students built many strong relationships with the youth, (2) middle school students youth reinforced their school studies and demonstrated what they've learned, and (3) Merrimack

College students became involved with the same agencies in initiatives outside of the Partnership program. Agency directors reported a few unexpected problems: youth attendance and retention, the fifth to eighth grade curriculum being less challenging for some, and variable youth commitment to completing weekly laboratory notebook entries. Observed program benefits were summarized, as shown in Exhibit 6.1; these included the benefits of good role models and positive interactions with adults, the excitement and joy of learning, and the increased exposure to, appreciation of, and enhanced skills in carrying out and communicating science content.

In the third year of the Partnership, executive directors from the agencies assembled as a focus group, reviewed the three-year program, and strategically planned for the future. Community stakeholders agreed with one agency director's sentiment:

> The relationship between the college and the youth is essential in closing the achievement gap cited in national studies. Prior to the LMSP many middle school students had never been encouraged to think about college and careers. The program provides opportunities for the youth to be exposed to careers in science and technology. Through visiting the College they are exposed to various aspects of a campus and this encourages the youth to do well in school. Most importantly, through the interaction with faculty and administration at Merrimack College as well as the weekly mentoring relationship with college students, it encourages the youth to become life-long learners and place education as a priority in their life. (LMSP, 2006)

The Partnership agencies share a responsibility to build the capacities of their programs and the community they serve, and during this focus group representatives were adamant about how best the LMSP could support these goals and their needs. The Lawrence Math and Science Partnership was established to strengthen the STEM skills of Lawrence youth, and it received accolades for its alignment with the literature on effective after-school program practices and for facilitating close mentoring relationships among the youth and undergraduates (LMSP, 2006).

Findings

The inquiry-based STEM curriculum featured in the LMSP and delivered by trained and engaging undergraduate mentors fulfills the recommendations of the National Science Board (NSF) and the National Science Teachers Association. This 2003–2006 study reports the significant progress made toward the Partnership's measurable goals of advancing the practice of experiential learning and undergraduate and middle school student learning.

Merrimack College Undergraduate Student Background and Advances

Female undergraduates clearly outnumber the male mentors involved in the Partnership. Table 6.1 shows the percentage of just females and just males in each division and the overall percentage of males and females; this information is important to determine whether a mathematics and science-oriented curriculum attracts more females or males and from which division. Although the majority of respondents are female (83 percent), there are a smaller percentage of female mentors (53 percent) from the Division of Science and Engineering than males (77 percent). Conversely, consistent with the profiles and demographics for our education minors, there are a larger percentage of female mentors (40 percent) from the Division of Liberal Arts than males (6 percent), and a vast majority of those were reported to be education minors. Because the program provides and promotes early classroom and teaching experiences, it follows that education minors would become involved with the program. As shown in Table 6.2, the population and reason that was significantly different was the education minors' requirement to participate and their hope to gain teaching experience. Moreover, statistically significant findings were that students pursuing education as a profession would consider this program, which includes a teaching opportunity, to be contributing to their career development (see Table 6.4).

The majority of Merrimack College undergraduates rated this program as having enhanced their "personal development" (93 percent) and as an opportunity to make "contributions to society" (97 percent). Clearly, as shown in Table 6.3, they reflected on the importance of their role as mentors to these youth who are ordinarily limited by their disadvantaged circumstances, and the undergraduates now understand and appreciate their personal development gains on both social justice and academic fronts. Academically, respondents saw value in the opportunity to practice their scientific communication skills (71 percent) and the process of science (70 percent). "Making new college friends" was also important, with 77 percent of respondents rating it highly. Predictably, of those who selected this aspect 37 percent were freshmen, 20 percent were sophomores, 14 percent were juniors, and 6 percent were seniors: a total of 77 percent. Establishing a peer group and venturing out together in cocurricular and extracurricular venues is intentional and is a priority for many new students at Merrimack.

Ninety respondents to the survey offered additional comments. They cited the joys of working with children, and several illuminated personal and academic benefits: "It has furthered my desire to go into teaching," "a very good learning experience," and "wonderful opportunity for all to help others and learn about yourself." Several addressed the value of service-learning: "has a positive influence on the youth involved," and "a great way to reinforce my school work while giving back to the community." Finally, some comments extrapolated to the future: "I would recommend the program, " and "hope to do it again next semester."

Middle School Youth Perceptions of Science and Future Goals

When all middle school youth respondents were considered, the item "I put a lot of effort into my science work" changed negatively and significantly from entry to exit. The items "When I am older, I would like a job experimenting and testing things" and "When I am older, I would like a job in science or technology" were also both significant in the negative direction. As students become more aware of the effort required to be successful in science, they become more critical of their own efforts. Also developmentally as students move from early middle school (grades four, five, and six) to late middle school (grades seven, eight, and nine), they generally move in the direction of being more negative toward school and learning. An additional explanation may arise from one of the partnership sites that hosts 25 percent of the total youth population, in which older eighth grade students were dissatisfied with having the same activities as fifth graders and did not appreciate the opportunity to ask more complex and sophisticated questions of the system or model.

Of great interest were the differences between male and female middle school respondents and their change of attitudes and perceptions over time. Based on the entry and exit results between males and females, it appeared that girls moved in a more positive direction, from no to yes, more than boys, who seemed to have moved in the negative direction, from yes to no.

Over the life of the program, to a significantly greater extent than the boys, middle school girls discovered that "science classes are mostly fun"; they began to enjoy "figuring out problems and how things worked," and appreciated that science classes and activities had taught them the scientific process. To a significantly greater extent, girls in the Partnership plan to "take extra science and technical classes," study and discover "things no one else has ever found," and wish to become "a scientist or engineer." It is not clear why this change occurred for girls and not boys. Identification with the female undergraduate mentors (83 percent) and the value placed on those vibrant and engaging role models may explain the middle school girls' change in attitude over time. The appeal of hands-on discovery and the personal satisfaction of designing and testing may have also empowered the girls, leading to positive changes in perceptions and interest over time.

Impact on the College Community

Merrimack College continues to serve as a major educational resource for individuals and for the Merrimack Valley community, especially when one considers the effect of this Partnership and the extent of the outreach. This program's intentional integration of theory and practice, enriched by reflection and assessment, is ongoing and prepares our students to make life choices that are personally fulfilling, civically engaged, and socially responsible. Based on Andrew Furco's three-stage developmental steps toward institutionalization of service-learning practices, the college is assessed as "Stage Two—Quality Building"—midway in the continuum (Furco, 2003). The renewed focus on experiential education opportunities and on best practices that move our curriculum reform and institutionalization of service-learning forward in the Furco continuum, is timely.

The Education Department at Merrimack College considered the Partnership's initiatives and formally endorses the program as a superlative venue for both service and learning. They describe it as a well-suited venue for meeting their students' need to practice STEM content and process in an active learning environment. It gives them the opportunity to serve in an urban education setting and become aware of the plight of the urban poor. Involving pre-service education students in curriculum development and education research and as mentors in the LMSP program additionally fosters a knowledge base of service-learning and a new pedagogical approach to teaching and learning. The effect this will have on their future choices in pedagogy, their future classrooms, and the youth therein is exponential.

Appreciation of Cultural Diversity

Perhaps the greatest benefit of this program is that it provides the opportunity to bring together diverse groups of people working toward a common goal. The students and faculty at Merrimack are reported to be largely Caucasian and middle class. As reported by the undergraduate respondents, 185 were white (90 percent), 9 were Hispanic/Latino (4 percent), 7 were Asian (3 percent), 1 was multiracial (1 percent), and 4 were of other ethnic backgrounds (2 percent). Participation in this Partnership is an education in different lifestyles and cultural norms. The same is true for the participating youth and their community agencies. The majority of the middle school youth are either Latino or Asian (Cambodian, Vietnamese), with family incomes at or below poverty level. These youth are reported to live in disadvantaged situations and in neighborhoods that are not culturally or socioeconomically diverse. This program, by design, allows the mentors to more fully understand the inequities of our society, motivating them to seek change. It additionally introduces the youth to college students and the prospect of postsecondary education and college for themselves—raising their awareness and career aspirations.

Conclusion

Merrimack College supports experiential learning and it is mission-driven to provide community service. However, the faculty as a whole hosts a limited number of courses offering service-learning opportunities that intentionally ask students to do the following:

1. Research and consider the community-based need
2. Collaborate with community members
3. Find their student voice
4. Implement meaningful service

5. Reflect on and write about their experience

6. Discover how their service informs their learning and how their learning informs their service

The LMSP has brought about change, and since 2003 increasing numbers of undergraduates have enrolled in courses that were linked to the LMSP—doubling the number of undergraduates participating in service-learning campus-wide. Notably, the LMSP provides both community service and service-learning opportunities for Merrimack College undergraduates. Some mentors receiving service-learning credit return to the program and assume leadership and site coordinator positions. Some mentors return to fulfill a desire to serve and do so for no course credit. With or without credit, together they witness their effect as role models, and many make great efforts to return to their Partnership agencies in future semesters—developing lifelong service habits benefiting society.

Undergraduates identified as LMSP service-learning students report heightened awareness of the youth in Lawrence and the limitations associated with the school and after-school environment. Service-learning mentors report connections to their coursework with respect to STEM content, scientific literacy, and scientific method—and for some, in teacher education programs, connections to their future teaching careers.

The LMSP engages middle school youth participants at a critical time in their development—offering hands-on and inquiry-based STEM activities that ordinarily are not supported by the district schools or after-school programs. Two hours per week of enrichment, which includes puzzles and word searches linked to the experimental content area of the week, fosters both scientific literacy skills and scientific method skills for all participants. Interaction with undergraduate mentors captures the attention of the youth and focuses their sights on their academic future and career goals.

At the request of the community agencies, and in agreement with the college, the program will continue as a service-learning and community service mentor program. Although the lessons and materials will be offered and made available to the community agencies, the agencies maintain that their needs are not simply curriculum and supplies. Their expressed interests continue to be to host undergraduate role models and mentors to facilitate the activities and engage the youth in active learning that supports STEM skills and future vision.

Merrimack College faculty, students, staff, and administration are committed to change and seek to be transforming in response to the outcry of the external authorities, including the American Association for the Advancement of Science, the National Council for Research, and the National Science Foundation. The LMSP, by design, both is anchored by and mirrors our college-wide goals and values and our academic strategic plan. It recognizes the value of partnerships and a community of scholars engaged in learning and goals that foster critical thinking, communication, adaptability, cultural understanding, respect for diversity, and reflective thinking. The Merrimack College community involved in the Lawrence Math and Science Partnership is presented with a unique opportunity to redefine undergraduate STEM teaching and learning.

References

Accreditation Board for Engineering and Technology (2005). *Accreditation Criteria.* Baltimore, MD: Author. Retrieved from http://www.abet.org/criteria.html

Afterschool Alliance 2006. *New England After 3 PM.* Washington, DC: Author. Retrieved from http://afterschoolalliance.org/NE_after_3pm.pdf

Ahern-Rindell, A. J. (1999). Applying inquiry-based and cooperative learning strategies to promote critical thinking. *Journal of College Science Teaching,* 28(3), 203–207.

Ainsworth-Darnell, J. W., & Downey, D. B. (1998). Assessing the oppositional culture explanation for racial/ethnic differences in school performance. *American Sociological Review,* 63, 536–553.

American Association for the Advancement of Science (1990). *The liberal art of science: Agenda for action: The report of the Project on Liberal Education and the Sciences.* Washington, DC: Author.

American Association for the Advancement of Science (1991). *Investing in human potential: Science and engineering at the crossroads.* Washington, DC: Author.

Association of American Colleges and Universities. 2002. *Greater expectations: A new vision for learning as a nation goes to college.* Washington, DC: Author. (http://www.greaterexpectations.org/)

Astin, A. W., and Sax, L. J. (1998). How undergraduates are affected by service participation. *Journal of College Student Development, 39*(2) 251–262.

Balazadeh, N. (1996). *Service learning and the sociological imagination: Approach and assessment.* Paper presented at the National Historically Black Colleges and Universities Faculty Development Symposium, Memphis, TN.

Darling, N., Caldwell, L., & Smith, R. (2005). Participation in school-based extracurricular activities and adolescent adjustment. *Journal of Leisure Research, 37*(1), 51–76.

Eyler, J., & Giles, D. E., Jr. (1994). The impact of a college community service laboratory on students' personal, social, and cognitive outcomes. *Journal of Adolescence, 17,* 327–339.

Eyler, J., & Giles, D. E., Jr. (1999). *Where's the learning in service-learning?* San Francisco: Jossey-Bass.

Furco, A. (2003). *Self-assessment rubric for the institutionalization of service-learning in higher education.* New Orleans, LA: Tulane University. Retrieved from www.tulane.edu/~ServLmg/lsa/furcosrubric.shtml

Hufford, T. L. (1991). Increasing academic performances in an introductory biology course. *Bioscience, 41,* 107–108.

Lawrence Math and Science Partnership Agencies Executive Directors. Focus group. 10 Jan. 2006.

Lawrence Public Schools (2005). *Lawrence Public Schools MCAS district performance.* Retrieved from http://www.lawrence.k12.ma.us/

Markus, G. B., Howard, J.P.F., & King, D. C. (1993). Integrating community service and classroom instruction enhances learning: Results from an experiment. *Educational Evaluation and Policy Analysis, 15,* 410–419.

Massachusetts Department of Education (2001). *Curriculum frameworks for science technology and engineering.* Malden, MA: Author.

Massachusetts Department of Education (2004). *Curriculum frameworks for mathematics: Supplement grades 3, 5 and 7 grade level standards.* Malden, MA: Author.

McKenna, M. W., & Rizzo, E. (1999). Student perceptions of the "learning" in service-learning courses. *Journal of Prevention and Intervention in the Community, 18,* 111–123.

Merrimack College Experiential Learning Committee (2005). Davis Education Foundation grant proposal, November 2005.

Miller, B. M. (2003). *Critical hours: Afterschool programs and educational success.* Quincy, MA: Nellie Mae Education Foundation. Retrieved from http://www.nmedf.org/uploads/critical_hours_full.pdf

Moely, B. E., McFarland, M., Miron, D., Mercer, S. H., & Ilustre, V. (2002). Changes in college students' attitudes and intentions for civic involvement as a function of service-learning experiences. *Michigan Journal of Community Service Learning, 9*(1), 18–26.

Narum, J. (Ed). (1991). *What works: Building natural science communities.* Washington, DC: Project Kaleidoscope. Retrieved from http://www.pkal.org

Narum, J. (Ed). (2002). *Report on reports.* Washington, DC: Project Kaleidoscope. Retrieved from http://www.pkal.org

National Center for Education Statistics (2003). *Third international math and science study.* Washington, DC: Author. Retrieved from http://www.nces.ed.gov/TIMSS/

National Research Council (1996). *National science education standards.* Washington, DC: National Academy Press. Retrieved from http://www.nap.edu/catalog/html

National Research Council (1999). *Transforming undergraduate education in science, mathematics, engineering, and technology.* Washington, DC: National Academy Press. Retrieved from http://www.nap.edu/catalog/6453.html

National Science and Technology Council (2000). *Ensuring a strong U.S. scientific, technical, and engineering workforce in the 21st century.* Washington, DC: Author. Retrieved from http://www.ostp.gov/html/workforcerpt.pdf

Newman, B., Lohman, B., Newman, P., Myers, M., & Smith, V. (2000). Experiences of urban youth navigating the transition to ninth grade. *Youth and Society, 3*(4), 387–416.

Posner, J. K., & Vandell, D. L. (1994). Low income children's after-school care: Are there beneficial effects of after-school programs? *Child Development, 65,* 440–456.

Rutherford, F. J., & Ahlgren, A. (1990). *Science for all Americans.* New York: Oxford University Press.

Sugar, J., & Livosky, M. (1988). Enriching child psychology courses with a preschool journal option. *Teaching of Psychology, 15,* 93–95.

United States Bureau of the Census (2004). *Income, poverty and health insurance coverage in the U.S.* (Report P 60, p. 52). Washington, DC: US Department of Commerce. Retrieved from www.census.gov/prod/2004pubs/p60-226.pdf

United States Commission for National Security (2001). *Roadmap for national security: Imperative for change* (Hart-Rudman Commission). Washington, DC: Author. Retrieved from http://www.nssg.gov/Reports/reports.htm

United States Department of Education (2000). *Before it's too late: A report to the nation from the National Commission on Mathematics and Science Teaching for the 21st Century* (Glenn Commission). Washington, DC: Education Publications Center. Retrieved from http://www.ed.gov/americacounts/glenn/toc.html

United States Department of Education (2003). *International outcomes of learning in mathematics literacy and problem solving: PISA 2003 results from the U.S. perspective.* Washington, DC: Institute of Education Sciences, National Center for Education Statistics.

Zhang, J. (2002). Development of an evaluation scale to measure participant perceptions of after school enrichment programs. *Measurement in Physical Education and Exercise Science, 2,* 167–183.

7

School-Based Service-Learning as Action Research

Deborah S. Yost and Elizabeth Soslau

This chapter explores the unique connection between service-learning and action research and reflection in the context of a school-university partnership. The partnership plan, entitled "Project Achieve," advanced a model of urban professional development with the ultimate goal of increasing teaching effectiveness and student achievement. Two professors at La Salle University—a Catholic institution in Philadelphia with an enrollment of nearly eight thousand undergraduate and graduate students—developed Project Achieve in collaboration with the principal of an urban middle school. The plan targeted teaching development and skill; its premise was that increased teacher expertise in implementing the core curriculum would concomitantly increase student achievement as measured by the results of district-wide benchmark tests and statewide standardized tests. One aspect of this professional development plan was an action research component in which seven teachers volunteered to participate. These projects were based on the teachers' particular interests and were supported by mentors on the Project Achieve staff.

In addition to the project, numerous teacher candidates from the partner university were assigned to this school, some as student

---

Note: The My Voice© process published in-service materials are copyrighted 2001 by Need in Deed. Material reprinted and adapted with permission.

teachers and others as junior-level students working in classrooms one day per week. In this chapter we provide a chronicle of the project's processes and outcomes as well as our reflective accounts of the partnership experience. In addition, later in the chapter we address theoretical foundations of service-learning and action research, school-university partnerships, and reflection as inquiry.

Collaboration is the critical component of this discussion. Chapter coauthor Elizabeth Soslau studied the effects of service-learning on her fifth grade students' abilities to make meaningful connections to the core curriculum using an experimental research design; coauthor Deborah Yost served as Elizabeth's research mentor and the codirector of the Project Achieve grant. We highlight the service-learning–action research project's collaborative dimensions in order to answer a compelling question posed by the research literature: "Are service and/or learning better because of the quality of the partnership?" (Cruz & Giles, 2000, p. 31). Through subsequent investigations of our own experiences and of literature on service-learning, action research, and school-university partnerships, we concur that the service and learning were substantially enhanced through our partnership collaboration.

School-University Partnership Perspectives

The following sections provide an overview of Project Achieve and the service-learning action research project. Further, the teacher, Elizabeth Soslau, and university professor, Deborah Yost, describe the benefits of the partnership collaboration.

Overview of the Partnership Endeavor: Project Achieve

Project Achieve has evolved over the two-year grant cycle (2004–2006) as a teacher-leader model of professional development that served to enhance teaching effectiveness and student achievement at an urban middle school. The goal was achieved during the first year of the grant through the coaching and mentoring of fifth and eighth grade teachers, using Marzano's (1992) Dimensions of Learning model as a framework for research-based teaching. During the second year we trained six teacher-leaders to carry out the same model of professional development with all teachers at the school. Consistent with the professional development literature, Project Achieve focused on school-based, mentoring, and in-service education for teachers based on their needs. Observation and questionnaire protocols created from Marzano's model throughout the year were used to identify areas of need and to measure growth in instructional effectiveness over time. Student achievement data were collected from two middle schools, the host and a comparison school; the latter used a traditional professional development model. Each middle school serviced grades five through eight and together comprised approximately 2,400 students. Demographic data from both schools were similar in that 97 percent of the student body at both schools were students of color, and all were eligible for the free and reduced-price lunch program.

An important aspect of professional development for teachers during both grant years was an action research component designed to increase teachers' understanding and use of research-based teaching methods. During the 2004–2005 school year, Elizabeth Soslau, then a fifth grade teacher, designed and implemented—under the guidance of her university partner—a service-learning–action research project that measured the effects of service-learning on student achievement (see Soslau & Yost, 2007). Ms. Soslau was interested in discovering whether service-learning was a viable instructional method for teaching the mandated core curriculum. After receiving service-learning training from Need in Deed, a Philadelphia-based non-profit service-learning organization, Elizabeth designed a study using experimental and control groups. This study measured the extent to which service-learning helped students make personal, real-life connections to content, increased their motivation to learn, and heightened their academic achievement.

The collaboration between Ms. Soslau and the university partner was significant; they communicated extensively about the cycle of action research and progress gained in Ms. Soslau's research throughout the year.

Overview of the Service-Learning–Action Research Project

Ms. Soslau taught literacy to two fifth-grade classes in the 2004–2005 academic year. The study used an experimental group and a control group to measure the effects of a service-learning project on the academic and motivational gains of urban middle school students. Two fifth grade classes, each with thirty-four students, participated in the study. The students were heterogeneously grouped by academic ability and behavior rankings. Ms. Soslau designated one class as the experimental group, exposing these students to the standard curriculum through their participation in a service-learning project. The control group experienced the same curriculum via traditional instructional methods. Data included the following:

- Student journals, in which students from both groups wrote monthly entries discussing the content and value of their learning

- District-wide benchmark (curriculum-based) test results in both reading and mathematics

- Students' attendance and suspension rates

Data were collected from October 2004 to March 2005, with the goal of recognizing differences between the experimental and control groups.

The results revealed that the experimental group showed more gains in making real-world connections between content and their personal experiences (see Soslau & Yost, 2007). Their mathematic and reading benchmark scores showed a higher rate of growth over time than that of the control group. Further, the experimental group showed better attendance and lower suspension rates than the control group. The study concluded that service-learning curricular approaches assist students in learning content on deeper and more meaningful levels, thereby increasing their achievement and motivation to learn.

The university partner provided intensive mentoring for Ms. Soslau in one-on-one meetings throughout each research phase. As part of the research cycle, Ms. Soslau recorded her progress in a personal journal. The journal served as a catalyst for conversations between Ms. Soslau and her university partner as well as an opportunity to reflect periodically on the project's results. The final action research report included research questions, hypothesis development, methods design, data collection, data analysis, and general topics related to the challenges of conducting action research while simultaneously teaching a full class schedule.

As mentioned earlier, prior to being selected to participate in the university-sponsored action research program, Ms. Soslau received intensive in-service and professional development from Need in Deed. She was one of approximately twenty other teachers trained by Need in Deed in the Philadelphia region and the only teacher selected to be mentored by a university professor through the La Salle University–urban middle school partnership. The university partnership granted a small stipend for the action research project.

Ms. Soslau's exposure to service-learning methodology through Need in Deed prompted her to select the My Voice process as a framework for the service-learning project. Using the process acronym VOICE (Value Your Voice, Outline Your Objectives, Investigate the Issue, Conduct Meaningful Service, and Express What You Learned), she guided her students through the service-learning project's essential components.

The students completed the Value Your Voice step through a series of activities that allowed them to identify themselves as individuals and then as part of the larger classroom community. Through class meetings, brainstorms, simulations, and issue identification activities, Ms. Soslau provided a forum that enabled her students to reflect on and voice their personal concerns about their community.

During the Outline Your Objectives stage, the students held structured debates about the importance of several issues. Ms. Soslau helped students build consensus in choosing the social issue of "disease" to explore. The students brainstormed all of the diseases that they knew of and received help in categorizing the list. Several categories resulted, such as STDs, cancers, pediatric illnesses, and diseases that confine sufferers to wheelchairs. She conducted classroom meetings that allowed students to discuss how diseases affected them personally. Many students discussed family members or neighbors who were sick, and several students discussed family members who used wheelchairs. Wheelchair use and accessibility issues became the discussion's focus. With Need in Deed's assistance, Ms. Soslau brought in local real-life news stories and wheelchair-bound guest speakers to provide living resources for the students to further their research.

The project then moved into the VOICE model's Investigate the Issue phase. Students met with a professor and her students from Drexel University's Hahnemann Programs in Rehabilitation Sciences to learn more about wheelchair use and mobility issues. Two quadriplegics visited the students and answered candid questions about their challenges and everyday lives as wheelchair-bound people. Students also used wheelchairs themselves to build empathy for wheelchair users. They created neighborhood maps, which showed accessible and inaccessible routes in their community. Students used the Internet and met with an emergency room nurse to research additional information about wheelchair users and mobility issues.

After thoroughly investigating the issue, students decided to plan and conduct their service project in the Conduct Meaningful

Service phase. Ms. Soslau elicited service ideas from the students and, as a result of their brainstorming, the students decided to conduct several mini-service projects. They wrote letters to the owner of one store that was not accessible to wheelchair users. Students made flyers and placed them on cars that were parked on the sidewalk, blocking access to wheelchair users. They also wrote letters to the editors of several newspapers alerting the community to the accessibility issues. Students created a public service announcement, and they surveyed, designed, and drew architectural plans for a wheelchair ramp for a local park. (Students completed the ramp the following year.)

Finally, the students progressed into the last phase of the My Voice framework, Express What You Learned. Throughout the year they created personal portfolios that tracked their progress and highlighted their work. Students used journal reflections as a way to make explicit connections between the curriculum content and their own lives, and they developed tangible portfolio pieces throughout the year. Portfolios were continually assessed using teacher-made rubrics that were aligned to the project or activity criteria.

Because Ms. Soslau wanted to publish the study's results, e-mail and telephone correspondence enabled the university partner, Deborah Yost, to provide coaching in the writing and manuscript publication process. This was a unique aspect of the partnership that underscores the school-university project's intensiveness, comprehensiveness, and potential for tangible outcomes.

One Perspective: A Teacher's Service-Learning Action Research Project

As a result of the close mentoring and the personal relationship that resulted from the collaboration and school-university partnership, I, Elizabeth Soslau, became a self-reflective practitioner who methodically and consciously strives to improve my teaching practice by applying pedagogical theories. By being immersed in service-learning research, I was forced to focus on *intended outcomes* of the research project and therefore to more consciously plan lessons with the end in mind. The research design stipulated that I had to collect incremental data, so I became accustomed to adjusting instruction throughout the year. Without the opportunity to participate in the action research project, I would not have thought to use formative data to design and change my instruction. Instead, I would have relied on purely summative results to decide whether the service-learning project was effective in improving my students' academic achievement and motivation.

The service-learning project conducted by my students, who were themselves the subject of my action research, was an exemplary model of service-learning. The essential components of service-learning (including student voice, meaningful service, reflection, connection to learning, partnerships, assessment, and evaluation) were all addressed throughout the year (Billig, 2000; George, 2004; Hope, 1999; Smith, 2005). My project also gained national recognition through its inclusion in promotional video and print material of Learn and Serve America. As well, the wheelchair accessibility service-learning project received the Need in Deed *My Voice* award (one of only three presented to the entire network). I attribute the success of the project to the service-learning training provided by Need in Deed and the research mentoring gained from the La Salle University partnership. I have discovered that when action research is combined with service-learning, students and their teachers are engaged in *dual* action research projects. We were simultaneously studying a phenomenon and arriving at appropriate solutions based on information and data gathered.

By reflecting on my relationships with Deb, my university mentor, and with my students, I learned several key things. First, I realized the benefit of the reflection process. Deb asked me to keep a journal as part of the action research project. Through my journal writing I was forced to continually reflect on my teaching practices. I recorded several types of information in my journal:

research-related thoughts, personal feelings, reflective records of my teaching practice, service-learning ideas, and questions for myself, my mentor, and my students. In turn, I asked my students to keep journals to record their connections between the curriculum and their personal lives and their thoughts and feelings throughout the service-learning project. My students and I benefited from the art of reflection. We simultaneously became conscious of the service-learning process and how it enabled us to learn and make contextual connections to the surrounding world.

Both the mentoring process and service-learning as an instructional strategy used nontraditional teaching practices. Traditionally, university professors teach from a preset syllabus, but in this case Deb acted as a mentor and guide, which allowed *me* to dictate the content that *I* needed to facilitate the research process. The goal was not for the university researcher to transmit information to the action researcher, but rather to provide a forum that enabled me to actively seek information that was relevant and pertinent to the study. Similarly, tradition dictates that a middle school teacher's primary role is to "teach" a prescribed curriculum; however, because of my involvement in this service-learning project, I chose to mentor my students by letting their voices dictate the learning content. Thus both my students and I acquired new knowledge using a constructivist approach: "As a method of knowledge creation and acquisition, action research derives from the best Deweyan tradition of democratic problem solving" (Harkavy, Puckett, & Romer, 2000, p. 113).

Another Perspective: A University Partner's Mentoring Experience

The professional mentoring partnership that I, Deborah Yost, established with Elizabeth Soslau began in the fall of 2004 and culminated with her final action research report in the spring of 2005. Throughout the year that followed, we extended our collaboration with the creation of two manuscripts: one article that detailed the results of the service-learning–action research project (Soslau & Yost, 2007) and the second, this chapter, on school-based service-learning as action research. The relationship has had a profound impact on Elizabeth then and now, and on my own thinking and work as a coordinator of a school-university partnership and as a university professor.

Through my work with Elizabeth, I discovered that for a professor to successfully mentor a school-based, action-researcher, the teacher must be motivated to complete the project and capable of carrying out the responsibilities it entails while teaching full-time. After the first meeting in which my codirector and I met with all seven teacher-researchers to discuss the project and to brainstorm ideas, I was assigned to work with Elizabeth as her research mentor. Throughout the year she sought my advice regarding her research questions and ideas, and she requested deadlines for completing different phases of the action research process. She was highly motivated to create a service-learning project that reflected relevant literature's theory and findings and that measured its own outcomes. It was through her diligence and effort that this project resulted in such excellent results, worthy of the *My Voice* award and a refereed journal publication.

Mentoring several teachers engaged in action research was a challenging task because the participants differed in their knowledge of the research and their motivation to meet the established timelines for completing their projects. Thus, unlike in a research course that I might teach at the university, a more constructivist methodology had to be used to teach and mentor people who had differing knowledge bases and writing skills as well as projects that were conducted during different time frames. However, as I worked with my teacher–action researchers, I observed professionals who not only made great strides in their understanding of a methodological practice but also became much more focused on student learning and achievement. Elizabeth was no exception. Everyone gained something from engaging in action research in service to their classroom communities.

Working in an urban middle school one day per week over two years on the Project Achieve grant, I learned important lessons about creating successful and sustainable partnerships with schools. First and foremost, the leadership team, including the principal, must regard the work as important and worthwhile, because the principal is the school's driving force. The principal of our partner middle school had a strong desire to increase teachers' expertise and professionalism in order to raise academic achievement to No Child Left Behind (NCLB) standards. Thus, as we worked toward this goal, the principal and his leadership team assisted us every step of the way. University partners must also gain the respect of the teachers and other staff members through informal meetings and collaborations. Our manner with teachers was nonjudgmental and helpful as we guided them to learn more about themselves and their teaching styles and to discover effective teaching strategies. Instead of being viewed as outsiders, my codirector and I were integrated into the school in a relatively short period of time.

The partnership also positively enhanced my work as a professor. The close involvement I have had since the fall of 2004 with urban middle school teachers and their students has made me more attuned to the need for novice teachers to understand global and multicultural issues. Further, now that I have been exposed to the realities of urban education, I have become better able to communicate the great challenges and rewards of urban teaching to my undergraduate and graduate students. I find that, having become personally involved in schools, I am better able to teach my students how to blend the reality of schools with theory and research-based practices.

Outcomes of Project Achieve

It is important at this point to revisit the notion that school-based action research is a form of service-learning, as the broad definition of service-learning is a "knowledge-generated activity" (Harkavy et al., 2000, p. 113). Teachers who contemplate action research projects in their classroom settings are actually performing a service for their learning communities by discovering new methods and techniques to improve teaching and learning. Similarly, our partnership plan was collaboratively developed with the school's leadership team with service in mind. Therefore it was important that our service work was outcomes-based—that we evaluated the extent to which our partnership influenced the school *and* the teacher education program.

In creating the Project Achieve partnership plan, the codirectors strongly believed that in order to increase the level of professionalism displayed by teachers in the school, three actions must occur simultaneously:

- First, professional development must be personalized to meet the teachers' needs.

- Second, teachers must begin to view their instruction as a science as well as an art. Teaching as a science requires teachers to take a close look at the effectiveness of their techniques in terms of student learning and to investigate research-based pedagogical practices.

- Third, the notion of teacher-as-researcher discussed by the research literature has shown that teachers who engage in action research learn more about their students, their schools, and methods of delivering instruction. As well, they gain ideas for improving their teaching practices (Berger, Boles, & Troen, 2005; Kelley, 2004; Wood, 2001).

Project Achieve's results (see Yost & Vogel, 2007; Yost, Vogel, & Rosenberg, 2007) demonstrated significant growth in pedagogical skill, student achievement, and teacher candidates' confidence as measured by the following:

- Pre-post questionnaire and pre-mid-post observations of participating teachers

- Student achievement as evidenced by improved test scores (both district-wide benchmark tests and statewide standardized tests) compared to a matched middle school using a traditional form of professional development

- Questionnaire data obtained from junior- and senior-level teacher candidates who gained greater confidence in their instructional and classroom management skills

In addition to these results, seven teacher-researchers participated in focus group discussions, which provided information on what they gained or learned through conducting action research. The results of this discussion revealed a major theme: action research helped teachers to be more reflective about their practice and more vigilant about students' academic progress. For several teachers, conducting action research was about looking closely at one's own work; for one teacher in particular, this process made her more reflective. Others indicated that their action research endeavors made them more aware of how their work influenced student learning.

All teachers discussed the project's impact on their ability to understand and know their students. One indicated that her project helped her to really "see" what the students were doing in guided reading. Another teacher realized that he gained greater insight into his students by reading their journals, which expressed their deepest emotions regarding life's challenges. This teacher realized from his study that kids need to be able to express themselves in schools.

Another teacher learned that students benefit from being active participants in their own learning, as was demonstrated by her investigation into student self-monitoring during guided reading exercises. Her study showed very clearly that a self-monitoring procedure helped students become more reflective of their own learning processes.

One major implication of conducting action research, according to the participants, was that it forced them to examine processes of student learning as well as of their own teaching. According to one, "I think that being self-reflective made me a better teacher. I really focused on my teaching." The conclusion: for these teachers the process of conducting action research enhanced their abilities to analyze student learning needs and to develop innovative ways for motivating students. When asked whether they would like to conduct further research next year, all stated that they planned to pursue research in one form or another. They indicated that the results of their studies raised many new questions for which they would like answers.

It is interesting to note that four of the five teachers who finished their research projects chose to pursue unique professional opportunities. One teacher who conducted research on the writing process, using the Freedom Writer's Diary approach, went on to design a new research project that will culminate in a book cowritten with a Project Achieve codirector. Another teacher-researcher pursued National Board Certification following the completion of her action research project. The teacher who conducted a study using self-monitoring is now teaching undergraduates part-time at the partner university. Ms. Soslau has entered a doctoral program at the University of Delaware pursuing a doctorate in curriculum and instruction. These four teachers are pursuing higher levels of professional work as a result of being involved in action research in their classroom settings.

The partnership between a university and an urban middle school enabled change, innovation, and simultaneous renewal, which are appropriate goals of professional development schools (PDSs), service-learning, and action research. The school benefited, as significantly higher monthly benchmark scores were reached by the student population, and they subsequently attained adequate yearly progress in fulfillment of the NCLB standard; the latter may be linked to increases in student achievement across the core curriculum. Teachers benefited from their increased abilities in using research-based instructional strategies, which may be connected to heightened student achievement. The teacher–action research group benefited from engaging in projects that were designed to increase participants' levels of reflection-for-action (Schön, 1987). University codirectors gained firsthand experience and knowledge regarding the challenges of urban education, which changed the content and manner they use to train novice teachers. In addition, the professors enjoyed a unique opportunity to measure the extent to which school-based and personalized professional development enhances teaching and student achievement. Results from a survey of juniors and seniors participating in partnership schools revealed high levels of confidence and knowledge gained by the majority as a result of enhanced teaching opportunities.

Research Perspectives

The following sections highlight research on the unique connection between service-learning and action research, PDSs, and critical reflection as important elements contributing to innovation and change in the context of partnership endeavors. As school-university partnerships seek to change existing practices through collaborative activities such as service-learning–action research projects, the literature points to the importance of reflection and communication as catalysts for mutually beneficial reforms.

Service-Learning and Action Research

There is a synonymous link between action research and service-learning, according to numerous authors (for example, Cruz & Giles, 2000; Harkavy et al., 2000; Reardon, 1998; Strand, 2000). Harkavy et al. (2000) conclude: "The action research model for service-learning embeds research as a part of the activity of service in such a way that can create bonds between the university and the surrounding community" (p. 117). These authors are calling for a definition of action research that features both pedagogy and service, as well as partnerships between schools (or communities) and universities. Hence, according to Harkavy et al. (2000), service should be a "knowledge-generated activity" (p. 113), because action research is a form of service-learning. Although only one teacher out of seven at the middle school designed a service-learning–action research project under the auspices of the Project Achieve grant, this expanded definition of service-learning could encompass all projects in which teachers investigate and solve classroom-based problems.

Action research is teacher-initiated classroom research that results in improvements in classroom practices, whereas service-learning is "a pedagogy which involves academic study linked to community service" (Elwell, 2001, p. 2). These definitions underscore the importance of service-learning as both a pedagogical learning tool and a way to gather data for the purpose of addressing community needs.

Hendricks (2006) distinguishes among four types of action research, providing a further link between service-learning and action research:

1. *Collaborative action research:* Multiple researchers within a school-university partnership work together on an action research project. Collaborative action research provides a service to both the school and the university by improving

pedagogical practices in a mutually investigative setting.

2. *Critical action research:* A wider range of individuals—teachers, professors, administrators, community representatives—participate in action research for the purpose of solving social issues that these individuals mutually determine, thereby enabling synergistic learning by and for all participants.

3. *Classroom action research:* This type of research is conducted by teachers for the purpose of improving classroom practice through a structured reflective process.

4. *Participatory action research (PAR):* PAR is a social and collaborative process that focuses on transformational, community changes whereby both the service and service recipients design solutions and assess project outcomes.

These four definitions of action research focus on research in the context of community; collectively, they are what many service-learning providers use to accomplish their partnership goals. Strand (2000), for example, contends that service-learning provides not only a means of solving community-based dilemmas and problems, but also a tool for learning. Strand advocates a service-learning approach that focuses on doing research "*with* the community rather than *on* the community" (p. 85). The problem being investigated must therefore stem from community concerns, and community members must work collaboratively to address them. This is a form of participatory action research in that the community members serve as partners in the design and outcome of the service-learning project (Kinnevy & Boddle, 2001; Reardon, 1998). The collaborative research process was demonstrated by Knight, Wiseman, and Cooner (2000) in a study that involved school-university partnership teams working together to evaluate teacher and student learning over a two-year period. Thus it is clear that service-learning combined with appropriate analysis can positively impact community practices.

Cruz and Giles (2000) developed a four-part model for professional development school partnerships and service-learning research. An important aspect of this model is that the school-university partnership should be the primary unit of any research analysis. They base this notion on the fact that the partnership is the "infrastructure that facilitates the service and learning" (p. 31). With this shift in focus, researchers can measure the impact of service-learning based on activities that flow from the partnership. The change in research emphasis would therefore answer this question posed by Cruz and Giles: "Are service and/or learning better because of the quality of the partnership?" (p. 31).

We embedded the service-learning–action research project in a professional development school partnership. This way, the researchers could influence data-based outcomes of the service-learning projects relating to student learning and achievement. Project Achieve staff were also able to assess outcomes of the larger university partnership project, viewed as a school-based, collaborative service project (see Yost & Vogel, 2007; Yost, Vogel, & Rosenberg, 2007).

School-University Partnerships

Similar to service-learning scholarship, the PDS literature focuses on accountability. Many years ago, Zeichner (1992) wrote that the purpose of PDS is to "ground theoretical studies in the practice of teaching" (p. 303). Despite this early emphasis, research on the effects of PDS work has been minimal at best (Abdal-Haqq, 1998; Mariage & Garmon, 2003; Teitel, 2003). Outcome measures are now included in the standards for PDSs developed by the National

Council for Accreditation of Teacher Education. Teitel (2003) explains:

> The purpose of Professional Development Schools is to promote student learning. PDS's do that by improving schools, preparing new teachers in better ways, supporting the growth and development of all educators, and using inquiry and research to see what is working well and what is not. (p. xviii)

John Goodlad's (1994) concept of simultaneous renewal underscores the need for collaboration among university faculty, preservice teachers, cooperating teachers, and school leadership teams as they engage in mutual reforms. Stevens and Boldt (2004) note that beyond the rhetoric of simultaneous renewal lies the real challenge of school-university partnerships regarding policies, practices, and, ultimately, relationships. The authors contend that these challenges arise from lack of knowledge and experience in implementing the PDS model.

Research demonstrates that strong collaborations require a great deal of time, and those partnerships unable to devote this level of effort often fail (Goldring & Sims, 2005). Much of the failure results from differences in school and university cultures relating to "tempo of work, professional focus, career reward structure, and incongruent power and efficiency" (p. 225). Further, few partnerships are willing to delve into the complicated issues presented by both schools and teacher education programs (Stevens & Boldt, 2004); instead, they provide short-term solutions to complex problems (Peel, Peel, & Baker, 2002). These partnerships fade away rather quickly and leave schools with a more cynical attitude towards partnerships in general. Moreover, many school administrators and teachers view university partnerships as short-term, satisfying only the universities' desire for research and publication to the exclusion of the schools' needs (Smith & Trexler, 2006). Building lasting partnerships is not an easy endeavor, and it requires long-term commitments on projects that are mutually beneficial (Harkavy, 2005).

What is the difference between a quality partnership and a poor one? A successful partnership that is focused on staff development and school leadership requires extensive collaboration if it is to positively impact student learning (Peel et al., 2002). Thus these authors contend that effective communication among all stakeholders is needed to foster enhanced collaboration and empowerment. Further, all stakeholders in the partnership should be reform-minded and nurture a willingness to enact change. The concept of growth and improvement through change should be embedded in the culture of the school as well as the partner institution.

Influencing the culture of a school toward the idea of *innovation and change* was the subject of a study by Goldring and Sims (2005). Their focus on leadership training reflects the realization that traditional education for administrators does not emphasize *leadership for change*. The project outlined an alternative curriculum that helped administrative candidates understand how to develop and lead teachers through the change process. They hypothesized that the more closely partner institutions are aligned in their goals, the easier it is to maintain the partnership. Hence having a shared culture that is focused on *innovation and change* is an important criterion for simultaneous renewal.

Even though few studies have examined the impact of PDS work on student learning, there is some research that points to positive learning effects from school-university partnerships. A study conducted by Knight et al. (2000) used a collaborative teacher research model to evaluate the effects of PDS activities on the achievement of elementary-aged students. The study's quantitative and qualitative data revealed that students' writing and mathematics skills increased after exposure to interventions that the university and participating teachers selected collaboratively.

Another study, by Mariage and Garmon (2003), focused on the goal of collaboration among teachers for the purpose of enhancing their professional development, thereby increasing students' learning opportunities. As participant-observers, the university researchers worked with teachers and the leadership team to collect data. The results demonstrated how a school-university partnership advanced both teacher and student learning at underperforming schools.

Reflection as Inquiry

Researchers have documented the benefits of partnerships in promoting a reflective stance in teacher education candidates and practicing teachers (Kelley, 2004; O'Donnell & Gallegos, 2006; Reardon, 1994, 1998; Robinson, 2000; Swick, 1999; Wood, 2001). Inquiry-based methods lead novice teachers to use data-based teaching practices, infuse reflection into problem-solving processes, and feature a strong commitment to student learning (Berger, Boles, & Troen, 2005; Darling-Hammond, Hammerness, Grossman, Rust, & Shulman, 2005; Kelley, 2004; Swick, 1999).

Action research has strong ties to the model of critical reflection proposed by Dewey (1910), in which the art of thinking closely parallels the research process by providing a structured framework for solving problems in a school or community setting (Yost, Sentner, & Forlenza-Bailey, 2000). When teachers combine action research with service-learning, students and their teachers are engaged in dual action research projects aimed at studying phenomena and arriving at appropriate solutions based on information and data gathered. By focusing on reflection, teachers and teacher candidates become more critically reflective and capable of solving classroom problems.

The link between the art of thinking and research is elaborated on by Dewey (1910) as a sequence of steps. The individual:

1. Experiences a dilemma or problem
2. Observes the location and definition of the problem

3. Suggests a possible solution to the problem based on evidence

4. Develops a hypothesis based on reasoning (both inductive and deductive)

5. Engages in further observation and experiment, which leads to acceptance or rejection of the initial conclusion

The cycle of thinking introduced by Dewey matches the action research–service-learning process in which the community engages by attempting to answer a question or to solve a problem. The model of critical reflection allows for flexibility, which is often needed as groups investigate complex community problems (Kinnevy & Boddle, 2001). Additionally, action research by novice and experienced teachers significantly enhanced reflective thinking and fostered teaching practices that were more student-centered and attentive to individual needs (Berger, Boles, & Troen, 2005; Darling-Hammond et al., 2005; Kelley, 2004).

Other models of reflection introduced by Van Manen (1977) and Schön (1987) have connections to the service-learning–action research process. Van Manen introduced three developmental stages of reflective thinking in teachers: (1) effective application of skills and technical knowledge (teachers analyzing the effects of strategies used), (2) reflection about the assumptions and consequences underlying specific practices (teachers assessing the educational implications of practice), and (3) reflection on the moral and ethical dimensions of decisions related to the classroom practice (teachers considering the broader social, political, and economic implications of using the practice). Action research addresses all stages of Van Manen's model because it investigates all aspects of teaching practice as they relate to student outcomes.

Schön (1987) introduced three stages of reflection. Reflection-on-action occurs after the teacher has taught a lesson; therefore the teacher engages in thinking about the success or failure of the lesson based on student learning outcomes. This information guides the teacher's selection of strategies for future lessons. Reflection-*in*-action occurs while the teacher is teaching the lesson. This mode of reflection, which is evaluative by nature, is often referred to as *vigilance*; a teacher carefully observes student responses and makes instructional changes when necessary. Reflection-*for*-action most closely parallels the service-learning–action research process, in that the teacher engages in deep reflection to guide further actions based on data gathered over time and in-depth thinking about the implications of the teacher's potential actions.

To accomplish reflection as defined here, a teacher must rely on evidence used in the analytical process. This process parallels the research cycle to a significant extent. Service-learning–action research evaluates not only classroom or community practices but also their implications and outcomes. Further, data-based practices enable teachers to test and analyze new methods of practice.

Service-learning–action research stimulates many forms of reflection, especially because of its ties to collaboration and data-based analyses. Stevenson (1995) points out that reflection is both internally and externally directed. Internally directed reflection is a personal self-examination of the individual's actions or practices. Externally directed reflection becomes part of the individual's collective community, in which all points of view are heard and expressed. The latter form of reflection has vast implications for developing critical thinking among teachers, both novice and experienced, through the sharing of multiple perspectives (Mosca & Yost, 2000; Yost & Mosca, 2002). Multiple perspectives enable teachers to broaden their experiences and understand alternative points of view. Externally directed reflection is especially germane to service-learning–action research, as it is a collaborative, communal endeavor. Furthermore, school-university partnerships explicitly foster externally directed reflection by routinely using multiple perspectives from the partnership's various constituents. The overview of research on service-learning action research, PDS, and critical reflection coalesces a solid rationale for developing service-learning action research projects in the context of school-university partnerships.

Partners' Reflection: Implications for Future Development of Service-Learning–Action Research

As Cruz and Giles (2000) concluded from their analysis of the unique connection between service-learning and action research, focusing research efforts on the infrastructure of the partnership plan enables one to answer the question: "Are the service and learning better as a result of the partnership?" (p. 31). The Project Achieve partnership plan did indeed achieve its goals of increased teacher effectiveness and professionalism through personalized professional development and action research projects. More important, significant gains in student achievement were evidenced by district-wide benchmark and statewide standardized test scores. These achievement gains enabled the middle school to make adequate yearly progress, a considerable achievement in light of the fact that none of the comparison middle schools in the district achieved this goal for the 2005–2006 academic year. Naturally embedded in action research is critical reflection, which leads teachers to greater awareness of methods and techniques that increase student learning.

The learning effects of this partnership were also evident at the university. It should be noted that the advent of Project Achieve coincided with a restructuring of the undergraduate curriculum at La Salle University, whereby course work was altered to connect directly to the real work of teachers. Through the partnership, teacher interns gained first-hand experience in planning and teaching units of instruction to urban students. They also gained much-needed confidence and professionalism through their year-long experiences working with both general and special education students at this school. The two professors who directed Project Achieve were able to apply what they learned from the urban teachers and the leadership team directly back to their own university courses. The professors also gained a unique opportunity to design, implement, and measure the effects of a school-based, teacher leader model of professional development on instructional growth and student achievement. Thus reciprocal benefits from the perspectives of both the school and the university were realized through this collaborative partnership endeavor.

We contend that the professional development school model has great potential as a holistic, service-learning entity that embeds several smaller service-learning projects in its partnership plan. Our goal in conceiving and implementing Project Achieve was first and foremost to increase the learning and achievement of urban middle school students over time. Our premise was simple: increased teacher skill, professionalism, and expertise would concomitantly increase student learning and achievement. Thus our service was to the school community and to measure outcomes relating to academic achievement. The school was reciprocally engaged in serving the university's needs as well. The service-learning projects, as we define them, were the teacher-directed, action research projects in which each teacher sought to develop and test teaching strategies in their classrooms to enhance student learning.

As future PDS partnerships contemplate service and learning, we recommend that they consider the following points, derived from our own experience and literature review:

- Develop projects that are outcomes-based and that serve the school *and* university communities.

- Jointly determine the needs of both the school and the university partner, and develop a plan that is collaboratively based and mutually beneficial.

- Expand the partnership's notion of service-learning–action research to ensure that all school-based projects are outcomes-based.

- Consider using either collaborative action research, critical action research, classroom action research, or participatory action research (Hendricks, 2006) in the design of the partnership plan.

- Ensure that the partnership remains flexible by looking closely at data generated to ensure that needed adjustments will be made as necessary.

- Ensure the flow of communication between the school and university, and address any concerns that the constituents may have from each side of the partnership.

To answer the question posed at the beginning of this chapter, "Are service and/or learning better because of the quality of the partnership?" (Cruz & Giles, 2000, p. 31), our answer is an emphatic "yes." The gains made by teachers involved in personalized professional development and action research projects and the increases in student learning as measured by scores on the district's benchmark tests and the state's standardized test, along with enhanced experiences in urban education gained by teacher candidates and their professors, all strongly suggest that the infrastructure of the partnership plan was successful in achieving its goals.

In order for urban or other schools to meet the challenging demands of No Child Left Behind for increased performance on standardized tests, PDSs should focus their efforts on service—to the school community and to their teacher education programs in a simultaneous renewal of both settings. Through school-university partnerships that advance service-learning as action research, it is possible for reciprocally beneficial reforms to occur.

References

Abdal-Haqq, I. (1998). *Professional development schools.* Thousand Oaks, CA: Corwin Press.

Berger, J. G., Boles, K. C., & Troen, V. (2005). Teacher researcher and school change: Paradoxes, problems, and possibilities. *Teaching and Teacher Education, 21,* 93–105.

Billig, S. H. (2000). Research on K–12 school-based service-learning: The evidence builds. *Phi Delta Kappan, 81*(9), 658–664.

Cruz, N. I., & Giles, D. E. (2000). Where's the community in service-learning research? *Michigan Journal of Community Service-Learning,* 28–34.

Darling-Hammond, L., Hammerness, K., Grossman, P., Rust, F., & Shulman, L. (2005). The design of teacher education programs. In L. Darling-Hammond and J. Bransford (Eds.), *Preparing teachers for a changing world.* San Francisco: Jossey-Bass.

Dewey, J. (1910). *How we think: A restatement of the relations of reflective thinking to the educative process* (2nd rev. ed.). Boston: D.C. Heath.

Elwell, M. D. (2001). Editors' choice: The efficacy of service-learning for community college ESL students. *Community College Review, 28,* 47–62.

George, P. (2004). Service-learning: Putting knowledge to work. *Middle Ground, 8*(2), 35–40.

Goldring, E., & Sims, P. (2005). Modeling creative and courageous school leadership through district-community-university partnerships. *Educational Policy, 19,* 223–249.

Goodlad, J. I. (1994). *Educational renewal.* San Francisco: Jossey-Bass.

Harkavy, I. (2005). University-assisted community school program of West Philadelphia: Democratic partnerships that make a difference. *New Directions for Youth Development, 107,* 35–43.

Harkavy, I., Puckett, J., & Romer, D. (2000). Action research: Bridging service and research. *Michigan Journal of Community Service Learning* (special issue), 113–118.

Hendricks, C. (2006). *Improving schools through action research.* Boston: Pearson.

Hope, W. (1999). Service-learning: A reform initiative for middle level curriculum. *The Clearing House, 72*(4), 236–239.

Kelley, L. M. (2004). Why induction matters. *Journal of Teacher Education, 55,* 438–448.

Kinnevy, S. C., & Boddle, S. C. (2001). Developing community partnerships through service-learning: Universities, coalitions, and congregations. *Michigan Journal of Community Service-learning, 8*(1), 44–51.

Knight, S. L., Wiseman, D. L., & Cooner, D. (2000). Using collaborative teacher research to determine the impact of professional school activities on elementary students' math and writing outcomes. *Journal of Teacher Education, 51*, 26–38.

Mariage, T. V., & Garmon, M. A. (2003). A case of educational change: Improving student achievement through a school university partnership. *Remedial and Special Education, 24*(4), 215–234.

Marzano, R. J. (1992). *A different kind of classroom: Teaching with dimensions of learning.* Alexandria, VA: Association for Supervision and Curriculum Development.

Mosca, F. J., & Yost, D. S. (2000). Controls from within: Developing tools for reflecting on counter-aggressive responses to troubling behavior. *Reclaiming Children and Youth, 10*(2), 100–105.

O'Donnell, J., & Gallegos, R. (2006). Project MOVEMOS: A university-public school collaboration. *Action in Teacher Education, 27*(4), 12–22.

Peel, H. A., Peel, B. B., & Baker, M. E. (2002). School/university partnerships: A viable model. *International Journal of Educational Management, 16*, 319–325.

Reardon, K. M. (1994). Undergraduate research in distressed urban communities: An undervalued form of service-learning. *Michigan Journal of Community Service Learning, 1*, 44–54.

Reardon, K. M. (1998). Participatory action research as service-learning. *New Directions for Teaching and Learning, 73*, 57–64.

Robinson, T. (2000). Service-learning as social justice advocacy: Can political scientists do politics? *Political Science and Politics, 33*, 605–612.

Schön, D. A. (1987). *Educating the reflective practitioner.* San Francisco: Jossey-Bass.

Smith, D. (2005). Accountability for academics and social responsibility through service-learning. *Middle School Journal, 36*(4), 20–25.

Smith, M. H., & Trexler, C. J. (2006). A university-school partnership model: Providing stakeholders with benefits to enhance science literacy. *Action in Teacher Education, 27*(4), 23–34.

Soslau, E., & Yost, D. S. (2007). Urban service-learning: An authentic teaching strategy to deliver a standards-driven curriculum. *Journal of Experiential Learning, 30*(1), 36–53.

Stevens, D., & Boldt, G. (2004). School university partnerships: Rhetoric, reality, and intimacy. *Phi Delta Kappan, 85*, 703–708.

Stevenson, R. B. (1995). Action research and supportive school contexts: Exploring the possibilities for transformation. In S. E. Noffke & R. B. Stevenson (Eds.), *Educational action research: Becoming practically critical* (pp. 197–209). New York: Teachers College Press.

Strand, K. J. (2000). Community-based research as pedagogy. *Michigan Journal of Community Service Learning* (special issue), 85–96.

Swick, K. J. (1999). Service-learning in early childhood education. *Early Childhood Education Journal, 27,* 129–137.

Teitel, L. (2003). *The professional development schools handbook.* Thousand Oaks, CA: Corwin Press.

Van Manen, J. (1977). Linking ways of knowing with ways of being practical. *Curriculum Inquiry, 6,* 205–208.

Wood, A. L. (2001). What does research say about teacher induction and IHE/LEA collaborative programs? *Issues in Teacher Education, 10*(2), 69–81.

Yost, D. S., & Mosca, F. J. (2002). Beyond behavior strategies: Using reflection to successfully manage youth in crisis. *The Clearing House, 75,* 264–267.

Yost, D. S., Sentner, S. M., & Forlenza-Bailey, A. (2000). An examination of the construct of critical reflection: Implications for teacher education programming in the 21st century. *Journal of Teacher Education, 51,* 39–49.

Yost, D. S., & Vogel, R. (2007). Successful teachers, achieving students: What works in urban professional development. *Middle School Journal, 38*(3), 34–40.

Yost, D. S., Vogel, R., & Rosenberg, M. (2007, April). Constructing and evaluating a teacher leader model of professional development that leads to student achievement. Paper presented at the American Educational Research Association, Chicago, IL.

Zeichner, K. (1992). Rethinking the practicum in the professional development school partnership. *Journal of Teacher Education, 43,* 296–307.

8

Experiencing Engineering While Helping Others

UMass Lowell's Assistive Technology Design Fair

Douglas Prime and Donald Rhine

In 2002 the University of Massachusetts (UMass) Lowell's College of Engineering launched the Assistive Technology Design Fair (ATDF) program for high school students. This unique educational outreach program gives high school students the opportunity to engage in real-world engineering design problems aimed at helping people with disabilities or special needs. Working with their teacher-advisers, design teams—typically four to six students—must identify people in their community who have needs that can be met using technology. Over a period of four months, teams learn and use the engineering design process to design an assistive technology product to help their disabled client. Each team has to define the requirements of a successful design, brainstorm and analyze possible solutions, justify their chosen design, and make a presentation outlining their design process and final solution. Their ultimate goal is to build a working prototype of their solution to present at the Assistive Technology Design Fair hosted at UMass Lowell each May—and ultimately, to deliver the project to their client. ATDF is a noncompetitive event, and all teams who enter projects receive awards.

In 2006, more than 30 design teams and 120 students from 10 Massachusetts' high schools participated in ATDF, and 60 percent of the teams actually delivered finished projects to their clients. Each high school has recognized the value of this type of service-learning opportunity for their students. Not only do students find they have the ability to use their creative and technical talents to help people in their community, but in the process they also learn a lot about engineering, disabilities, and assistive technology. The success of our ATDF program is the result of strong partnerships among the university and many community and industry partners. Working with community organizations that serve disabled people has provided a strong AT educational component to our program and often results in clients for projects. Finally, the significant growth in our ATDF program has been made possible by committed industry partners—Tyco Electronics, 3M Touch Systems, Philips Medical Systems, and Teradyne—who have provided funding for this program, as well as engineers who volunteer to conduct design reviews and often mentor student teams.

Background

The Assistive Technology Design Fair for high school students was a logical outgrowth of the college's longstanding focus on service learning and assistive technology and of our more recent K–12 science and engineering educational outreach efforts. In 1990, UMass Lowell's College of Engineering launched an NSF-funded Assistive Technology Program to provide real-world capstone design projects for electrical engineering seniors. Since 1998, the College of Engineering has also been developing educational outreach programs for middle school and high school students and teachers to help enrich science and technology education in Massachusetts, to increase the visibility and status of engineering as a profession, and to interest more students in science and engineering careers.

The Assistive Technology Design Fair for high school grew out of these efforts and is modeled after the college's assistive technology program, originally established by electrical engineering professors Donn Clark and Alan Rux. As the success of middle school engineering outreach programs grew, there was an apparent need for more advanced, more realistic design experiences to nurture the technology and engineering interests of students throughout high school. The college decided to create a design experience that would give students a good understanding of what engineering is about and also help them to view engineering as a rewarding career that benefits society. The college's goal was to develop a service-learning program that would:

- Engage students in an authentic, meaningful engineering experience

- Be noncompetitive

- Teach students the engineering design process

- Connect with high school academics as much as possible

- Help students realize the relevance and utility of academic and technical skills

- Help students learn real workplace skills (decision making, project management, teamwork, communication, and presentation skills)

- Allow students to feel empowered as engineers and problem solvers

Although the ATDF program grew out of some unique initiatives at UMass Lowell, the authors believe it is possible for other engineering colleges, technical schools, and perhaps even some high schools to adopt this program model or institute a similar program at their institution.

Examples of ATDF Projects

Since 2003, over sixty-five assistive technology (AT) projects designed by high school students have been presented at our ATDF fairs. The students who participate are typically high school juniors and seniors who are taking technology, engineering, or physics courses. We have had students from several vocational-technical high schools who have done ATDF projects as capstone design projects in their technical courses. The following projects have been chosen to illustrate the variety and varying complexity of design problems solved by students.

Profile #1: A leg-exercising device adapted from a skateboard

High school students from Swampscott worked with a fellow student who has a chronic muscle disease. This student requires daily physical therapy to encourage the use of his legs. The team's challenge was to design a device that would allow the boy to exercise his legs often, by himself, while sitting in his wheelchair. Their final solution was to mount a skateboard to a frame using a pivot at the center so it rocked back and forth. It was ingenious, because although the boy can extend his legs, he has trouble pulling them back toward his body — but their pivoting design enabled him to do just that.

Profile #2: A modified video game controller for a boy with cerebral palsy

A team from Tyngsborough High School designed a specially adapted video game controller for a young boy with cerebral palsy. This boy has very limited use of his right arm and cannot do anything requiring two hands. He loved to watch his friends play video games; however, he could not participate. This team's solution was to design a large platform controller that sits on the floor in front of the boy. The platform supports the boy's weak right arm, and his hand is attached to the joystick using a Velcro strap. He operates the gaming functions with his left hand, using oversized pushbuttons mounted on the platform. They reported that on the afternoon that they delivered his modified game controller, the boy proceeded to play video games for six hours straight — just like most other kids!

Profile #3: A wrist support cradle designed to help an elderly woman drive

A team from Greater Lawrence Technical High School worked with a woman with carpal tunnel syndrome in her wrists as a result of fourteen years of sewing. Her car has a manual transmission, and it is painful and difficult for her to shift gears. This team designed an adjustable support cradle that fits behind the shift handle to immobilize their client's wrist while driving. The woman's wrist brace attaches to the cradle using Velcro. The cradle provides support and stability for their client's wrist while driving, and it allows her to move her hand more comfortably when shifting.

Profile #4: Using voice recorders for assisted communication

A team from Hanover High School worked with a severely disabled boy to help him communicate more easily. Their client is confined to a wheelchair and cannot talk — he could only move his fingers on one hand. This boy uses a communication board to spell words by pointing to letters, which is a slow and difficult way to communicate. This team used five simple, inexpensive voice recorders activated by large buttons to create a talking box to store the common messages that the boy most often needs to communicate.

Profile #5: A modified keyboard for a young boy with cerebral palsy

Students from Dracut High School designed a modified keyboard for a five-year-old boy who has cerebral palsy. Their client has difficulty with fine motor skills; he struggles to use a computer because he hits more than one key at a time, and he types so slowly that he gets repeated characters from each keystroke. These students were able to purchase a colorful adaptive keyboard that had built-in software to solve the problem of typing repeated characters. Then they fitted the keyboard with a plastic cover with holes over each letter, so the boy could use a stylus to type one letter at a time successfully.

Profile #6: A custom reading magnifier and light for specific vision loss

A team from Fitchburg High School helped a woman who had vision loss and difficulty reading as a result of a brain tumor. They had to design a portable light and magnifying device that could help her keep her place while reading. Their attractive design used a bar magnifier with super-bright LEDs, set in a housing machined from plastic door molding. Sadly, their client, the mother of one of these students, passed away in September 2006.

Profile #7: An automatic door opener designed for a boy in a wheelchair

Two future engineers from Dracut High School designed an automatic door opener for a young boy in a wheelchair. This boy, the cousin of one of the engineers, simply wanted to be able to enter his house without help when he gets home. Their unique solution involved using two garage door openers with cable systems to open both front doors. The boy operates the door openers using a remote control mounted to his wheelchair. This was an amazing project for high school students to accomplish; their design was completely successful and is still being used by their client.

In many cases the resulting student projects are impressive with respect to their creativity as well as their execution. Clearly, some designs are very original; others involve uniquely applying or adapting existing technology or modifying assistive devices to meet the specific needs of clients. Quite a few projects might be viewed as reinventing existing technology; these types of projects still provide a valuable learning experience for students and provide clients with free AT products, which are usually expensive to purchase. All of these approaches are appropriate and lead to successful projects as long as students focus on their clients' needs and work to solve real problems.

The ATDF Model

The Assistive Technology Design Fair program strives to achieve four major goals:

- To give students an intimate understanding of the design process and firsthand experience solving a real-world engineering problem

- To encourage more teachers to implement engineering design projects as part of the courses they teach or as after-school clubs

- To help students see engineering as a profession that directly benefits both individuals and our society, by helping develop a greater understanding and appreciation of people with disabilities

- To further nurture students' interest in science and engineering with the hope of encouraging more students to pursue scientific and technical careers

Realizing these goals takes a true K–12-university-community-industry partnership. UMass Lowell's primary partners are the teachers and students who participate (and, in some sense, the clients they serve). Their work is facilitated by university staff, community organizations, and industry engineers who help mentor student design teams. Industry sponsors also provide funding to pay for project materials and teacher stipends and to cover the cost of ATDF events held at the university. Since 2005, contributions from Tyco Electronics, 3M Touch Systems, and Philips Medical Systems have made our program possible. In 2006 the direct costs were about $16,000 to fund 10 schools fielding 30 teams with 120 students.

Getting Started

Each September, ATDF invitations are mailed to the superintendents, principals, and high school science and technology department heads of many Massachusetts school districts. The ATDF season begins informally in November when we invite interested teachers to attend an informational meeting at the college. At this meeting, we present project goals, requirements and benefits; share exemplary past ATDF projects and AT resources; introduce the design process and provide suggestions for successfully managing projects; and give teachers ideas for finding ATDF clients and problems. The requirements for each team participating in our ATDF program are as follows:

- Find a client and submit a formal problem statement for approval (due late January).

- Research, brainstorm, and evaluate possible design solutions.

- Participate in a design review with volunteer engineers from industry and UMass Lowell (scheduled in late February to early March).

- Build and test a working prototype of their final solution.

- Prepare both a Microsoft PowerPoint and a poster presentation describing the team's client and problem, outlining their design process, and describing the final solution (prepared in late April for the Design Fair held in early May).

In November and December, teachers form teams and assist students in finding clients and defining problems that are realistic to solve within a three- to four-month time frame. According to a recent Census Bureau report, 51.2 million people (18.1 percent of the population) in the United States had some level of disability and 32.5 million (11.5 percent of the population) had a severe disability (Steinmetz, 2002). Given these statistics, it is clear that students anywhere should be able to find clients in their own schools and communities. However, this is a challenging part of the process and presents an obstacle for many teams. Working with an actual client on a real problem is the most important and fundamental requirement for participating in ATDF. If students don't work with a real client, then their project becomes little more than a contrived classroom exercise—although such "invented" projects may still be hands-on and may have academic value for the teachers, they lack the dimensions that make ATDF a powerful learning experience. Without a client, students do not have an emotional investment in their work, and the projects do not have nearly the same impact for them—and projects without real clients are not service-learning. Students are encouraged to look for clients within their own schools, families, and communities. Many teams find clients who are relatives or students who attend their school. Potential clients can be found by contacting special education teachers, nursing homes, hospital rehab clinics, and other organizations that serve people with disabilities.

The Kick-off Event

For students, the ATDF design season officially begins on the first Saturday in January with the ATDF kick-off event and culminates with the design fair, usually held on the first Saturday in May. To help students and teachers achieve success and to make the ATDF a rich learning experience, the kick-off event includes components aimed at educating teachers and students about assistive technology and disabilities, the engineering design process, and the project management skills needed for complex, long-term projects. Several exemplary ATDF projects are used as case studies to lead students through the entire engineering process and illustrate the important aspects of solving assistive technology problems. This part of the program helps students develop an understanding of how to identify appropriate clients and projects, how to manage a client relationship, and how to successfully manage their project given technical, cost, and time constraints.

Each year the kick-off event also highlights a community organization that works with the disabled. This community partner gives a presentation to inform students about the nature of the disabilities with which they work, followed by demonstrations and hands-on activities that give students firsthand knowledge about the disability and the technology used to help overcome it. These community partners also become resources for the student teams to use as potential sources for clients or for general advice. For example, in 2005 the Lowell Association for the Blind gave an excellent presentation on blindness and visual disabilities at the kick-off event. They set up a series of stations that allowed students to simulate the experience of being blind. Wearing blindfolds, students learned to use a walking cane, experienced descriptive videos, played beep baseball and checkers, and tried out an assistive device used to pour drinks. They also saw demonstrations of AT devices that help people with visual disabilities. In 2006, we joined with the Kennedy Day School, part of the Franciscan Hospital for Children in Boston. The director talked about many issues involved in caring for and teaching severely disabled children and showed the assistive technology they use in their work. As a result of this partnership, several ATDF teams worked on projects for the Kennedy Day School. Finally, each year students are shown an outstanding documentary film, *Freedom Machines*, which gives students a broad overview of various disabilities and the challenges that disabled people face. This program shows many examples of how assistive technology helps to break down barriers for these people.

Supporting Student Teams During the Design and Build Process

After the ATDF kick-off event, the college takes several steps to support student teams and help steer them toward success. First, students must submit formal problem statements that are reviewed by program staff to determine the legitimacy of the problem and whether or not it is feasible for students to accomplish (or whether it is too easy). In virtually all cases, problems are either accepted or accepted pending revision—rarely is a problem declined. The approval process allows us to give suggestions to help students write clear and effective problem statements and develop detailed design requirements, which is very important to the outcome of any design problem. Once a team's problem is approved, their teachers have authorization to spend up to $150 per team for project materials; in special cases, teams may be approved for additional funding depending on the nature of their project.

The next hurdle that students must pass is the design review. The college recruits volunteer engineers from several companies, and they contact teachers to schedule dates for design reviews. The reviews are generally conducted four to six weeks after the problem statements are approved. The volunteer engineers meet with students to review their problem statement, the design alternatives they have considered, and the design they are proposing as their final solution. The engineers ask critical questions about the team's problem and their designs and suggest ideas that students may not have considered. Prior to these meetings, the college provides an orientation for the engineers, so they will know how to conduct the meetings and how to provide effective and positive feedback to students. Almost all students have reported that the design review experience was positive and helpful, and the volunteer engineers find it rewarding to work with the high school students in our program. Many of these dedicated engineers stay in contact with their design teams throughout the duration of the program.

Beyond design reviews, the only other help we provide to students and teachers is done via email, or occasionally with site visits. Several members of our AT staff are available to respond to student questions and to provide technical support and resources to help them with their problems. It is largely the teacher's role to facilitate ATDF projects. Their jobs include making visits with students to find clients, ordering project materials for each team, helping students build prototypes, and attending the ATDF events. Because teachers spend many additional hours outside of class supporting student teams, UMass Lowell provides ATDF teachers with nominal stipends of $250 per team for up to four teams.

How High Schools Implement the ATDF Model

The teachers who have been involved in ATDF have said that they get involved to offer their students engaging real-world projects that enhance their curriculum or extracurricular enrichment opportunities. Our ATDF program provides an authentic learning experience for students, one that allows them to learn and experience the engineering design process, apply some academics skills in a real-world context, and develop and hone important workplace skills (decision making, project management, teamwork, presentation skills, communication, and so on). Our ATDF teacher-advisers are physics and technology/engineering teachers who teach at comprehensive and vocational-technical high schools. Figure 8.1 shows a profile of teachers who have been involved in ATDF and how they have implemented projects at their schools. In 2006, 80 percent of ATDF projects were done in conjunction with high school courses. For the past two years, 60 percent of participating teachers have been technology/engineering teachers, who have fully integrated ATDF projects into their curriculum. The other 40 percent of our teachers are physics teachers. Half of them incorporated ATDF

# Teachers / # Projects	ATDF 2005		ATDF 2006	
	7 schools and 22 teams		10 schools and 30 teams	
	After School	Part of Curriculum	After School	Part of Curriculum
Physics teachers	2 / 4	1 / 1	2 / 6	2 / 6
Technology and engineering teachers	0	4 / 18	0	6 / 18

Figure 8.1. Profile of ATDF Teachers and How They Implement Projects.

projects into their classes, and the others have offered ATDF as an extracurricular enrichment opportunity, mostly for honors and AP students.

Our ATDF program integrates naturally into any high school engineering or technology class. It is a powerful and authentic way to teach the design process and achieve many of the learning outcomes specified by the Massachusetts Science and Technology/Engineering Curriculum Frameworks and High School Standards (Massachusetts Department of Education, 2001, 2006), and the Standards for Technological Literacy (International Association of Technology Education [ITEA], 2000). To date, our physics teachers have mainly used ATDF projects as ancillary projects in their classes, because for them the academic content connection is not as strong and is not guaranteed. However, we continue to encourage more physics teachers to tie ATDF projects to their curriculum because they have proven to be a valuable learning experience for students on many levels. In the last section, we discuss some ideas for program improvement including ideas for insuring that ATDF projects offer stronger academic connections. It is also important to encourage more physics teachers to become involved with ATDF because they are almost entirely responsible for the number of girls who have been involved with our program. Since 2005, 25 percent of participants were girls, and most of them were physics students.

Implementation Case Study: Tyngsborough High School

Tyngsborough High School is a small but fairly typical high school in Massachusetts with approximately 650 students. Tyngsborough was one of the original schools that piloted ATDF in 2002–03, and it has been involved ever since. Coauthor Donald Rhine uses ATDF as part of a Projects in Engineering course that he developed to allow juniors and seniors to take skills learned from math and science classes and apply them to hands-on design projects. ATDF projects now constitute one of the major units in this curriculum each spring, although they are not a full-time in-class effort. The nature of the project dictates that the students must complete parts of the program on their own time. Students use 15 percent of class time on a weekly basis to work on their projects. This time is used to coordinate team activities and provide progress reports to the class. Blocks of several class periods are allocated to ATDF work when teams are preparing for design reviews, working on final construction, and preparing for the final presentation.

Finding and Working with Clients

ATDF teams in Tyngsborough usually comprise three or four students. They begin by surveying parents, neighbors, and friends to find potential clients; however, Tyngsborough does not allow students to use their own relatives as clients, because one of the course goals is for them to learn how to establish a "business" relationship with a client. They must have a final client selected and a formal proposal ready to send to UMass Lowell by the end of January. As a class, students brainstorm other potential resources in the community and discuss how to prepare for client interviews. Students must dress appropriately, be sensitive to the needs of their clients, and talk to them with respect. Students usually ask potential clients this key question: Is there an everyday task, game, or hobby that you want to do or to participate in, but cannot?

Because many organizations may be wary of strangers showing up unannounced, the students must write a business letter to introduce the team and their purpose.

Finding the right client and project takes time and requires some judgment on the part of students and teachers. The goal is to find a real problem that is not too hard or too easy and can be accomplished within three months. Often students come back with a proposal to invent an almost-magical multipurpose device that would solve a myriad of problems (the "grabber–back scratcher–can opener–TV remote device"). The teacher should allow students to exercise creativity but also steer them away from inadvisable projects. Usually teams end up contacting two or more potential clients before settling on a final client with a workable need. Safety and risk are key factors in determining acceptable projects. For the safety of the student and the client, students are usually prohibited from undertaking any projects that require the direct use of household line voltage or contact with 120V AC circuits (unless they are working with a vocational or engineering teacher who is an electrical expert). Students typically purchase wall transformers or use battery power to overcome this design constraint.

Defining the Problem

Once students find a client, they prepare a formal problem statement, which includes background on their client and their need, a specific statement of the problem to be solved, and the design criteria that will define a successful solution. This is a challenging and crucial step in the design process for students. It requires teams to interview their client and get to know him or her personally. It is important for students to learn as much as possible about their client's disability and specific needs; often it is important to study the client's living environment if it is a factor in solving the problem. Students also do background research on existing and available assistive technology that relates to their problem.

An effective problem statement requires students to consider a range of design requirements and constraints—including safety, cost, size and weight, comfort, ergonomics, ease of use, reliability, aesthetics, and so on—and to determine the specific requirements and constraints for their problem. Many teams not only state the problem and design requirements but also suggest or define the solution they have in mind at the outset. Without even considering design alternatives, students tend to jump to quick conclusions. Another common problem is that students develop design criteria that include unnecessary constraints. It is important to help students overcome both these tendencies, as they will hinder the design process and will not result in the best solution.

Developing and Evaluating Design Alternatives

At this point in the process the students can finally unleash their creative energy and let out the solutions they have been trying to hold back. For homework, students develop and sketch several potential solutions to the problems; this is followed by a whole-group brainstorming session in which all share their initial ideas. Effective brainstorming requires that students listen to and consider all ideas initially without judgment and not become fixated too quickly on only one solution, which is often their own. Often the best ideas derive from what seem to be crazy, off-the-wall ideas and from combinations of aspects of several design ideas contributed during brainstorming.

After allowing a day or two for design ideas to percolate, the students discuss and compare their ideas in order to reduce their list down to three to five of the most promising designs. A simple method is to put all ideas on the board or on the wall and allow each team member to cast a predetermined number of votes. At this stage, teams revisit their design criteria and work to develop each design idea in detail. To do this, teams produce more detailed drawings and descriptions of key design features, develop a list of materials and parts needed along with a cost estimate, judge how well each design will meet the stated design requirements and constraints, and compare the pros and cons of each.

After students develop each of the design alternatives to a sufficient degree, the students need to use a rational method to select the optimal design. One method commonly used is a decision matrix—a table that matches each design alternative against the design specifications and desired attributes. Students use a grading scale to rate how well each design meets each specification or attribute, based on their best judgment given their research. The design alternative with the most favorable score is chosen as the solution to prototype.

The next step is design reviews, in which students summarize their work in a ten-minute PowerPoint presentation that they give to the volunteer engineers who visit from industry. This is a great opportunity for students, as it approximates what they will encounter in their future careers. Each team's goal is to convince the engineers that they have considered several viable alternatives and made a sound decision on which design to prototype. The engineers are trained to ask critical questions (in a gentle manner) and make positive suggestions to help students refine their designs or possibly consider other alternatives.

Building and Testing a Prototype

Once students have considered and incorporated the engineers' feedback, they are ready to build a prototype. Students should try to build a rough working prototype, if time permits, and then a final version of their product; this will minimize the risk of their final design not working as planned. Students usually are able to modify and improve their initial prototype to produce a final product. During the prototyping phase, students should continue to communicate with their client to ensure that the final product will be a success.

During this final project phase, there is a lot of work to be done in a short time frame, and high school teams find it difficult to manage their time effectively. To achieve success, it is crucial for teams to allocate tasks and responsibilities among all team members. Tyngsborough students select one team member to handle the purchasing parts and materials; other students are responsible for scheduling and managing team activities. Each team creates a master schedule to plan the last two months of their work and to outline what needs to be done to deliver their product on time. Typically, despite planning efforts, much of the work slips into the last week of the project, and then the rush is on—just like in the real world! Students often find creative ways to fabricate their products. In many cases, students have had local businesses donate parts and materials.

Once the project is complete, students bring their device to their client to ensure that it works effectively and to obtain feedback on needed modifications or desired improvements. Inevitably, some teams fall apart as they try to complete the process. The typical reasons for team meltdown include the failure of one or more team members to pull their weight; the failure of the design to come together as planned, with no backup plan to fall back on; and procrastination. Usually when things go awry these issues can be mitigated with good planning and mediation by the teacher. Not all projects end up being deliverable to the clients. In some cases, the product may present safety issues; in others, the quality of the project is not what students had hoped for and not suitable for delivery. Even in these cases, the ATDF process is still a valuable learning experience for students.

Sharing and Celebrating Ideas and Hard Work: The Design Fair at UMass Lowell

Students present their final products and their design ideas to the ATDF community at the design fair in May. This is an amazing experience that allows students to share their design work with their peers, their parents, and UMass Lowell staff, as well as visitors from industry and other community partners. The process of preparing for the design fair requires students to reflect on their service-learning experience in many ways. Teams present their final solution and the development of their designs with a poster board presentation and a brief PowerPoint presentation. They also write an article that can be published in the school newspaper or local newspaper, along with thank-you letters to industry sponsors. The fair itself allows students to celebrate their accomplishment (in most cases) and to be inspired by the work of other students.

Student Outcomes

In 2006, the college surveyed ATDF students for the first time and conducted in-depth interviews with three design teams to determine what students were getting out of their ATDF experience. Most questions on this survey were open response, because of uncertainty about the range of possible responses. We did not want to prompt students to consider any particular answers. The questions sought to assess what value students derived from their experience in terms of academic connections, new skills learned, and changes in career interests. We also wanted to assess how the ATDF experience affected them on a personal level, if at all.

Surveys were solicited from five out of ten participating schools, which represented a fair cross-section of participants. We collected thirty-four surveys from twelve design teams, so the data represent 27 percent of the students and 40 percent of the teams who participated in 2006. Although these are the first data the college has gathered, the results begin to give a picture of our program's impact on students (see Figure 8.2). Based on surveys and interviews conducted in 2006, it is clear that not all students participating in ATDF were interested in engineering careers, and not all of them may even be college bound. Only 42 percent of participants said that they were really interested in engineering at the outset of the project, and 21 percent were not at all interested (however, responses from one school heavily influenced this latter statistic).

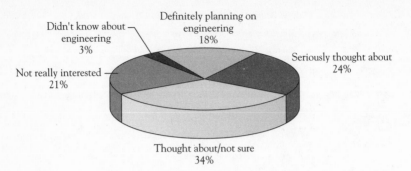

Figure 8.2. Participants' Interest in Engineering Prior to ATDF.

There is evidence that the ATDF program helps to increase students' interest in engineering and technology. After having participated in ATDF, 70 percent of students surveyed said they were "much more interested" or "somewhat more interested" in pursuing engineering or technology careers (see Figure 8.3); more important, 50 percent of these students had been initially unsure about their interest level or not really interested in pursuing a technical career.

However, the most surprising finding is that over 90 percent of students surveyed—even those students who had not expressed an interest in engineering—said they felt that ATDF was a "very

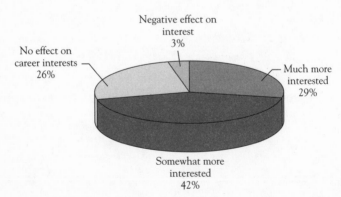

Figure 8.3. Change in Engineering Career Interest as a Result of ATDF.

valuable" or "reasonably worthwhile experience." Why such a dramatic change? Clearly these numbers are not linked to whether students became more interested in engineering and technology careers, and they seem to indicate a much broader emotional and educational value for many students.

Successfully completing projects for the Assistive Technology Design Fair is a challenging undertaking for any student, and it requires a considerable amount of work (not all of which happens in school, even for teams who are doing ATDF as part of a class). So for those who aren't really interested in technology and engineering, it is interesting to know what they are getting out of this experience. We can suggest, based on our surveys, that the majority of students find working with disabled people to be an eye-opening experience. It is clear that many students are connecting with their clients on a personal level and are really invested in their projects on an emotional level. As supporting evidence, note that 70 percent of students surveyed said that their ATDF experience affected them in a personal way. A few of these students said that the experience changed their outlook on careers, but virtually all the rest of these students gave explanations such as these:

- "How lucky we are to be able to complete simple tasks on our own. Not everyone is as fortunate, and this project taught me that."

- "It was a great feeling to know that I contributed to a product that will help a person's life, and maybe even more people's lives."

- "This was a great experience for me. It showed that hard work paid off, and it gave us a good feeling of completion when it was over."

- "I feel a great pride in being able to make someone's life easier."

- "This project affected me in a way no one knew. I helped someone less fortunate than me, and that made me change for the better. I now have great respect for all people who do this work for a living."

- "This project did affect me because it made me a better person. It showed me there are other people we should consider and help." (This is from one of those students who was not really interested in engineering.)

One may wonder whether the students were just telling the authors what they wanted to hear. However, the surveys were done anonymously and mailed back to the university, and students were not required to write any comments at all. Considering that similar comments were made by almost all of the students who said they were personally affected by the project, the authors have to assume they are sincere. We believe that these comments and many more like them illustrate one of the most important outcomes for students—that ATDF represents one of the first truly meaningful and worthwhile pieces of work in most students' academic careers. This may be true of many types of service-learning projects; however, it seems the lessons and the feelings may be even more powerful when they involve creating assistive technology for disabled people. This may be why so many students have found our ATDF program to be a satisfying experience.

The survey asked two other questions of students, in an effort to determine the extent to which their ATDF projects connect to and reinforce academics and to see what other types of skills they learned from their project work. Figure 8.4 shows the general academic connections made by students during the course of their ATDF projects. The data on academic connections are reported in broad categories because they were elicited using an open-response question. Many more students reported applying lower-level

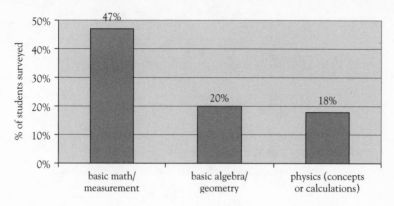

Figure 8.4. Academics Applied in ATDF Projects.

academic skills, and fewer students reported applying higher-level skills. The authors believe these numbers would be even higher if the students responded on a checklist-type questionnaire, which would prompt students to reflect on the various skills they may have applied in their design problems.

The results do suggest that most ATDF projects are not too technical, and that the academics applied to the problems are often at a middle school level. Some teachers have expressed this concern, and it may be one barrier that prevents greater integration of ATDF projects into physics classes. However, students learn many other things by participating in ATDF, which makes it a very valuable project. When asked about other skills and lessons learned during their ATDF experience, significant numbers of students talked about the technical skills they learned (drawing, building, and tools skills) and also about learning the design process (see Figure 8.5). Many students indicated that problem solving and teamwork were important aspects of their ATDF projects, and almost one-fifth of students identified other business and workplace skills they used, such as time management, budgeting, presentation, and communication skills.

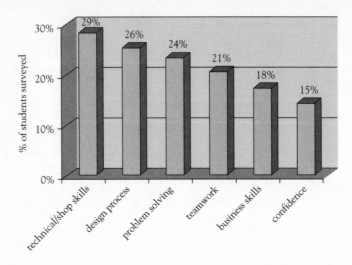

Figure 8.5. Other Skills Students Learn from ATDF Projects.

Reflections on Program Improvements

Considering service-learning in its broadest sense, our ATDF program is certainly "a form of experiential education in which students engage in activities that address human and community needs together with structured opportunities intentionally designed to promote student learning and development" (Jacoby & Associates, 1996, p. 5). As described earlier, our program builds in a series of structured educational components to help students and teachers explore the nature of disability and assistive technology, learn the engineering design process, and learn workplace and project management skills. However, other service-learning practitioners have created more specific definitions of service-learning that emphasize the need for a solid academic content connection (Howard, 1993; Tsang, Martin, & Decker, 1997). The authors of this chapter, as well as the editors of this book, subscribe to a more comprehensive view that service learning is "a credit-bearing educational experience in which students (a) participate in an organized service activity that meets identified community needs and (b) reflect on the service activity in such a way as to gain further understanding of course content, a broader appreciation of the discipline, and an enhanced sense of civic responsibility" (Bringle & Hatcher, 1995, p. 112).

ATDF projects fulfill all the requirements of service-learning, except that they are not always undertaken for course credit and do not necessarily include a high-level academic connection. The authors have shown that students are applying some academic skills and certainly gaining a greater sense of civic responsibility from their ATDF experiences. The issue is the degree to which ATDF projects provide a rigorous academic connection for students in any given course. Clearly this is less likely to happen when ATDF projects are implemented in physics courses, as opposed to technology/engineering courses, in which learning and applying the design process is a central goal. Given the open-ended nature of design itself, combined with the uncertainty of outcomes associated with this type of service-learning model in which students select their own problems, it is difficult for teachers to make an a priori determination of the exact academic content involved in a particular project. In the authors' view, this issue should not deter physics teachers from trying to at least loosely integrate ATDF projects into their curricula. Teachers might offer ATDF as an optional graded project for interested students, then use their work to provide shared lessons that benefit the entire class. The idea is that each team would document high school math and science skills applied to their design project and then present the most substantive applications to the class in the form of a mini lesson. Teachers could periodically provide some class time for students to present the higher-level applications that arise from their work, as shared lessons for the entire class. This concept of *shared lessons* is one way to increase the academic content connection for all involved—even if only a few teams use higher-level concepts and skills, everyone will get something out of it. At UMass Lowell, we may also consider adding a shared lessons session to our fair to increase its academic value.

Aside from finding strong academic connections, it is clear that the process of reflection can help to achieve the greatest benefit from any service-learning project. Tsang (2000) observes that the integration of service and engineering design projects in capstone coursework is not a new practice, but it is distinguishable from conventional projects primarily due to its emphasis on reflection. This is perhaps a bit overstated; although reflection does enhance and clarify students' learning, it is the act of working on a real problem with a real client in the community that is the cornerstone of service-learning. Other engineering service-learning practitioners suggest that the value of service-learning lies in the fact that students, in their problem-solving processes, must consider ambiguities that are inherent to complex social issues, and that their success and learning depend on the quality of their reflection sessions in the classroom, which should familiarize students with various perspectives and nurture appreciation of engineering's potential social impact (Moffat & Decker, 2000).

It is important to build in opportunities for reflection, especially when doing service-learning with high school students. This is why our ATDF program includes a structured kick-off event and formal problem submission and design review processes as key components of the student learning experience. Performing design reviews with professional engineers forces students to look critically at their own work and to consider a range of ideas that they may not have otherwise thought of. The ATDF kick-off event helps prepare students to work with disabled people. The presenters coach students on how to find clients, how to interview them and their care providers, and how to effectively define their needs. The kick-off event also forces students to look at the nature of disabilities and issues disabled people face; it begins to give them an appreciation of the promise of assistive technology and the impact that technology can have on people who experience barriers in their lives.

However, usually the greatest impact is realized by those students who present successful projects to their clients and see firsthand how the assistive devices improve the lives of these people. To the authors, it seems that assistive technology projects naturally lend themselves to built-in reflection, and thus are one of the best types of service-learning projects in the sense of helping students gain perspective on the societal impact of technology. As the survey data showed, many students seem to be genuinely affected by their ATDF experience and seem to gain a real appreciation of their clients' situations. It is unclear how much of this impact would have been realized as a natural result of this type of project and how much of it resulted from the structured reflection experiences built into our ATDF program. Nevertheless, these opportunities for structured reflection do add value to the students' overall experience. In fact, the ATDF program could be improved still further by creating a more formal process for students to receive feedback on their final projects from the volunteer engineers and our AT staff, and also from their clients when projects are delivered. As Jacoby (1996) states, "Reflection should include opportunities for participants to receive feedback from those persons being served, as well as from peers and program leaders" (p. 7). This is a key learning issue that the college has yet to fully address with the program's service-learning model.

Other barriers that can make ATDF difficult to implement include the need for a project space and tools for building prototypes, as well as the need for someone who knows how to use power tools safely and can teach students to do so. These are significant issues for science teachers who want to be involved in ATDF. Some teachers have solved this problem by partnering with a technology teacher or by finding a parent volunteer with a home shop space that students can use. The only other way to get around this is to work with a local machine shop or manufacturer who could volunteer to build student prototypes. One school involved in our program has outsourced the prototyping work, but in our view this is the least desirable solution, as it takes an important part of the project away from students. Actually building their designs to present to clients is one of the most motivational aspects of the project for students; if this is removed, they would likely be less invested in the project, and they may not realize the same personal satisfaction that has been reported by most students.

The issue of teaching proper tool use and safety to students is very important and should not be underemphasized, as it could cause a liability problem for schools. Wherever students work, and whomever they work with, there must be somebody working with them who is knowledgeable about shop safety and the proper use of the tools. Our college always recommends that schools have parents sign liability waivers for students involved in this project, unless it is part of a technology/engineering class. This is because technology/engineering instructors are certified to teach technology education programs, which means they are experienced with teaching the safe use of power tools and have access to labs or shops at school. As such, the liability issues regarding any accidents using tools would be no different than for their high school technology education classroom. However, if this project is being overseen by a science teacher who is not certified in tool use and safety, there could be a liability issue in the event of an accident.

Another major hurdle that hinders some teams from completing successful ATDF projects is the need for technical support beyond what teachers can provide. When students embark on projects, they cannot predict the complexity of design ideas they will pursue, and they often think of ideas that they cannot execute. Some of UMass Lowell's engineering and AT staff have been able to provide teams with advice and consultations via e-mail; in addition, our staff has made occasional site visits to help teams. Obviously, it is not practicable for our staff to be involved on a large scale with teams on a one-to-one basis. The only way to implement the formal design review process with so many teams is to recruit a cadre of industry engineers to help out. Although it might be more advantageous to conduct a series of design review meetings with students, this does not seem feasible given the short time frame of the project and the time involved in recruiting and scheduling volunteer engineers. So it is still largely left up to teachers to monitor and review students' progress and to help steer students to projects that they are likely capable of completing.

Finally, the foremost challenge that prevents many teams from actually entering our ATDF program each year is that of finding clients and good problems. Asking high school students to call and meet with people from different community organizations on their own time is a tall order. However, this is one of the "adult" aspects of our program that makes it such a rich learning experience. Even so, the college is considering ways to make the problem-finding process more manageable for students.

First, the program may in the future include a central, web-based client registry that we would share with participating schools. The program might develop a short online form that could be filled out by staff of any schools or community organizations that serve disabled people. The form would simply provide the client's name and location, a very short description of their need or problem, and a person to contact if an ATDF team wants to work with this client. Each team would still have to meet with and interview their client and test their prototypes with the client. Creating a client registry could simplify the problem-finding process for teachers and students, while retaining the most important student-client interactions. However, unless the client registry was geographically extensive, it would not work well for all teams. It is difficult for teams to work with clients who live too far away. Also, we encourage ATDF teams to work with clients in their own community, so everyone will realize and recognize the benefit of their work. A better solution might be to encourage participating high school teachers to team up with a local organization in their community that serves disabled people—the easiest being the special education departments in their own schools (several of our schools have done this). This option requires more initial work on the part of teachers, but it would certainly make the problem-finding task easier for students, and it would get them one step closer to success.

Reflections on Replication and Sustainability

Any true service-learning project will take more time to implement and more work to sustain, compared with ordinary classroom projects or textbook-based learning. Service-learning projects also require external support and partnerships. In the authors' opinion, this type of project is so valuable that it is very much worth the effort. Our ATDF program model has evolved into an intensive experience for students and quite an involved partnership. As such, other institutions may be overwhelmed by the details and the apparent expertise needed to implement it. However, it is important to realize that ATDF did not start out this way.

In 2002, we piloted the program with only six design teams from two local high schools and with a small internal budget. Originally it was a much less formal and less intensive experience, and obviously it did not provide all the same learning benefits that teams realize today. The faculty and staff met with teachers to introduce the project and provide them with some initial coaching and resources; then the teams showed up with their projects in May. Teachers and teams also received support via e-mail and participated in informal design reviews.

ATDF is a service-learning model that could be implemented in different ways, on different scales, and still provide students with a valuable, authentic learning experience, even without a large university or industry partnership—although clearly both increase the scope and benefits of the experience for all involved. One certainly does not need to have a college-based assistive technology program to support a high school ATDF program. We believe that many other engineering colleges, technical schools, or community-industry partnerships could establish an ATDF program in the same fashion as has been done at UMass Lowell. If there is enough national interest, the authors could even produce a program manual and provide training sessions for program leaders that would ensure the ease and success of program replication at other colleges.

It might even be possible for high schools to implement small-scale ATDF programs on their own, even without the support of a university or industry partnership—especially if organized by a technology/engineering teacher. Teachers could work with a local community organization to find clients, and the design reviews could be either conducted by the teachers or structured as a peer-to-peer student process. However, teachers would have to have some experience with the engineering design process. Schools would also have to find funding for project materials on the order of $150 per team. If high schools are enthusiastic about implementing ATDF programs locally, it is not unrealistic to assume that many could find technical support and funding from local companies or even recruit the help of individual engineers within the community. Developing an Assistive Technology Design Fair program is worth all the effort because of the many benefits it provides to students, teachers, and people with disabilities—and we have found companies are very willing to support such a worthwhile endeavor.

References

Bringle, R. G., & Hatcher, J. A. (1995). A service learning curriculum for faculty. *Michigan Journal of Community Service Learning, 2,* 112.

Howard, J. (Ed.). (1993). *Praxis I: A faculty casebook on community service learning.* Ann Arbor, MI: OCSL Press.

International Association of Technology Education. (2000). *Standards for technological literacy: Content for the study of technology.* Reston, VA: Author.

Jacoby, B., & Associates (Eds.). (1996). *Service learning in higher education: Concepts and practices.* San Francisco: Jossey-Bass.

Massachusetts Department of Education (2001). *Science and technology/engineering curriculum frameworks*. Boston, MA: Author.

Massachusetts Department of Education (2006). *Massachusetts science and technology/engineering high school standards*. Boston, MA: Author.

Moffat, J., & Decker, R. (2000). Service-learning reflection for engineering. In E. Tsang (Ed.), *Projects that matter: Concepts and models for service-learning in engineering*. Washington, D.C.: American Association for Higher Education.

Steinmetz, E. (2002). *Americans with Disabilities: 2002*. Washington, D.C.: U.S. Census Bureau.

Tsang, E. (2000). Service-learning as a pedagogy for engineering: Concerns and challenges. In E. Tsang (Ed.), *Projects that matter: Concepts and models for service-learning in engineering*. Washington, D.C.: American Association for Higher Education.

Tsang, E., Martin, C. D., & Decker, R. (1997). Service-learning as a strategy for engineering education for the 21st century. In Proceedings of the 1997 American Society for Engineering Education Annual Conference, Milwaukee, WI, June 23–26, 1997. Washington, D.C.: American Society for Engineering Education.

9

Program Theory

A Framework for Collaborative Measurement of Service-Learning Outcomes

Joannie Busillo Aguayo and Joyce Munsch

Service-learning is rapidly becoming an integral component of undergraduate education at the university and college level (Campus Compact, 2002) and is increasingly being embraced by faculty as a pedagogically sound approach to enhance student learning and to help instill a sense of civic responsibility. However, the development of service-learning experiences that meet the rigorous academic standards of higher education while at the same time providing measurable benefits to K–12 students at the partner schools is a complex process that involves careful planning and collaboration between the academic department and the community organizations (Albert, 1996; Bringle & Hatcher, 2002; Eyler & Giles, 1999; Long, Larsen, Hussey, & Travis, 2001).

One of the inherent strengths of service-learning partnerships is that there are multiple participants in the process and therefore multiple beneficiaries. However, this strength is also one of service-learning's greatest challenges. By design, service-learning

An earlier version of this paper was presented by the first author at the 2006 California State University Conference on Community-Based Teaching and Research.

partnerships are extremely complex and multidimensional in their structure (Holland, 2001). At a minimum, there are five groups of stakeholders: (1) the undergraduate students who provide the direct service in the community; (2) the faculty who supervise and oversee the placement of the undergraduates; (3) the university administration, which values the community visibility engendered by these partnerships; (4) the community schools that benefit from the additional resources (such as time and expertise) that university students provide to their campus; and (5) the students in the classrooms who receive direct services from the university students. Each of these stakeholders has a specific set of needs, desires, and perspectives that must be identified and integrated into the program design and evaluation process.

The Need for Evidence-Based Practice and Accountability

When forging a partnership between a university and community organization such as a K–12 school, the inclusion of both participants from conceptualization through evaluation should promote a sense of ownership and therefore increase the likelihood that participants will be equally committed to ongoing program improvement (Christie, 2003; Patton, 1997). To accomplish this, the service-learning partnerships must be developed and evaluated from multiple perspectives through an ongoing and collaborative process. Program theory or theory-based evaluation is a useful participatory framework that can ensure that programs—such as service-learning partnerships between institutions of higher education and K–12 settings—are conceptualized and evaluated using criteria valued by all relevant participants. The ultimate outcome should be a partnership that better meets the needs of all the partners.

In spite of the documented benefits of a theory-based evaluation approach, it is not widely known or used outside of the evaluation field. This chapter provides the rationale for using program theory evaluation as a tool for planning and evaluating service-learning partnerships, describe the components of program theory evaluation, and provide an example of its application. Although a theory-based evaluation approach is useful for any service-learning partnership, this chapter focuses specifically on partnerships between higher education and K–12 settings.

Rationale for Program Theory-Driven Evaluation and Logic Models

Program theory evaluation, incorporating logic models, provides a framework with which academic faculty and K–12 partners can conceptualize, measure, and evaluate learning outcomes based on criteria that have value for both the undergraduate and the K–12 students (Bickman & Peterson, 1990; Chen, 2005; Donaldson, 2003; Fitzpatrick, Sanders, & Worthen, 2004; Rossi, Lipsey, & Freeman, 2004; Wholey, Hatry, & Newcomer, 2004). Program theory has been defined as "the construction of a *plausible and sensible* model of how a program *is supposed to work*" (Bickman, 1987, p. 5; emphasis added) and as the rationale and blueprint for a program's theory of change and action (Chen, 2005). Accordingly, programs must focus not only on the outcomes desired by participants but also on whether these desired outcomes are realistic and achievable given the available resources, the proposed program, and the nature of needs to be addressed (Chen, 2005).

Proponents of program theory evaluation emphasize that a primary purpose of evaluation is not just to assess the merits of a program but also to "produce useful information that can enhance the knowledge and technology we employ to solve social problems" (Chen, 2005, p. 7). With this as the goal, an important aspect of evaluation is to determine not only whether a program is working, but also how and why it is working, and whether it is benefiting its participants in the way the program intended (Bringle, Phillips, & Hudson, 2004; Fitzpatrick et al., 2004; Rossi et al., 2004).

Drawing on the work of many notable evaluation researchers (Bickman & Peterson, 1990; Chen, 1990; Donaldson, 2003; Rossi et al., 2004; Weiss, 2000; Wholey, 1987), program theory emphasizes collaboration and participation by all key participants (Greene, 1988; Chen, 2005) and the use of evaluation to promote stakeholder empowerment (Fetterman, 2003). Proponents of program theory evaluation believe that such evaluations more closely reflect the concerns and needs of participants and thus are more useful to them (Guba & Lincoln, 1987).

According to Donaldson (2003), program evaluation should strive to provide both users and providers of the service with a continuous feedback loop to determine whether the program is meeting the needs of the partners and doing so efficiently and within the framework of standards of professional practice. To provide such a continuous feedback loop, program evaluation must be viewed as an integral and ongoing activity that will provide both university faculty and K–12 personnel with useful information to make decisions about the design, implementation, and ultimate effectiveness of the service-learning partnership (Rossi et al., 2004). Given the multiple stakeholders involved in service-learning endeavors and the complexity of such programs, we need evaluation methods capable of integrating multiple perspectives and sources of data. Program theory in general, and logic models in particular, offer practical and useful tools for designing and evaluating service-learning programs.

Although the terms *program theory* and *logic model* are often used interchangeably, program theory is a more detailed, *narrative* description that underlies the implicit and explicit explanation of the rationale and plan of a program's intended outcomes and how these outcomes are expected to be achieved. The two components that form the structure for the overall program theory are the program's *impact theory* and *process theory* (Bickman, 1987; Chen, 1990, 2005; Christie, 2003; Donaldson, 2003; Rossi et al., 2004).

A logic model, on the other hand, is a *graphic* description of the program theory that specifies a chain of causal assumptions that link program resources, activities, and intended program outcomes (Chen, 2005; Cooksy, Gill, & Kelly, 2001; Wholey, 1987).

Components of Program Theory Evaluation

This section further describes the program theory approach by addressing its two components: impact theory and process theory.

Program Impact Theory

The first component of a program theory is the impact theory, which involves identifying and evaluating the short-term, intermediate, and long-term outcomes that are expected from the program. Both in developing a program's impact theory and in evaluating a program's impact theory, planners determine long-term outcomes before the short-term objectives and intermediate goals, to ensure their alignment and to increase the likelihood that objectives and goals will lead to the desired outcomes (Chen, 2005; Rossi et al., 2004).

Long-term outcomes specify the ultimate impact expected to result in a benefit to all of the participants. Long-term outcomes typically are not expected to be achieved before three to five years. *Intermediate goals* are the observable, measurable behaviors that are expected following implementation of the program, whereas *short-term objectives* refer to the knowledge and skills needed so that the desired goals and outcomes can be achieved (Chen, 2005).

Program Process Theory

Once outcomes have been developed, the activities and strategies necessary to achieve these outcomes are determined, as well as the resources needed to support these processes (Rossi et al., 2004). The program's *process theory* refers to how the program is to be implemented and the organizational structure that must be in place so that the desired activities and experiences can occur. Additionally, it specifies the human, financial, and material resources and institutional support needed to implement the program. This is essential, because without adequate resources, service-learning programs are doomed to fail, regardless of how well the program theory is developed or implemented (Albert, 1996; Bringle & Hatcher, 2002; Bucco & Busch, 1996; Campus Compact, 2002).

Program Theory as Both Impact and Process

Program theory is the sum of its impact theory and process theory dimensions. It manifests the program's rationale and blueprint for desired outcomes and the causal links between the program's resources, activities, and outcomes (Chen, 2005).

The use of a program theory approach during the initial planning stages of program development helps to embed evaluation into the program design; as such, it forms a continuous feedback loop that supports sustaining, improving, establishing, or terminating program elements, as needed. Because all participants are involved in the process of developing the program's theory of intended outcomes as well as how and why the program will achieve these outcomes, it is more likely that participants will accept and apply information obtained from the program evaluation (Fetterman, 2003; Mark & Shotland, 1985; Patton, 1997). Furthermore, program theory evaluation ensures that the program's outcomes can be attributed to the program's activities. Together, program theory development and evaluation help program evaluators avoid "black box" evaluations in which there is no logical connection between the program's impact and the program's processes (Chen, 2005; Cooksy et al., 2001; Donaldson, 2003; Rossi et al., 2004).

This is essential because significant resources are required to implement and sustain service-learning programs, so a program evaluation must demonstrate not only *whether* a program is working, but *how* and *why* the program is working (Bringle et al., 2004; Chen, 2005).

Limitations of Program Theory

Although program theory and the use of logic models can significantly strengthen the likelihood that program outcomes are logically connected to program resources and activities and thus increase the probability of achieving program outcomes, there are some limitations to adopting this approach.

First, the process of developing a program theory and its accompanying logic model can be time- and resource-intensive (Stufflebeam, 2001). However, because program theory evaluation is highly flexible, it can be scaled up or down to meet the needs of the program. In the long run, this ability to tailor an evaluation to meet a specific set of needs can save valuable resources. By focusing evaluation on only those areas of greatest mutual interest, program evaluation using a program theory model can be cost-effective because it can prevent costly outcome studies for programs that are not yet ready for a full-scale outcome assessment (Wholey, 1987). It also can help determine whether an evaluation question is even related to outcome assessment (Rogers, Petrosino, Huebner, & Hacsi, 2000).

Also, planners can minimize concerns about the amount of resources required to develop a program theory by resisting the urge to try to develop a "perfect" program theory or to try to evaluate the entire program theory at one time (Chen, 2005; Rossi et al., 2004; Weiss, 2000). The development and modification of the program theory is meant to be an ongoing process that should be repeated many times over the life of the program. In fact, it is highly desirable that partners develop a culture of seeking continuous feedback that can be used to improve the program implementation and outcomes (Chen, 2005; Donaldson & Lipsey, in press; Rogers et al., 2000). As an iterative process, it requires a commitment from all vested stakeholders to continue dialoguing until a version of the program that satisfies all sides is developed. Rather than being a limitation, this actually becomes a strength, because it means that the program is seen as an organic entity that grows, develops, and changes over time (Weiss, 2000).

Another possible limitation is that program theory evaluation may not meet what could be considered the "gold standard" of evaluation: the randomized trial experimental design. However, because program theory evaluation is not method-driven, but needs-driven (Kalishman, 2002), it can use both experimental and nonexperimental research designs and both qualitative and quantitative data gathered through multiple methods (including surveys, focus groups, observations, and interviews) (Donaldson & Lipsey, in press; Fitzpatrick et al., 2004; Wholey et al., 2004). This is a significant advantage because it allows program evaluators to use the research design and data collection methods that are most likely to provide the desired information at the appropriate stage of program development (Chen, 2005; Rossi et al., 2004) and that are most useful to the program's stakeholders (Christie, 2003; Patton, 1997).

Development of a Program Theory and Logic Model for a Service-learning Course in K–12 Settings

To illustrate the application of a program theory approach to an actual higher education K–12 partnership, in this section we describe how we used a program theory evaluation approach with an undergraduate service-learning course at California State University, Northridge (CSUN). This course is a senior seminar for Child and Adolescent Development majors that has a 150-hour service-learning component in a community-based setting. Internship sites include preschools, elementary, junior and senior high schools (both public and nonpublic), and a number of other agencies that serve children and families.

Similar to backward design approaches, development of program theory and logic models begins with the end in mind by first identifying what is needed by stakeholders. As noted previously, this step is crucial when designing service-learning programs to ensure that there is consensus among stakeholders as to what each group perceives as the need for the service-learning partnership (Leigh, 2004; Rossi et al., 2004). As such, we wanted to ensure that the needs of our community partners for serving their children were balanced with our needs for the university students to participate in meaningful learning experiences. Without explicit agreement on this issue, it is unlikely that the service-learning partnership would be successful.

To achieve consensus, we held several meetings between faculty and representatives from our partner schools over a period of several months. At these meetings, each group had the opportunity to express their needs and desired outcomes from the proposed partnership. We also obtained input from the university students who would participate in the partnership, through focus groups and surveys.

We conducted a review of the literature in the areas of child and adolescent development, learning theory, and supervision, as well as models of service-learning and service-learning partnerships, to be sure that the rationale and design of our program was grounded in scientific and evidence-based principles. After collecting data using multiple methods from multiple stakeholder perspectives, we had the framework for our program theory: a *program impact theory* of desired and intended outcomes and a *program process theory* that stipulated the processes we believed would be required to success-fully achieve these outcomes (Chen, 2005; Rossi et al., 2004).

As a part of developing our program impact theory, we identified the long-term, intermediate, and short-term outcomes for the university students participating in the service-learning experience, as well as the long-term, intermediate, and short-term outcomes for the participating community K–12 partners. *Long-term outcomes* for the university students participating in the service-learning program included the extents to which they (1) experienced the enhancement of their career goals, (2) felt they had an opportunity to make a meaningful contribution to the community, and (3) demonstrated commitment to ongoing professional development. For the K–12 school partners, long-term outcomes included improving student achievement or increasing the likelihood that students would complete school through grade twelve and beyond.

Intermediate goals for the university students reflected traditional course goals and the actions that students might be expected to perform as a result of their experience. For example, students were expected to be able to show that they (1) could apply theory to practice, (2) had developed a personal philosophy of working with children, and (3) could communicate effectively and work collaboratively with others. For the school partners, one intermediate goal was improved performance on assignments and test scores as a result of increased opportunities for K–12 students to interact with university students acting as role models, mentors, and tutors during class and after-school activities.

And finally, the stakeholders identified *short-term learning objectives* or the knowledge and skills the partners would need to reach the intermediate goals. Short-term learning objectives for the undergraduate students focused on determining whether students acquired knowledge of how community programs and systems operate; had an increased awareness of personal biases, strengths, and weaknesses; or had gained an understanding of various theories and their appropriate application in a practical setting. For the school partners, one short-term learning objective was increasing the K–12 students' understanding of subject matter content.

While long-term outcomes for a service-learning program were not expected to be fully realized until three to five years or later after participation in the program, the short-term objectives and intermediate goals for the students in our program were expected to be demonstrated by the end of the academic year, and reflect observable and measurable knowledge, understanding, and performance (that is, student learning outcomes) (Albert,

1996; Bringle et al., 2004; Eyler & Giles, 1999; Fink, 2003; Holland, 2001).

Figure 9.1 illustrates an impact theory for a higher education K–12 program such as ours. The logic model depicted in Figure 9.1 is read from left to right as a series of "if . . . then" relationships. For example, *if* students develop the knowledge, understanding, and

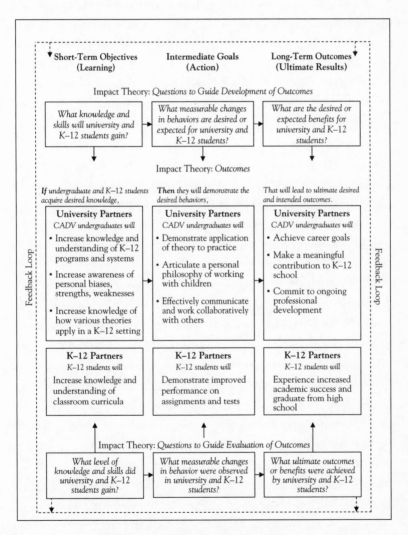

Figure 9.1. A Model of Impact Theory.

skills necessary to apply theory to practice in a "real world" setting, *then* students will ultimately be able to achieve their career goals (or be prepared to enter a graduate program, and so on). Or, *if* K–12 students increase their knowledge and understanding of subject matter content and can apply this knowledge effectively through classroom activities, *then* students will ultimately attain higher levels of academic achievement, higher test scores, and increased likelihood of completing their education through twelfth grade and beyond. The boxes at the top of Figure 9.1 contain questions that we used to guide the development of the program *impact theory elements*. The impact theory elements are the short-term objectives, intermediate goals, and long-term desired and intended outcomes shown in the boxes in the middle of the figure. The questions that guided the *evaluation* of the impact theory are located at the bottom of the figure. The answers to the evaluation questions help form the feedback loop for the impact theory by identifying whether the program achieved the desired and intended outcomes. Readers are encouraged to see Chen (2005) or Rossi (2004) for further information to guide program impact theory development or evaluation.

Figure 9.2 uses a logic model to illustrate a *process theory* for our higher education K–12 partnership, with the questions that assisted us with developing the program's process theory to guide the implementation of activities and the identification of the resources needed to implement those activities. For example, the students in our program participated in a seminar, in addition to their community service in the schools. At this point in developing our process theory, the university partner considered the number of on-campus classes the undergraduates would attend, the number of hours of service they would provide in the community setting, and the activities they would engage in. The community schools considered how to best integrate undergraduates into their school setting, how many days or hours students should be at the schools to maximize benefits to the K–12 students, how to create meaningful

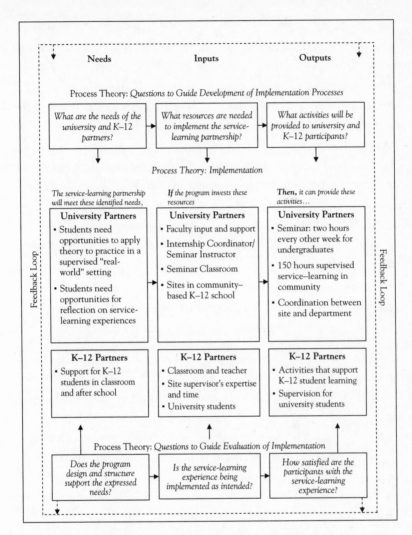

Figure 9.2. A Model of Process Theory.

activities for the undergraduates, and the mechanisms that would be used to supervise the university students in the classrooms.

As in Figure 9.1, the process theory is read as a series of "if ... then" relationships and is combined with the impact theory: *If* the necessary resources are invested to produce meaningful service-learning experiences and activities, *then* students will gain the knowledge and skills needed to apply theory to practice in a real-world setting and thus will be able to achieve their career goals. The boxes at the top of Figure 9.2 include some questions that were used to guide the *development* of the process theory, and the boxes under the process theory elements (in the middle of the figure) contain the questions used to guide *evaluation* of the process theory. The answers to the evaluation questions helped to form the feedback loop for the process theory by identifying whether the program had adequate resources to implement the program and whether the program had been implemented as intended. Readers again are encouraged to see Chen (2005) or Rossi (2004) for further information to guide program process theory development and evaluation.

Conclusion and Recommendations

The most promising aspect of program theory evaluation is its usefulness in explicitly showing how intended outcomes are linked to program resources and activities (Weiss, 2000). It is a framework that fits particularly well with the challenges of evaluating service-learning programs, because it is a participatory approach that promotes collaboration and consensus building around a shared vision. Furthermore, when the starting point for program design is determination of the desired and intended outcomes, evaluation is already embedded into the program design. Thus program theory evaluation fosters evaluation at multiple points in the lifecycle of a program as a formative process, to improve programs, as well as a summative process, to demonstrate effectiveness and efficacy (Chen, 2005; Rogers et al., 2000; Rossi et al., 2004). Program theory evaluation is an approach that can help programs to improve effectiveness and efficiency, not just establish a program effect.

In today's academic environment, resource-intensive programs such as service-learning programs are being asked to do more than to demonstrate their effectiveness through outcome assessment. They are increasingly being asked to empirically show explicit *links* between program resources and outcomes (Bringle et al., 2004; Bucco & Busch, 1996; Long et al., 2001), to demonstrate the value and benefit of such programs to all participants (Bringle & Hatcher, 2002; Bringle et al., 2004; Eyler & Giles, 1999; Fink, 2003; Werner, Voce, Openshaw, & Simons, 2002; Young & Baker, 2004). Unfortunately, this creates considerable anxiety around the issue of evaluation, which ultimately can hinder the collection of crucial information about what is working or not working, as well as valuable information that can guide program improvement (Donaldson, Gooler, & Scriven, 2002).

It has been our intent in writing this chapter to encourage all participants involved in service-learning programs to consider adopting a program theory framework. We have tried to emphasize that if a program-theory framework is used during the initial design and development phase of service-learning programs, evaluation is built into the program from the start, rather than being added on later in the process; as such, it can help to guide program development and improvement as well as to assess outcomes (Chen, 2005; Donaldson & Lipsey, in press; Rossi et al., 2004).

Our program has been a direct beneficiary of this approach. We have continued to gather information from the university students participating in the service-learning experience and their supervisors at the various K–12 partner sites to gauge the success of the program. As a part of the iterative process described in this chapter, we periodically revisit our program model to assess our effectiveness in reaching our objectives and goals. We know from the discussions that happen in the campus seminar and the evaluations we receive for the course that the students participating in this service-learning program continue to feel that (1) it is meeting their goals of preparing them for careers in the community working with children and families, and (2) they are developing their ability to apply theory to practice in community settings. Although our students have other options for meeting their degree requirements, about 60 percent of all Child and Adolescent Development majors continue to choose the option of participating in this community service program, based on the perceived value it adds to their educational preparation.

The program also continues to receive strong support from the K–12 community partners; in fact, they routinely request more university students for their schools than we can provide. During the first three years of operation of this program, our community partners have had to reexamine the preparation and training they provide to the university students before placing them in the classrooms so that the students are better equipped to participate in meaningful ways. They also have had to reexamine the amount and type of ongoing supervision that the university students receive. However, changes such as these have occurred with minimal disruption because we continue to maintain good lines of communication between the campus and the community, to treat all participants as vital and contributing members of a partnership, and to use a program theory framework to guide the evolution of the program.

References

Albert, G. (1996). Intensive service-learning experiences. In B. Jacoby & Associates (Ed.), *Service-learning in higher education: Concepts and practices* (pp. 182–207). San Francisco: Jossey-Bass.

Bickman, L. (1987). The functions of program theory. *New Directions for Program Evaluation, 33*, 5–18.

Bickman, L., & Peterson, K. A. (1990). Using program theory to describe and measure program quality. *New Directions for Evaluation, 47*, 61–72.

Bringle, R. G., & Hatcher, J. A. (2002). Campus-community partnerships: The terms of engagement. *Journal of Social Work, 58*(3), 503–516.

Bringle, R. G., Phillips, M. A., & Hudson, M. (2004). Understanding service learning. In *The measure of service learning: Research scales to assess student experiences* (pp. 3–9). Washington, DC: American Psychological Association.

Bucco, D. A., & Busch, J. A. (1996). Starting a service-learning program. In B. Jacoby & Associates (Ed.), *Service-learning in higher education: Concepts and practices* (pp. 231–245). San Francisco: Jossey-Bass.

Campus Compact. (2002). *Essential service-learning resources brochure (2002).* Retrieved March 11, 2006, from http://www.compact.org/resource/SLres-definitions.html

Chen, H. T. (1990). Issues in constructing program theory. *New Directions for Program Evaluation, 47,* 7–18.

Chen, H. T. (2005). *Practical program evaluation: Assessing and improving planning, implementation, and effectiveness.* Thousand Oaks, CA: Sage.

Christie, C. A. (2003). The user-oriented evaluator's role in formulating a program theory: Using a theory-driven approach. *American Journal of Evaluation, 24*(3), 373–385.

Cooksy, L. J., Gill, P., & Kelly, P. A. (2001). The program logic model as an integrative framework for a multimethod evaluation. *Evaluation and Program Planning, 24*(2), 119–128.

Donaldson, S. I. (2003). Theory-driven program evaluation in the new millennium. In S. I. Donaldson & M. Scriven (Eds.), *Evaluating social programs and problems: Visions for the new millennium* (pp. 109–141). New Jersey: Erlbaum.

Donaldson, S. I., Gooler, L. E., & Scriven, M. (2002). Strategies for managing evaluation anxiety: Toward a psychology of program evaluation. *American Journal of Evaluation, 23*(3), 261–273.

Donaldson, S. I., & Lipsey, M. W. (in press). Roles for theory in contemporary evaluation practice: Developing practical knowledge. In I. Shaw, J. Greene, & M. Mark (Eds.), *The SAGE Handbook of Evaluation.* London: SAGE.

Eyler, J., & Giles, D. E., Jr. (1999). *Where's the learning in service learning?* San Francisco: Jossey-Bass.

Fetterman, D. (2003). Empowerment evaluation strikes a responsive chord. In S. I. Donaldson & M. Scriven (Eds.), *Evaluating social programs and problems: Visions for the new millennium,* (pp. 63–76). Thousand Oaks, CA: Sage.

Fink, L. D. (2003). *Creating significant learning experiences: An integrated approach to designing college courses.* San Francisco: Jossey-Bass.

Fitzpatrick, J. L., Sanders, J. R., & Worthen, B. R. (Eds.). (2004). *Program evaluation: Alternative approaches and practical guidelines* (3rd ed.). Boston, MA: Pearson.

Greene, J. C. (1988). Stakeholder participation and utilization in program evaluation. *Evaluation Review, 12*(2), 91–116.

Guba, E. G., & Lincoln, Y. S. (1987). The countenances of fourth generation evaluation: Description, judgment, and negotiation. In D. Palumbo (Ed.), *The politics of program evaluation* (pp. 203–234). Thousand Oaks, CA: Sage.

Holland, B. (2001). A comprehensive model for assessing service-learning and community-university partnerships. *New Directions for Higher Education,* *114,* 51–60.

Kalishman, S. (2002). Evaluating community-based health professions education programs. *Education for Health, 15*(2), 228–240.

Leigh, D. (2004). Conducting needs assessments: A step-by-step approach. In A. R. Roberts & K. R. Yeager (Eds.), *Desk reference of evidence-based practice in health care and human services.* New York: Oxford University Press.

Long, A. B., Larsen, P., Hussey, L., & Travis, S. S. (2001). Organizing, managing, and evaluating service-learning projects. *Educational Gerontology, 27*(3), 3–21.

Mark, M. M., & Shotland, R. L. (1985). Stakeholder-based evaluation and value judgments. *Evaluation Review, 9,* 606–626.

Patton, M. Q. (1997). *Utilization-focused evaluation: A new century text* (3rd ed.). Thousand Oaks, CA: Sage.

Rogers, P. J., Petrosino, A., Huebner, T. A., & Hacsi, T. A. (2000). Program theory evaluation: Practice, promise, and problems. In P. J. Rogers, T. A. Hacsi, A. Petrosino, & T. A. Huebner (Eds.), *Program theory in evaluation: Challenges and opportunities* (Fall 2000 ed., Vol. 87, pp. 5–13). San Francisco: Jossey-Bass.

Rossi, P. H., Lipsey, M. W., & Freeman, H. E. (2004). *Evaluation: A systematic approach* (7th ed.). Thousand Oaks, CA: Sage.

Stufflebeam, D. (2001). Evaluation models. *New Directions for Evaluation, 89,* 38–39.

Weiss, C. H. (2000). Which links in which theories shall we evaluate? *New Directions for Evaluation, 87,* 35–45.

Werner, C., Voce, R., Openshaw, K. G., & Simons, M. (2002). Designing service-learning to empower students and community: Jackson Elementary builds a nature study center. *Journal of Social Issues, 58*(3), 557–579.

Wholey, J. S. (1987). Evaluability assessment: Developing program theory. *New Directions in Program Evaluation, 33,* 77–92.

Wholey, J. S., Hatry, H. P., & Newcomer, K. E. (Eds.). (2004). *Handbook of practical program evaluation* (2nd ed.). San Francisco: Jossey-Bass.

Young, D. S., & Baker, R. E. (2004). Linking classroom theory to professional practice: The internship as a practical learning experience worthy of academic credit. *Journal of Physical Education, Recreation, and Dance, 75*(1), 22–30.

Afterword

Ira Harkavy

The chapters in this book tell many different stories, but they are united by three general themes, all indicative of a recognition that service-learning is serious business; that is, that it can and should contribute to making a genuine difference in communities, schools, and higher education.

The appropriate goal for service-learning is no less than helping to significantly improve the quality of life and learning across the schooling system and society. In effect, the volume calls for a Baconian-inspired strategy for the development and advancement of a comprehensive approach to service-learning. To Bacon, the first principle for progress is "know thy goals." As he wrote in 1620: "It is not possible to run a course aright when the goal itself is not rightly placed." As such, service-learning should be evaluated by the extent to which it actually advances democracy in our classrooms, communities, and society.

For service-learning to realize that goal, colleges and universities need to be involved in democratic, mutually beneficial, and respectful partnerships with community groups and schools. Partnerships in a university's local ecological community, I would assert, have the greatest potential for producing long-term, serious, collegial collaborations that result in significant change on campus and in the community. Making connections and forming meaningful partnerships based on accountability (broadly conceived) is one of the three themes that run through the entire volume, calling to mind E. M. Forster's powerful, reverberating epigraph to *Howards End*: "Only connect!"

Calling on colleges and universities to connect and form democratic partnerships is relatively easy to do. A much harder and more significant challenge is *how* to make the right kind of connections—the second common theme. The chapters in this volume illustrate that service-learning is a useful and successful means for forming effective, democratic university-community partnerships. By and large, the chapter authors describe an active, problem-solving form of service-learning that goes beyond mere reflection on a service experience. They argue for an approach that integrates research, teaching, and service and involves working to solve real-world problems, such as inadequate education, as well as improving the learning of college students.

The third common theme, which serves as a subtext of the volume, is that the democratic transformation of colleges and universities is crucial to the democratic transformation of America into a genuinely democratic society—and that service-learning can significantly contribute to that transformation. As I write this in the opening decade of the twenty-first century, it seems to me nearly axiomatic that universities are the most influential institution in advanced societies. As John Gardner, Ernest Boyer, and Derek Bok, among others, have noted, universities possess enormous resources (most significantly, human resources), play a leading role in developing and transmitting new discoveries and educating societal leaders, and significantly shape the schooling system. A number of the chapters argue, in effect, that as the American higher educational system currently operates, it is not realizing its full potential for contributing to the development of democratic communities and schools. Among other defects, American universities have tended to contribute to a schooling system that is elitist and hierarchical.

As John Dewey emphasized, democratic schooling is the basis for a participatory democratic society. Simply put, unless the schooling system from prekindergarten through undergraduate education is transformed into a democratic schooling system, America will continue to fall far short of functioning as a decent, just, participatory democracy. The transformation of higher education, as the most influential, strategic, powerful component of the schooling system, is crucial to the transformation of the entire schooling system and the education of democratic, creative, caring, societally contributing democratic citizens. This argument animates much of the discussion in *Partnerships for Service-Learning* and provides this excellent book with energy and direction. And this argument, in my judgment, should help animate the service-learning movement to fulfill its potential and help America fulfill the democratic promise of America for *all* Americans.

Index

A

Abdal-Haqq, I., 223
Academic engagement, 173
Action research: four types of, 221–222; future development of, 229–231; outcomes of Project Achieve, 216–220; overview of Project Achieve/research project, 207–214; Project Achieve as, 206; reflection and, 226–229; service-learning and, 221–223; teaching practice improved by, 212–214
Adams, B., 140
Adams, M., 10
Addams, J., 37–39, 45, 75
Afterschool Alliance, 39, 168
After-school programs, 37–40, 39, 168, 169–170
Aguayo, J. B., 267
Ahern-Rindell, A. J., 166
Ahlgren, A., 166
Ainsworth-Darnell, J. W., 169
Akujobi, C., 104
Al Otaiba, S., 5
Albert, G., 267, 272, 276
Alexander, W., 105
Amanti, C., 149
Anderson, J. B., 3, 4, 24, 25, 26
Anzaldúa, G., 137

Assistive Technology Design Fair (ATDF): background on, 236–237; description of, 235–236; examples of ATDF projects, 238–241; four goals of, 241; model for, 241–247; reflections on, 258–265; student outcomes, 253–257, 258; at Tyngsborough High School, 248–253
Astin, A. W., 104, 105, 132, 173

B

Bacon, F., 285
Bailis, L., 105
Baker, M. E., 224
Baker, R. E., 281
Balazadeh, N., 173
Barber, B., 141, 149
Bass, S., 105
Batchelder, T. H., 104
Battistoni, R., 63, 68
Beaumont, E., 100
Belief in a Just World, The, 58
Bell, L. A., 10
Benson, L., 44
Berger, J. G., 217, 226, 227
Bickman, L., 269, 270
Bilingual education, 148–149
Billig, S. H., 104, 132, 213
Boddle, S. C., 222, 227
Bok, D., 286
Boldt, G., 224

Boles, K. C., 217, 226, 227
Boyce, K., 47
Boyer, E., 139, 286
Boyle-Baise, M., 5
Boyte, H., 45
Bradshaw, W., 80, 97
Bringle, R. G., 132, 259, 267, 270, 272, 277, 281
Brookes, J., 75
Brown, K., 131
Brumberg, J., 138
Bucco, D. A., 272, 281
Burkhardt, J., 141
Busch, J. A., 272, 281
Butler-Pascoe, M., 139

C

Calabrese Barton, A., 148
Caldwell, L., 169
Callahan, J., 5, 37, 55
Campus Compact Benchmarks, 28, 33
Campus Compact, 41, 104, 267, 272
Carger, C. L., 148
Casey, M., 152
Catelli, L. A., 106
Cejudo, M.A.R., 75, 82, 83, 94
Center for Community-Based Learning (CCBL), 76–77, 79, 81, 91
Center School, The, 4, 13, 14–18, 31
Chambers, T., 141
Charles Stewart Mott Foundation, 40
Chen, H. T., 269, 270, 271, 272, 273, 274, 275, 277, 280, 281
Child Opportunity Zone (COZ), 48
Christie, C. A., 268, 270, 274
Cigna, J., 61
City Year, 47
Civic learning theory, 141
Clark, D., 237
Classroom action research, 222
Cochran-Smith, M., 142
Colby, A., 100
Collaborative action research, 105, 221–222
College-based service-learning program, 37–71

Community fragmentation, 64
Community Technology Empowerment Project (CTEP), 82
Comunidades Latinas Unidas en Servicio (CLUES), 81–83, 94, 95, 99
Conrad, D., 45
Cooksy, L. J., 271, 272
Cooner, D., 222
Cooper, E., 148
Costello, J., 106
Credit Recovery Program, 50, 53
Critical action research, 222
Cruz, N. I., 207, 221, 223, 229, 231
Cultural diversity, appreciation of, 200
Culturally responsive pedagogy, 141–142
Curtis, K., 109, 111
Cutforth, N., 140

D

Daikos, C., 3
Darling, N., 169
Darling-Hammond, L., 226, 227
Decker, R., 258, 260
Delgado-Gaitan, C., 148
Denner, J., 137
Dewey, J., 41, 141, 226, 227
Diamond, R., 140
Dick, F., 136
DiFilippo, J. E., 165
Dinsmore, J., 5
Do no harm rule, 46
Doheny, O., 132
Donaldson, S. I., 269, 270, 272, 273, 274, 281
Donohue, P., 140
Downey, D. B., 169
Drake, C., 148
DuPaul, K., 75
Dyson, A., 149

E

Ehrenreich, B., 14
Ehrlich, T., 100

Eifler, K., 5
El Paso, Texas, 134–135
Elwell, M. D., 221
Erickson, J. A., 4, 24
Esek Hopkins (EH) middle school, 49–50, 52–53, 71
Experiential learning theory, 140–141
Eyler, J., 172, 173, 267, 277, 281

F

Feinstein Institute for Public Service, 41, 42. *See also* University-school partnerships
Fern, E., 152
Fetterman, D., 272
Fink, L. D., 277, 281
Fish, S., 100
Fitzpatrick, J. L., 269, 270, 274
Foote, L. C., 165
Forlenza-Bailey, A., 226
Forster, E. M., 286
Freeman, H. E., 269
Fresno County Office of Education (FCOE): description of, 104, 107–109; partnership between RLS program and, 111–125
Furco, A., 173, 199
Furman, G., 64, 66

G

Gallegos, R., 226
Gardner, J., 286
Garmon, M. A., 223, 226
Gender, youth attitudes and, 188–191, 192
Gender-equity and service-learning: assessment of Project ACE, 149–150; community members and, 156–157; conclusions on, 157–158; context and setting for, 132–135; description of Project ACE, 129–131; foundations of Project ACE, 135–136; pre-service teachers and, 150–155; theoretical framework for, 139–142; University

of Texas El Paso (UTEP) and, 129, 130, 132–133, 155–156
Genishi, C., 149
George, N., 26
George, P., 213
Geschwind, S., 41
Giles, D. E., 84, 172, 173, 207, 221, 223, 229, 231, 267, 277, 281
Gill, P., 271
Gilligan, C., 138
Goldring, E., 224, 225
Gonzalez, J. L., 136
Gonzalez, N., 149
Goodlad, J., 224
Goodman, P., 67
Gooler, L. E., 281
Granados-Greenberg, J., 3
Gray, M. J., 41
Greene, J. C., 270
Greenleaf, R., 67
Greer, F., 111
Griffin, P., 10
Grossman, P., 226
Guba, E. G., 270
Guzman, B., 137

H

Hacsi, T. A., 273
Halpern, R., 39
Hammerness, K., 226
Harkavy, I., 44, 75, 84, 100, 105, 132, 214, 217, 221, 225, 285
Harry Kizirian (HK) Elementary School, 42–49, 51–52, 70
Harvey, K., 93
Harwood, A. M., 7, 29, 33
Hatcher, J., 132, 259, 267, 272, 281
Hatry, H. P., 269
Hedin, D., 45
Hendricks, C., 221, 231
Hergenrader, D., 105
Hernandez, V., 109, 111
Hildreth, R., 45
Hill, D., 25
Hironaka-Juteau, J. H., 105, 106
Hofschire, L., 132

Holland, B., 268, 277
Homework Help Center, 87, 88, 89, 90
Honeycutt, J., 132
Hope, W., 213
Horn, L., 133
Housing and poverty in Rhode Island, 60–62
Howard, J. P., 104, 173, 258
Huber, M., 140
Hudson, M., 270
Huebner, T. A., 273
Hufford, T. L., 175
Hunt, S., 26
Hussey, L., 267
Hutchings, P., 140

I
Ikeda, E., 104
Ilich, I., 66, 67
Ilustre, V., 173
Information Works!, 71
Irvine, J., 138

J
Jackson, R., 45
Jacoby, B., 258, 261
Jenkins, D., 131
John Marshall Transition Center (MTC), 4, 13, 20–23
John Stanford Public Service and Political Science Academy (JSPSA), 4, 13, 18–20
Journals, data from, 209, 210, 213–214

K
Kalishman, S., 274
Katula, R. A., 104
Kelley, L. M., 217, 226, 227
Kelly, P. A., 271
Kezar, A., 141
Kielsmeier, J., 45
King, D. C., 105, 173
Kinnevy, S. C., 222, 227

Klein, S. P., 41
Klute, M. M., 104
Knight, S. L., 222, 225
Kohlberg, L., 58
Kolb, D., 141
Kolvenbach, P.-H., 28
Kraft, J. A., 105
Kraft, R. J., 45
Kretzmann, J., 45
Kromer, T., 4
Krueger, R., 152

L
Larsen, P., 267
Lawrence, Massachusetts, 170
Lawrence Math and Science Partnership (LMSP): assessment instruments for, 179–180; assessment results for, 181–196; conclusions on, 200–202; description of, 165, 170–172; expectations and initiatives of, 174–176; findings from, 196–200; Merrimack College and, 165, 172–174; participants in, 177–179, 182, 183
Lawson, R., 7, 29, 33
Lee, D., 91
Leigh, D., 275
Lerner, M., 58
Library partnership: conclusions on, 98–101; history and background of, 78–80; impacts of, 84–98; Metropolitan State University and, 75–77; Saint Paul Public Library (SPPL) and, 77, 78, 79, 80; staffing for, 80–81; as unique partnership, 77–84
Lincoln, Y. S., 270
Lipsey, M. W., 269, 273, 274, 281
Literature on service-learning, 4–9, 104–106
Livosky, M., 173
Lohman, B., 169

Long, A. B., 267
Lyness, L., 26

M

Macias, E., 131
Madriz, E., 152
Maier, M., 135
Manson, R., 47, 55
Mariage, T. V., 223, 226
Mark, M. M., 272
Markus, G. B., 104, 173
Martin, C. D., 258
Marullo, S., 140
Marzano, R. J., 208
Mathematics in the elementary class-
    room, 147–148
May, M., 137
Maybach, C., 156
McFarland, M., 173
McGill, I., 141
McKenna, M. W., 173
McKnight, J., 45, 66
Meier, D., 60
Melchior, A., 105
Mercer, S. H., 173
Meritz, D., 135
Merrimack College: description of,
    172–174; Lawrence Math and
    Science Partnership (LMSP) and,
    165, 170–172; partnership's impact
    on, 199–202; STEM literacy and,
    165–168, 176; undergraduates' rat-
    ings on service-learning, 196–197
Merz, C., 64, 66
Metropolitan State University,
    description of, 75–77. See also
    Library partnership
Mewborn, D. S., 137
Meyer, S., 132
Middle school partnerships, 49–50
Migliore, S., 84
Miller, B. M., 169, 170
Miron, D., 173
Mitchell, B., 66
Moely, B. E., 173

Moffat, J., 260
Moll, L., 149
Morrill Act, 75
Morton, K., 37, 42, 45
Mosca, F. J., 228
Mother-Daughter Program, 135–137,
    143, 148–149, 157–158
Multicultural education for secondary
    teachers, 146–147
Munsch, J., 267
Munter, J. H., 129, 141, 148
Myers, M., 169
Myers-Lipton, S., 105

N

Narum, J., 166, 167, 168
Nathanel Greene (NG) middle
    school, 50, 53–54, 70
Need in Deed, 208, 210, 213
Newcomer, K. E., 269
Newman, B., 169
Newman, P., 169
Nieto, S., 133, 142
Nisbett, N., 103
Nixon, D., 26
No Child Left Behind Act, 60, 64,
    216, 220, 231
Noddings, N., 138

O

Oakes, J., 133
Obesity, childhood, 109–111
O'Donnell, J., 226
O'Meara, K., 140
Ondaatje, E. H., 41
Openshaw, K. G., 281
Ortiz, R., 26

P

Padovano, K., 106
Padrón, Y., 138
Panthofer, N., 132
Parks, S., 58
Participatory action research (PAR),
    222

Patton, M. Q., 106, 152, 268, 272, 274
Payne, C., 105
Peel, B. B., 224
Peel, H. A., 224, 225
Peregrino, S., 129
Pérez Carreon, G.., 148
Perez, M., 109
Perry, W., 58
Peskorz, A., 85, 91, 92, 93
Peter, K., 133
Peterson, K. A., 269, 270
Petrosino, A., 273
Phillips, M. A., 270
Pickeral, 4, 6, 7, 31
Pinzon-Perez, H., 110
Porter-Honnet, E., 84
Posner, J. K., 169
Potthoff, D., 5
Poverty in inner cities, 168–170
Poverty in Rhode Island, 60–62
Preservice teacher education: The Center School and, 14–18; Franklin High School and, 18–20; John Marshall Transition Center and, 20–23; reflection on, 28–34; review of literature on, 4–9; SCSC partnership and, 9–13; Seattle University MiT program and, 23–28
Preservice teachers and Project ACE, 150–155. See also Project ACtion for Equity (Project ACE)
Price, J. N., 106
Prime, D., 235
Professional development schools (PDSs), 220, 223–226, 230, 231
Program impact theory, 271, 277–278
Program process theory, 271–272, 278–280
Program theory: accountability and, 268–269; components of program theory evaluation, 271–272; conclusions on, 280–282; evaluation and logic models, 269–271; for K-12 settings, 274–280;

limitations of, 273–274; stakeholders and, 267–268
Project Achieve: defined, 206; future developments and, 229–231; mentoring experience from, 214–216; outcomes of, 216–220; overview of, 207–209; research perspectives and, 220–229; as research project, 209–214; teaching practice improved by, 212–214
Project ACtion for Equity (Project ACE): assessment of, 149–150; community members and, 156–157; conclusions on, 157–158; context and setting for, 132–135; defined, 129–131; foundations of, 135–136; pre-service teachers and, 150–155; theoretical framework for, 139–142; UTEP faculty members and, 155–156
Project Connect, 7, 8
Project Kaleidoscope (PKAL), 166, 167
Providence After School Alliance (PASA), 54, 55
Providence College's Feinstein Institute for Public Service, 41, 42. See also University-school partnerships
Puckett, J., 105, 214

R
Rasmussen, E., 86, 87
Reardon, K. M., 221, 222, 226
Recreation Administration and Leisure Studies (RLS) program: description of, 103–104, 106–107; partnership between Fresno County Office of Education (FCOE) and, 111–125
Reflection, as inquiry, 226–229
Reflections on service-learning: individual learning, 55–59; institutional learning, 59–64
Reyes, R., 129
Rhine, D., 235, 248
Rice, J., 137, 140

Rivera, H., 138
Rizzo, E., 173
Robinson, T., 226
Robyn, A., 41
Rogers, P. J., 273, 280
Romer, D., 105, 132, 214
Root, S., 5, 55, 104
Rosenberg, M., 217, 223
Rossi, P. H., 269, 270, 271, 272, 273, 274, 275, 277, 280, 281
Rust, F., 226
Rutherford, A., 3
Rutherford, F. J., 166
Rux, A., 237
Ryan, R., 75, 82, 83

S

Sadker, D., 133
Sadker, M., 133
Sagor, R., 105, 115
Sagor's five-step process, 115–117
Saint Paul Public Library (SPPL), 77, 78, 79, 80. See also Library partnership
Sanders, J. R., 269
Sax, L. J., 104, 173
Scholarship, redefining, 140
Schön, D. A., 220, 227
School-based service-learning as action research: future developments on, 229–231; mentoring experience from, 214–216; outcomes of, 216–220; overview of Project Achieve, 207–209; overview of research project, 209–214; research perspectives and, 220–229; teaching practice improved by, 212–214
School-university partnership perspectives, 207–220. See also University-school partnerships
Science, technology, engineering, and mathematics (STEM) programs of study, 131, 134. See also STEM literacy
Science careers, women in, 144

Science classes: gender and, 188–191, 192; middle school youth perceptions of, 198–199
Scientific literacy, 166
Scout Island Adventure Challenge, 108–109, 118
Scriven, M., 281
Seattle University Master in Teaching (MiT) program, 4, 11, 15, 23–28, 29, 30, 31, 32
Seattle University Master in Teaching Service Leadership Conference, 13
Sedlak, C., 132
Seidman, I., 152
Sentner, S. M., 226
Sepanski, J., 5
Service Matters, 41
Service-learning: defined, 132; literature on, 4–9, 104–106; reflections on, 55–64
Shapiro, H., 129, 141
Shotland, R. L., 272
Shulman, L., 140, 141, 226
Shumer, R., 75, 88, 89, 90
Shumer, S., 75
Sigmon, R. L., 85, 93
Silverstein, N. M., 105
Simmons, R., 104
Simons, M., 281
Sims, P., 224, 225
Sleeter, C., 142
Smith, D., 213
Smith, M. H., 224
Smith, R., 169
Smith, V., 169
Smither, B., 103
Social justice, defined, 10
Solis, C., 131
Soslau, E., 206, 207, 208, 209, 210, 211, 212, 215, 219
Spencer, D., 136
Stakeholders, five groups of, 268
Steinmetz, E., 243
STEM (science, technology, engineering, and mathematics) literacy, 131, 134, 165–168

Stephens, J., 100
Stevens, D., 224
Stevenson, R. B., 228
Stirtz, G., 5
Stoecker, R., 140
Strage, A. A., 105
Strand, K. J., 140, 221, 222
Student Coalition for Strengthening Communities (SCSC), 3, 9–13
Study Hard club, 50
Stufflebeam, D., 273
Sugar, J., 173
Surveys, as assessment instrument, 179–180
Sutton, P., 109, 110, 111
Swick, K. J., 4, 226

T

Tannenbaum, S. C., 103
Teacher education, pre-service: The Center School and, 14–18; Franklin High School and, 18–20; John Marshall Transition Center and, 20–23; reflection on, 28–34; review of literature on, 4–9; Seattle University MiT program and, 23–28; Student Coalition for Strengthening Communities (SCSC) partnership and, 9–13
Teacher education and Project ACE, 150–155. See also Project ACtion for Equity (Project ACE)
Teens Know Best (TKB) program, 84, 91, 92
Teitel, L., 142, 223, 224
Threnhauser, E., 104
Tinajero, J. V., 129, 135, 136
Title IX, 133
Tornatzky, L., 131, 139
Torres, J., 7, 28
Travis, S. S., 267
Trexler, C. J., 224
Troen, V., 217, 226, 227

Tsang, E., 258, 260
Twitchell, T., 44

U

University of Massachusetts (UMass) Lowell's College of Engineering, 235, 236. See also Assistive Technology Design Fair (ATDF)
University of Texas El Paso (UTEP), 129, 130, 132–133, 155–156. See also Project ACtion for Equity
University-school partnerships: after-school programs, 37–40; challenges of, 50–55; complications in, 41; conclusions on, 69–70; at elementary school, 42–49; framework for, 64–69; middle schools and, 49–50; reflections on, 55–64. See also Assistive Technology Design Fair (ATDF); Project Achieve; School-university partnership perspectives
Urban youth and poverty, 168–170

V

Valenzuela, A., 138
Van Manen, J., 227
Vandell, D. L., 169
Voce, R., 281
Vogel, R., 217, 223
Vogelgesang, L., 104, 105, 132

W

Wade, R., 4, 6, 24, 26
Walsh, T., 5
Waxman, H., 138
Weil, S. W., 141
Weiss, C. H., 270, 273, 274, 280
Werner, C., 281
White, W. S., 40
Wholey, J. S., 269, 270, 271
Wiburg, K., 139
Wiseman, D. L., 222
Wood, A. L., 217, 226
Wood, G., 60
Worthen, B. R., 269

Y

Yamauchi, L., 132
Yarbrough, D. B., 4
Yee, L., 104
Yff, J., 4
Yost, D. S., 206, 207, 209, 212,
  214–216, 217, 223, 226, 228

Young, D. S., 281
Youth surveys, as assessment instrument, 179–180

Z

Zeichner, K., 6, 223
Ziebarth, J., 5